# A GUIDE TO AN EFFECTIVE MIDDLE SCHOOL

IRVINGTON PUBLISHERS, INC.
551 FIFTH AVENUE NEW YORK, N.Y. 10017

ISBN 0-8290-1523-X (paper)
0-8290-1524-8 (cloth)

Printed in the United States of America

| Chapter | | Page |
|---|---|---|

THE MIDDLE SCHOOL--MORE THAN A NAME

Among the more noticeable educational changes
taking place in many communities today is the
transition to a middle school program. While this
trend is of such recent origin that its exact nature
and extent are still under scrutiny, enough evidence
has been gathered to identify it as having a widespread effect on educational organizational patterns.
For example, in a 1968 national study report,
Alexander found 1101 schools identifying themselves
as middle schools.[1] This was remarkable progress in
a period of less than ten years since the first
middle schools were established. Even more rapid
growth took place in the next decade as Brooks[2]
reported finding 4060 middle schools in that national
survey.

In seeking to learn the cause or causes for this
significant movement towards the middle school, it
is possible to identify several factors that motivate
such change.

1.  Problems of declining enrollments.
    Many school districts in the country are
    experiencing declining enrollments which are
    accompanied by empty or underused classrooms.
    Consolidation of the fewer students becomes
    necessary with older, less efficient
    buildings sometimes being closed, sold, de-
    molished or converted to other community
    uses. In the process, the rearrangement of
    student population makes it feasible to
    consider establishment of a middle school.

2.  Problems of crowding in existing buildings.
    School districts that are experiencing rapid
    growth in population sometimes turn to the
    middle school concept in seeking to provide
    relief in terms of needed classroom space.
    Rather than add to existing school buildings,
    needed classrooms can take the form of a
    new middle school.

3. Problems of desegregating schools now racially
   segregated.
   Where school attendance lines coincide with
   racially segregated living patterns, some
   districts turn to the middle school as a means
   of providing for more mixed racial populations
   in schools. In this way, a new middle school
   district can be superimposed on existing
   elementary school attendance areas which may
   be racially homogeneous.

4. Problems of hand-me-down, obsolete high school
   buildings no longer needed for secondary
   education.
   The completion of a new high school facility
   frequently presents a community with the
   problem of what to do with an obsolete
   building no longer needed for that purpose
   but one which, for a variety of political
   reasons, cannot be demolished. After all,
   that fine old high school building was probably the one many voters in the community
   attended in their youth. What realistic
   administrator would dare to demolish it! A
   common practice is to convert such a facility
   to a middle school.

5. The "bandwagon effect" or "faddism."
   We have popular "styles" in education just as
   we do in clothing, cars, etc. At present,
   middle schools are considered a sign of being
   in the forefront of educational change. Some
   communities simply change the name of an
   existing junior high school to "middle school"
   as a quick but superficial way of gaining
   public recognition for being "innovative."
   Such "innovation" is purely cosmetic, at best.

6. Problems of better meeting the needs of pre-
   adolescent or early adolescent youth.
   A change to a middle school provides a means
   for developing a program which better meets
   the needs of a unique group of students who
   are no longer children and not yet true

adolescents.  It also makes better use of
teacher talents and community resources in a
well-coordinated, soundly based educational
program.

In examining the above, it readily becomes apparent that there may be a number of factors in a community which prompt it to move towards a middle school
program.  These may frequently be of a purely
political or economic nature and serious questions
can be raised as to the appropriateness of such
reasoning.  The only valid reason for the adoption
of the middle school concept is that it provides the
best approach to meeting the unique needs of the
youth who constitute the population of such a school.
Also it is designed to recognise the true nature of
the present society in which these youth must live.

A further point which requires attention is in
the matter of terminology.  The term "Middle School"
is not intended as an exclusive term but rather as a
generic term.  It is not the intent of the authors
that the term "Middle School" is to replace completely
the established "Junior High School" since many
junior high schools have in the past and also in the
present carried on effective programs for the education of the "between-ager" or transescent student.
The term "Middle School" is used throughout this
book for the reason that it is a new term not
encumbered in the eyes of readers with stereotypes of
traditional education so often proven inadequate.
While in time it is hoped that the term "Middle
School" will become firmly established as the terms
"Elementary School" and "Secondary School," for the
present, as least, the ideas set forth in this book
are to be considered equally applicable to creating
viable junior high school programs as well as
middle school programs per se.

## What is the Middle School Concept?

The middle school concept logically draws its
major strengths from the very nature of the transescent individual and his interaction with the society

in which he lives. There are three elements which
become apparent as the transescent and his society are
studied in an effort to find the bases for a truly
relevant educational program.

1.  As we observe and analyze the ways in which
    the child grows and develops, we conclude that
    the physical maturation of children, particu-
    larly in the years from 11 to 14, has been
    considerably accelerated. Improved diet and
    upgraded health care have seen to this.
    As a result, children today are larger,
    stronger and in many ways more mature physi-
    cally than children of the same ages in pre-
    vious generations. These observations are
    further substantiated by reports of anthro-
    pologists based on statistical evidence they
    have gathered.

2.  Along with these physical changes, we also
    note socio-psychological differences between
    transescent children of today and those of
    previous generations. Increased travel by
    families contributes to this, not only travel
    within this country but abroad as well. Then,
    more numerous cultural and informational re-
    sources provided by more extensive mass media
    are also a factor. Books are available today
    in quantities never present before. The paper-
    back revolution is apparent everywhere.
    Reading material and the information, ideas,
    and stimulation that these provide contribute
    significantly to the more rapid social devel-
    opment of children. The almost universal
    availability of television is also a factor
    in the environment of the transescent. The
    many hours spent in viewing TV often exceed
    those spent in the actual classrooms.

3.  Educating larger and larger numbers of students
    has become necessary as our population has
    grown. Unfortunately, there has been a
    growing impersonalization of education as

well. The individual has lost his identity
in many schools. This lies at the heart
of much of the present dissatisfaction with
schools and is nowhere more true than in
the middle grades. Growing recognition
is being accorded the basic principle of
education which stresses the importance of
providing differentiated treatment of young
people at varied maturity levels. This leads
to consideration of the differences inherent
in transescents as against younger and older
children and follows with an examination of
the kinds of educational programs called for
by such identified developmental characteristics.

In an effort to provide general guidelines for
use by educators in planning middle school programs,
several tasks are necessary. First, the growing
body of literature dealing with the middle school
concept* must be examined to identify important
principles essential for these programs. Secondly,
educational leaders prominent in developing and
carrying on successful middle school programs must
be interviewed for their views on what are important
elements in a successful middle school program.
Thirdly, observations of actual middle school programs in operation will be necessary as these will
provide additional input for the development of needed
guidelines. Next, and certainly not the least important, is the consideration of the nature, the
characteristics of the youth to be served and the
kind of society in which he lives. As in any worthwhile educational program, this is a most important
consideration. The findings of several studies have

---

*Included in the literature were several doctoral
studies concerned with characteristics of successful
middle schools. These were done by Jack Riegle,
James Hawkins and William Powell, all at Michigan
State University, East Lansing, Michigan, as well as
Thomas Bohlinger, G. Wayne Swezig, Shirley Scholl at
Miami University, Oxford, Ohio, and others.

led to the identification of varying numbers of characteristics of the middle school.  For the purposes
of this book, sixteen characteristics have been identified as being most viable and of representing the
scope of a desirable set of guidelines for planning
new or revised programs as well as being useful in
evaluating existing middle school or junior high
school programs.

## Sixteen Criteria for Evaluating the Middle School

1.  Is Continuous Progress Provided For?
    Regardless of chronological age, students should
    be allowed to progress at their own individual
    rates.  This transescent state of growth is one
    where individual differences are most pronounced.
    Forcing students into a rigid chronological
    grouping pattern ignores this important develop-
    mental characteristic and defeats the effective-
    ness of educational plans.  Instead, the curri-
    culum must be built on continuous progress per-
    mitting each student to move through sequential
    learning activities at his own rate.

2.  Are Class Schedules Flexible?
    In the traditional school, rigid time schedules
    often interfere with learning rather than serving
    it.  Logically, the schedule should be based on
    instructional needs for various activities.  To
    do this, the schedule should be varied and flexi-
    ble with changes made in class periods where
    these are necessary to fit the kinds of study
    activities being carried on.

3.  Is Team Teaching Used?
    Every teacher possesses certain teaching strengths
    as well as weaknesses.  In addition, transescent
    students benefits from a carefully planned sched-
    ule which puts them in contact with more than one
    teacher.  However, they are not yet ready for the
    highly departmentalized approach of the high
    school.  Therefore, a team teaching approach

which utilizes teacher strengths in working with
students individually and in groups is the logical way to meet the transescent's needs.

4.  Is a Multi-Material Approach Used?
    While the basal text approach to teaching is the
    dominant approach today, it has disadvantages
    which give cause for serious concern.  One of
    the major disadvantages is its inflexibility
    since it assumes that all students respond to
    the same approach equally and progress through
    the text at the same rate.  More consistent
    with the nature of the transescent is the use
    of a wide range of easily accessible instruc-
    tional materials and a variety of activities
    to appeal to varied abilities and interests of
    students.  The multi-material approach is con-
    sistent with the wide intellectual and physio-
    logical range of middle school age students who
    may compare with seven to nineteen year olds.

5.  Is there Provision for Basic Skill Repair and
    Extension?
    Because of individual rates of growth, some
    youngsters have not entirely mastered the basic
    skills.  These students require an extension
    of the program of basic skills development begun
    in the elementary school.  There should be many
    opportunities to practice reading, listening,
    map and arithmetic skills, questioning, debate,
    etc.  In some instances, the special services
    of remedial teachers may be necessary for some
    students.

6.  Are Exploratory and Enrichment Studies Provided
    For?
    The transescent has a strong interest and curios-
    ity in the world in which he lives.  To provide
    for this, the middle school should offer a wide
    range of educational opportunities for the
    student.  Electives should be part of the pro-
    gram of every student so that his unique needs
    can be met.  Time should be spent in enriching
    the student's concept of himself and the world

around him rather than confining him to learning
only required subject matter in traditional form.

7. **Are There Activities for Creative Experiences?**
The creative talents of transescents require
opportunities for expression.  Students should
be free to explore interests in many areas and
to do so without pressures.  Student newspapers,
dramatic activities, art, musical programs, and
others should be carried on in such a way that
they encourage students to select, conceive,
plan, and carry out activities in these areas.

8. **Is There Provision for Independent Study?**
Strong individual interests and curiosity char-
acterize the transescent.  This serves as a
highly effective motivational force when there
is adequate provision for independent study by
the student with the teacher available for
assistance in planning and as a resource person.
The value that this has in fostering self-dir-
ection by students makes it an important provision of the middle school.

9. **Is There Full Provision for Evaluation?**
The middle school program should provide a system of evaluation that is personal and positive
in nature.  If an individualized program is to
be carried on, then the evaluation should be
individualized.  The student should be encouraged to assess his own progress and plan for
future progress as well.  The present common
grading system using letters provides little
information useful in understanding progress and
areas of needed improvement.  As part of an
effective evaluation system, student-teacher
conferences on a regularly scheduled basis are
available.  Additional conferences including
parents can aid in reporting progress.  The
whole atmosphere in conducting evaluation should
be constructive and positive rather than critical and punitive.

10. <u>Is Planned Gradualism Provided For?</u>
Another characteristic of the transescent
is his eagerness to make more of the decisions concerning his own behavior, his
own social life and choice of friends, his
learning activities. While he is ready for
some decision-making at this stage, he is
not quite ready for assuming the full bur-
den of such planning as the high school
student must do. The transescent still
requires some security and continues to
depend heavily upon adult guidance. Therefore, the program of experiences in the
middle school should satisfy the transescent's needs for more independence while
it also continues to offer the assurance
of sound adult guidance.

11. <u>Is There an Appropriate Program of Physical Experiences and Intramural Activities</u>?
Highly competitive athletic programs are not
appropriate for transescents who are generally unprepared for the serious pressures
these activities generate. Instead,
physical education classes should center
their activity on helping students understand and use their bodies. A strong intramural program which encourages widespread
participation is greatly preferred to a
competitive, selective program of athletics
which benefits only a few in a "star" system. The stress would be on the development of body management skills.

12. <u>Are Appropriate Social Experiences Provided
For?</u>
Some middle school age students are still
children, immature and not yet ready for
more sophisticated social activities.
Others are already adolescents with strong
interests in social contacts with members
of the other sex. Many are in transition
between these two stages. Therefore, a
program of social activities based on a

high school model is inappropriate. Instead,
there should be a program which provides for
the unique needs of the transescent. These
include wholesome social contact with members of the other sex through interaction
in small groups, large group activities in
common areas of the school, club activities,
dancing of the "mixer" type such as square
dancing, and others. Serious dating and
pairing off of couples is more appropriate
at later ages.

13. Are There Adequate and Appropriate Guidance
    Services?
    The transescent has many problems troubling
    him and these often stem from the rapid
    physical changes he is experiencing. These
    problems require careful counseling from
    teachers and from trained guidance counse-
    lors. Group and individual counseling
    services are an important part of a success-
    ful middle school program.

14. Is There Adequate Provisions for Student
    Services?
    Every community has many human resources
    that can be useful in a school program.
    The middle school recognizes this and seeks
    to utilize people from the community in
    many ways. Volunteer parents, teacher
    aides, clerical aides, student volunteers,
    and others can do a great deal to facili-
    tate the operation of the middle school
    program.

15. Are There Adequate Provisions for Student
    Services?
    Providing adequately for the many needs of
    middle school students calls for a broad
    spectrum of specialized services. These
    should include health services, counseling
    services, testing services, and opportu-
    nities of both a curricular and a co-curri-
    cular nature. The important point is that

the major needs of every student should be
met by the school through its own services
available to schools.

16. Does the Program Emphasize Community
    Relations?
    The truly effective middle school is
    community-minded. It seeks to develop and
    maintain a varied program of community
    relations. Programs to inform, to enter-
    tain, to educate and to understand the
    community are part of the basic operation
    of the school.

Many communities today are considering the development of middle school programs. Other communities have begun programs which they feel are
middle school programs. Unfortunately, the
pressures of time and an inadequate understanding of
the true nature of a sound middle school program may
result in a disappointing or inappropriate programs
in some of these communities.

In each of the chapters which follow, one of
the sixteen criteria outlined above has been used
as the focal point for discussion and recommendations to guide educators in planning and evaluating
educational provisions dealing with the particular
criterion of that chapter. A general discussion of
the criterion is developed so as to establish it in
a context of the all-school setting. Then specific
recommendations are made for consideration in specific planning for educators. In instances wherever
it is appropriate, sample materials used in middle
school which have been recognized as successful,
quality institutions are also included as examples
of the kind of ideas which might be useful to
planners. By no means are the possibilities for
planners limited to those set forth in this book.
There are no limitations to the creative planning
which is possible for a group of dedicated, imaginative and informed planners.

It is hoped that the materials in this book will

stimulate several kinds of activities. One of these
is an analysis and discussion by faculty of the importance of a particular criterion as it relates to
the development of a total school program, of which
it is an important element. Secondly, it is hoped
that the specific ideas set forth will also stimulate thought and discussion of ideas which are
appropriate to a particular school body in a particular and unique setting.

Whether a school program is in actual operation
or whether it is still in the planning process, it
is felt that these suggestions will prove useful
not only in the development of worthwhile programs
but also in the strengthening of faculty understanding of the nature of their tasks and of their
particular, individual roles in carrying on the
accomplishment of these accepted tasks.

## CONTINUOUS PROGRESS

As has been described in the initial chapter, one
of the cornerstones of the middle school philosophy is
to meet more adequately the physical, social, emotional
and intellectual needs of the transescent.  The purposes of this chapter are to review some of the characteristics of the transescent, to examine the continuous progress movement, and to indicate advantages and
disadvantages of implementing continuous progress.
The chapter closes with guidelines for launching a continuous progress program.

### Behavioral Characteristics
### of the Middle School Student

The rapid physiological changes which take place
in the transescent result in certain behavioral characteristics typical to the middle school student:

1. Awkwardness in bodily movements due to bone
   growth preceding muscle growth

2. Concern with irregularities in physical development such as obesity, scars, acne, and much
   attention to physical appearance

3. Conformity to popular styles in clothing and
   hair

4. Talkativeness

5. A great need to release physical energy as
   denoted by extreme restlessness

6. Willingness to respond to a variety of non-
   structured and leisure activities

With their concern for appearance and popular
styles, yet with a need to be themselves, students of
middle school age exhibit certain social behaviors and
attitudes:

1. A desire to conform to peer standards while aware of adult standards of acceptable behavior

2. Concern for "right" and "wrong"; stirrings of active altruism and worries about those less fortunate than themselves

3. A strong need to belong to a peer group

4. A desire for opportunities to exercise choice in food, recreational, friendship selections with frequent changes in friendships

Enmeshed in their uncertainties and conflicts, middle school students have a tendency to:

1. Act impulsively in terms of language usage and in tasks; are impatient to get things done in a hurry

2. Want to become independent, yet desire limits to be set

3. Desire approval and acceptance from adults

4. Need frequent success and recognition for personal efforts and achievements

5. Exhibit instability in moods: anxious then confident, calm then boisterous

6. Often delay action on suggestions by adults

7. Be easily offended and sensitive to criticism

8. Be anxious about their intellectual and physical development, social relationships and adult authority

In terms of their intellectual and physical development, middle school age students:

1.  Are interested in both concrete and abstract exercises and are better able to deal with abstractions than formerly

2.  Desire opportunities to participate in practical problem-solving situations

3.  Are interested in making fuller use of basic skills learned in elementary school

4.  Display an interest in cultures and races other than their own

5.  Are curious and inquisitive

6.  Prefer an active to a passive role in learning activities

7.  Have short-term goals, and rarely sustained intense interests in various pursuits

8.  Prefer interaction with peers during learning activities

9.  Desire opportunities to express originality

10. Want to evaluate their personal capabilities in terms of their attributes and limitations

These are generalizations only. The individual student of the pre- and early-adolescent years will vary to some degree from these descriptions. Planners for a continuous progress program, however, must keep these generalizations in mind as they build programs to meet the general and individual needs of the middle school students.

Given these characteristics and needs, what kind of program might best meet them? To begin with, it is obvious that the program should provide optimum individualization of instruction for a population characterized by such wide variability. The program should feature continuing development with a

curriculum which provides for a) sequential concept
development in general education areas, b) major
emphasis on learning how to learn (skills for
continued learning), c) balancing exploratory experiences with activities and services for personal
development, d) values development. The program
should also promote continuous progress.

## Continuous Progress Education

Robert Anderson and John Goodlad published
The Nongraded Elementary School (Revised) in 1963
ushering in more than a decade of debate and writing
on continuous education.[1] Their thesis was that
rigidly enforced age-grade school organization inhi-
bited learning of pupils regardless of considerations of ability and interest.

Research in the behavioral sciences has continued to emphasize the uniqueness of the individual while educators have stressed the need for
greater individualization of instruction. The
philosophical basis of individualized instruction
rests on the following assumptions:

1. Schools ought to be accountable for the
   maximum development of each individual.

2. Each individual has learning styles and
   rates that are characteristic of himself.

3. Each person selects from the learning
   environment those experiences best utilized
   in the learning process.

4. Active participation in learning processes
   enhances learning effectiveness.

The continuous progress movement is a complex

------------

[1]John I. Goodlad and Robert H. Anderson, The
Nongraded Elementary School, New York: Harcourt,
Brace and World, Inc., 1963.

set of ideas as most great movements are. Goodlad and Anderson are the first to admit that the movement toward continuous progress education is stalled because of a lack of understanding. Part of the problem stems from inadequate and incomplete conceptualizations. Not enough attention has been paid to how the components of schooling are affected when continuous progress values are applied. Properly implemented, continuous progress can result in significant improvement in a school's potential for fostering desirable cognitive, affective and psychomotor growth in children and youth.

A valid continuous progress program in a middle school must grow out of the needs and characteristics of middle school age students and is based on a belief in and a commitment to the following:

1.  Success in school is based on progress in learning rather than on attainment of prescribed standards of achievement within a prescribed length of time. Within this definition almost all students can be successful in school.

2.  The school's program in terms of methods, materials and extracurricular activities must be designed to encourage, support, and reward progress in learning at whatever pace a student can sustain.

3.  Learning objectives must be stated with enough flexibility so that all students can achieve them at a level sufficient to maintain self respect.

4.  Specific behavioral objectives must be defined in such a way that progress can be visible to both student and teacher.

5.  Continuous progress requires that evaluation by teacher and student be continuous in order that the student's needs be defined

and prescriptions made.[2]

The continuous progress idea is not new to American education. The one-room rural school was a
place where the idea was actually lived. But with
urbanization and population increase, schools became larger and continuous progress education, once
facilitated by a low pupil-teacher ratio, gave way
to larger group instruction with children separated
into age levels with a high pupil-teacher ratio.

Recent studies of the learner, of our culture,
and of organized knowledge have renewed questions
concerning the purposes of schools and their relations to the larger, rapidly changing society.
Goodlad emphasized that developing the learner as
an individual and as a member of society is the
primary function of the continuous progress school.[3]
Mastery by all learners of a specific body of
knowledge or a set of skills is not the intent of
these schools. Rather, knowledge and skills are
valuable as a means by which individuals develop
into fully participating members of society.

The continuous progress movement has its roots
in the non-graded movement, a movement which was
relatively short-lived, yet useful in that it stim-
ulated discussion and debate about the rigidities of
the lock-step approaches which are built into the
age-graded, self-contained model. The term "nongraded" is giving way to the term "continuous
progress," a term which suggests a broader concept
of education. Included in this broader concept are

---

[2]Carlos M. Watson, Vanita Gibbs, and Ralph H.
Jones, "Continuous Progress: An Idea, a Method, an
Organization." Contemporary Education, Volume 42,
April, 1971, p. 247.

[3]National Education Association, Project on the
Instructional Program in the Public Schools, Planning and Organizing for Teaching (Washington, D.C.),

prescriptive approaches to teaching; vertical growth; and horizontal approaches, defined as cooperative or collaborative endeavors among the teaching staff.

## Advantages of
## Continuous Progress Education

1.  Better teaching and learning opportunities occur when learning skill sequences are operationally defined to meet the needs of the learner.

2.  Students are taught skills in learning sequences which range from readiness to competency or mastery; skill development is fostered.

3.  The elimination of passing or failing does away with much of the threat that brings unhappiness in school.

4.  Learners can move at their own pace without penalty of being failed simply because they haven't covered as much in a given year as is usually defined by "grade." Faster students are not held back by their classmates. When multiaging is used in skill development programs, older students tend to become leaders when working with slower or younger children.

5.  Multiaging frees students to make more contributions in relevant problem-solving work.

6.  Repetition of material is avoided since the student begins the new year or term where he left off.

7.  Gaps in instruction are avoided since there are no grades to skip.

8.  Team work among faculty members is facilitated; collaborative planning allows faculty

to evaluate and treat needs of individual
students.

9.  The greater flexibility in grouping procedures allows for more appropriate placement of youth for instructional and counseling purposes.

10. Since continuous progress programs focus
more on the learning needs, the social
needs, and emotional needs of the students,
the programs are problem-solving in nature,
and result in a substantial reduction in behavior problems.

11. There is greater awareness of student individuality since meeting the individual needs
of students is at the heart of the continuous progress program.

12. Where team teaching is used, there are
greater opportunities for sharing insights
on learner needs and progress.

13. There is no limit for the learning aspira-
tions of students in a continuous progress
program.

14. There is no fear of encroachment on materials supposedly reserved for another grade.

15. The "norm" in the continuous progress program is the individual student. Pressures
for meeting end-of-term goals normally found
in the age-graded programs are avoided. The
placement of the student depends upon his
readiness, capacity, competence, and
social/emotional needs.[4]

---

[4]Maurie Hillson and Ronald T. Hyman, eds., Change
and Innovation in Elementary and Secondary Organization. Chicago: Holt, Rinehart, and Winston,
Inc., 1971 (Second Edition), pp. 35-36.

Disadvantages of
Continuous Progress Education

As with any program, there are disadvantages.
The disadvantages are not cited by those engaging
in continuous progress education but are enumerated
by those who have a stake in maintaining the status
quo. Those who have been involved in continuous
progress programs are more likely to view difficulties in innovative programs as problems to be
overcome. As the reader surveys the disadvantages,
listed below, it should be remembered that such
disadvantages can be overcome by adequate leadership in the central administration and at the local
school level.

1. Parents and teachers have been brought up
   in a graded atmosphere, and have a grade-
   mindedness bias.

2. Establishing continuous progress programs
   requires development of new curricula or
   the programs will develop into mini-grades
   called levels.

3. There is a greater need for program articulation in such a design; otherwise, the
   student could suffer discontinuity as a
   result of going from an open system to a
   closed one.

4. School curricula are still organized around
   graded textbooks and topics. The effort
   required to create curriculum materials
   based on a continuum of skills and concepts
   is excessive.

5. The teaching in a continuous progress pro-
   is more demanding and difficult.

6. Special teacher preparation is required,
   including development of inservice programs.

7. Continuous progress requires greater staff

diversity in order to be successful.

8.  Continuous progress requires new record-
    keeping and reporting practices since the
    traditional marking systems are no longer
    consistent with the aims of continuous
    progress education. These new developments
    take additional time. Record-keeping and
    reporting practices are sensitive areas.[5]

This list of disadvantages contains pitfalls to
be avoided. It is certainly true, for example,
that the lay public and many of the professional
educators have "grown up" on the age-graded mode of
organization. The graded organization has been
with us for over 100 years. Its continued viability
rests on its simplicity. It is easier to administer
a staff of forty or more if the staff members are
separated (divided) into single classrooms, given
separate teaching supplies, and mass-purchased textbooks which can be bought for a cut rate. Easier
and cheaper are equated with better.

Administrators who are saying continuous progress is too difficult may be saying that they don't
believe teachers and administrators are dedicated
enough to make it work. But is the age-graded
school, begun at Boston's Quincy Grammar School in
1848, really the appropriate organization for
schools of the 1980's? Playing one teacher or department off against the other, a common practice in
age-graded schools, stifles professional and program development. Further, the age-graded model
has no research basis whatever. It continues
because it is easier, and its continued presence
is a manifestation of culture lag. This condition
can be overcome by a conscious, long-term public
education effort, inservice programs for the professional staff, and hiring policies which have
continuous progress programs in mind.

_____

[5]Ibid., p. 38.

## Making Continuous Progress a Reality

Before starting, the school leader needs to realize that the movement toward continuous progress education will be a time-consuming one. The message conveyed by school principals and supporting staff in central offices is basically the same; "It takes <u>years</u> to develop the staff and adapt curricular models and school organization to reach the continuous progress level of functioning."

Daniel Purdom in <u>Exploring the Nongraded School</u>[6] has set forth a list of propositions for the conceptual model of the continuous progress school:

1.  The school assists each learner in developing his potential to the maximum.

2.  The curriculum emphasizes the development of the broad structural concepts and modes of inquiry in the disciplines.

3.  Learning opportunities are provided on the basis of individual needs, interests, and abilities.

4.  All phases of human growth are considered when making decisions about how to work effectively with a learner.

5.  Learning opportunities are paced so that each child can progress in relation to his own rate of development in each area of the curriculum.

6.  An evaluation of all phases of human growth is made for each individual.

---

[6]Daniel M. Purdom, <u>Exploring the Nongraded School</u> (Dayton, Ohio: Institute for the Development of Educational Activities, Inc., 1970).

7. Evaluation of each learner's progress is carried on almost constantly.

8. The adequacy of each child's progress is an individual matter determined by appraising his attainments in relation to estimates of his potential.

9. The school is organized to facilitate continuous and cumulative learning for each learner throughout his schooling.

10. The school is so structured that there are alternate learning environments available to the individual and alternate opportunities within their environments to progress at different rates and work at different levels in each area of the curriculum.

11. Each learner uses his own interests and needs to help establish the objectives he will pursue. [7]

These propositions about the continuous progress school are excellent descriptions of an ideal, but how does a staff begin to approximate these functions?

Assessing the current status of the school program is a necessary first step. It would be reasonable to assume that a given school would be strong in some areas, perhaps approaching the ideal, and traditional in other areas, closer to the age-graded model.

The extent to which a school is approximating continuous progress functions can be assessed by using an instrument created by Donald Purdom. [8]

---

[7] Ibid. p. 16.

[8] Donald M. Purdom, A Conceptual Model of the Nongraded School, unpublished Ed.D. dissertation, U.C.L.A., 1968, pp. 92-143.

The information derived would do much to clarify
whether a school is approximating the ideal, or only
claiming to be.

The best way to ensure that the school will
function this way is to hire staff who accept this
definition of school purpose and who will work to
implement such a program. Without such acceptance
of purpose, much conflict and little success will
result.

It is an unusual circumstance which allows
wholesale hiring of new staff for a new program. It
is more likely that the success of the change to
continuous progress will hinge on the hiring of some
new staff members and inservice training of others.
The most crucial factor in making an innovation
function at the instructional level is staff reedu-
cation, and the kind of program called for in this
instance is one carried on intensely and continuously over a period of time, such as two or three years.

Preparatory to launching the change program,
local school leadership must gain a fundamental
understanding of school purpose, defined as helping
the learner fully develop his potential. The following sources should be examined carefully:

1.  B. Frank Brown, The Appropriate Placement
    School: A Sophisticated Nongraded Curricu-
    lum. West Nyack, New York: Parker Publish-
    ing Co., 1965.

2.  B. Frank Brown, The Nongraded High School.
    Englewood Cliffs, New Jersey: Prentice Hall,
    1963.

3.  John Goodlad and Robert Anderson, The Non-
    graded Elementary School. New York:
    Harcourt Brace and World, Inc., 1963
    (Revised).

4. Glen Heathers, "School Organization: Non-grading Dual Progress, and Team Teaching" in The Changing American School, Sixty-Fifth Yearbook of the National Society for the Study of Education, Part II, ed. J. I. Goodlad. Chicago: University of Chicago Press, 1966.

5. Virgil Howes, et al., Individualization of Instruction: A Search. Los Angeles: Educational Inquiry, Inc., 1967.

Next, the school staff must develop the broad conceptual framework for the curriculum. An understanding of the nature of key concepts and discipline structure can be gleaned from the following sources:

1. Jerome Bruner, The Process of Education. Cambridge: Harvard University Press, 1962.

2. Stanley Elam, ed., Education and the Structure of Knowledge, Fifth Annual Phi Delta Kappa Symposium on Educational Research. Chicago: Rand McNally and Co., 1964.

3. Dorothy M. Fraser, "Deciding What to Teach." Planning and Organizing for Teaching. Washington, D. C.: National Education Association, 1963, pp. 53-70.

4. John I. Goodlad, The Changing School Curriculum. New York: The Fund for the Advancement of Education, 1966.

The curriculum planner will need to use several techniques in identifying the broad concepts and inquiry modes in the various disciplines. These include consultation with subject matter specialists, investigating new curricular projects and materials developed by scholars, and surveying publications of learned societies.

In order to achieve the capability of diagnosing and prescribing appropriate instructional procedures

and materials for the learner, attention must be given
to developing a greater range of instructional resources.

The following considerations are essential:

1. Study budgeting and purchasing procedures with
   an eye toward reallocation of resources.
   Textbook money might be used to purchase
   trade books, some textbooks, audio-visual
   aids, and special reference materials,
   rather than numerous copies of the same
   textbook.

2. Establish a central resource area in order to
   reduce duplication and make a wider range
   of resources available.

3. Identify community resources such as places
   to visit and people with special skills.

4. Purchase self-teaching materials to enhance
   the self-pacing aim of continuous progress
   programs. Programmed learning materials seem
   most likely examples, with special map
   skills, study skills and reading kit materials now on the market which have self-
   checking features. Computer-assisted
   instruction looms on the horizon as break-
   through in this area, but costs are currently
   high for total application.

Establishing an adequate record-keeping system
which can record all phases of human growth is
essential if such data are to be used in working with
the learner and in reporting to parents and other
staff members. For example, data on social development, intelligence, aptitude, peer relationships,
teacher observation, interest inventories, and
attitudes ought to be included.

The prime consideration in development of a
record-keeping system for continuous progress edu-

cation is <u>simplicity</u>. The system must be simple
enough for students to enter and leave learning
activities, whether these be short units, learning
centers, laboratory areas, or learning packages
without the need to reorganize whole classes or
roomfuls of students.

Figure 1 is an example of such simplicity in
terms of student progress individualized learning
pacs. There are two main components to this simple
system: a wall chart and a notebook using a single
sheet for each pupil. Both wall chart and notebook
have the advantages of being accessible and allowing
students to be added or deleted as movement occurs.
Note that the wall chart has the students listed
alphabetically on the left with the pac titles
listed at the top of the chart. As the student
completes the package, his square under the appropriate pac is marked in some way indicating that it
is completed. In the teacher's notebooks, the
individual student's progress on a given pac is duly
recorded.

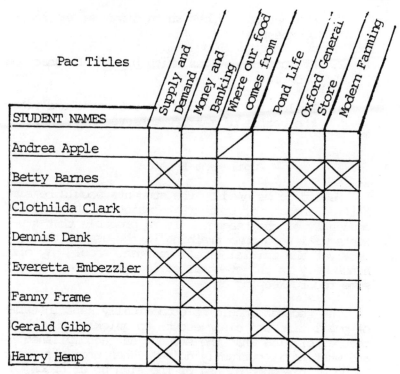

Figure 1:  Wall Chart[9]

| STUDENT NAMES | Supply and Demand | Money and Banking | Where our food comes from | Pond Life | Oxford General Store | Modern Farming |
|---|---|---|---|---|---|---|
| Andrea Apple | | | / | | | |
| Betty Barnes | X | | | | X | X |
| Clothilda Clark | | | | | X | |
| Dennis Dank | | | | X | | |
| Everetta Embezzler | X | X | | | | |
| Fanny Frame | | X | | | | |
| Gerald Gibb | | | | X | | |
| Harry Hemp | X | | | | X | |

Some records should be kept by the students themselves, others by teachers.  In preparing the record-
keeping system, the teacher must ask himself two
questions.  (1) "What must I know about the student?"
(2) "How often do I need to know this?"  The answers
to these two questions will enable the teacher to
design different kinds of record-keeping devices for
the students and the teacher to keep.  Instructional
pacs which take several days to complete require
an evaluation-record keeping system which contains
the following:

[9]McLean, Harvard W. and Killian, David L., How
to Construct Individualized Learning Pacs.  Dubuque:
Kendall/Hunt Publishing Company, 1973, p. 50.

1.  Evaluation devices which diagnose and record
    weaknesses.

2.  Evaluation devices which provide feedback on
    progress.

3.  Evaluation devices which determine and record
    the degree of mastery achieved.

## Pupil-Kept Records

Record forms used by the students should be simplified enough for students to maintain them independently of the teacher.  It is probable that students will need some training in the use of the system, yet the initial time investment should pay off
handsomely in the eventual saving of teachers from
some record-keeping chores.

The records should be economically kept in terms
of pupil time and clear enough to quickly show the
teacher or aide what the student has accomplished
and what he is currently doing.  When projects are to
be done in sequence, use of the sign up or check
sheet can be maintained easily by the student:  he
merely checks off the learning tasks completed.  In
a different kind of program where students have the
option to select activities in any order, a control
sheet or card can be used, with the activity titles
listed and the student circling the title he is
currently working on.  Later, upon finishing the
activity, the student may place an X through the
circle as shown in Figure 2.

| John Brent (name) | CONTINUOUS PROGRESS--Science | |
|---|---|---|
| Pollution | Food Chain | Volcanism |
| Oceans | Ice Age | Pond Life |
| (Metamorphic Rocks) | Galileo | Tycho Brahe |

Figure 2: Student's Control Sheet[10]

Figure 2 illustrates the individual student's control card. The teacher (or aide) can tell at a glance what the student has done and is currently working on.

Missing from these examples are indicators as to whether objectives have been met and to what extent pupils are experiencing success. Bar graphs are an excellent means of showing scores on activity post-assessments. If the teacher and pupils think it desirable (and the best forms of evaluation grow out of cooperative processes), the student's control card could be altered to show post-assessment scores. As shown in Figure 3, the filled-in bar graph would indicate completion of the activity and the level of success on the post-assessment.

[10]Ibid., p. 51.

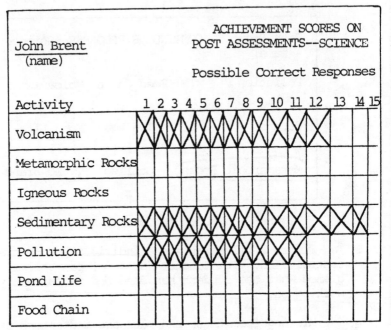

Figure 3:  Individual Student's Control Card[11]

[11]Ibid., p. 52.

The best forms of evaluation assess the extent
to which established goals and objectives have been
met.  Assuming the objectives can be assessed via
pencil and paper, the response items on the post-
assessment instrument could be grouped by objectives
so that the teacher and student could readily tell
which objectives have been met and which ones may
require "recycling."  Figure 4 illustrates a chart
showing this kind of feedback.

By grouping response items by objective and
charting them as in Figure 4, both student and
teacher can quickly ascertain that Objectives I and
III were attained, but Objective II  with only three
correct responses out of five, was not.

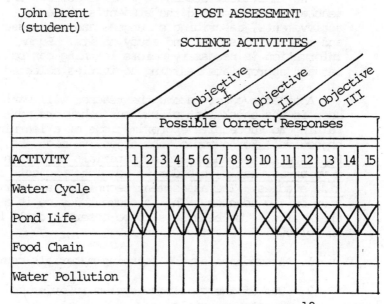

John Brent                    POST ASSESSMENT
(student)
                              SCIENCE ACTIVITIES

|  | Possible Correct Responses | | | | | | | | | | | | | | |
|---|---|---|---|---|---|---|---|---|---|---|---|---|---|---|---|
| ACTIVITY | 1 | 2 | 3 | 4 | 5 | 6 | 7 | 8 | 9 | 10 | 11 | 12 | 13 | 14 | 15 |
| Water Cycle | | | | | | | | | | | | | | | |
| Pond Life | X | X | X | X | X | X | X | X | X | X | X | X | X | X | X |
| Food Chain | | | | | | | | | | | | | | | |
| Water Pollution | | | | | | | | | | | | | | | |

Figure 4:  Student Achievement Card[12]

[12]Ibid.

The types of records kept by the pupil can also
include subjective rating scales whereby the student
can evaluate his own work and check whether he thinks
it is Very Good, Satisfactory, or Needs Improvement.

## Teacher-Kept Records

Carefully designed teacher-kept records are an
absolute necessity if teachers are to successfully
implement continuous progress education. Such
records enable the teacher to plan the individual
student's program. The design which a specific
record will take depends on the purpose for which it
is intended.

The individual student's profile assists the
teacher in determining the student's academic
achievements, describing strengths and weaknesses,
and indicating social and study habits. Such
information is necessary before learning can be
set and appropriate learning activities selected.

Another type of record the teacher will want to
keep is the check list of student behaviors pertaining to successive approximations of a learning
objective. For example, the objective might be,
Pupils will use the learning materials center on
a voluntary basis in order to complete projects and
side studies. The assessment technique is observation by the teacher. The assessment device is a
check list. The behaviors to be observed could be
as follows:

1. Attendance at the learning materials center.

2. Use of the catalogue system in order to
   locate materials.

3. Use of a variety of learning materials to
   complete a project.

4. Voluntarily going to the learning materials
   center when time is available.

Figure 5 illustrates the type of check list which would be useful in recording progress on this objective.

| BEHAVIORS: | Attendance | Catalogue System | Variety of Materials | Goes Voluntarily | Observer Comments |
|---|---|---|---|---|---|
| Jan. 5 | | | ⊠ | (Assigned by Teacher) | |
| Jan. 12 | ⊠ | | | (Assigned by Teacher) | Needed Assistance from Librarian |
| Jan. 17 | ⊠ | | ⊠ | (Assigned by Study Group) | Used Catalogue Well |
| Feb. 3 | ⊠ | | | (Assigned by Study Group) | No Reluctance—Worked Readily |
| Feb. 10 | ⊠ | | | | |

X = participation

Observer Summary: Excellent progress over a five-week period. Growth in independent use of materials. Last attendance was for individual study.

Figure 5[13]

In managing a system of records for groups and for individuals, the teacher still must keep a perspective on the overall progress of the class. For this purpose, a class profile sheet is indispensable in each academic area for the core team in

---

[13]Ibid., p. 54.

the middle school. The matter is simplified for the
secondary school subject-matter specialist. The
profile sheet can be in the form of a chart based
on the teacher's class list and provide spaces for
subject-matter data. These data could be depicted
as check lists, graphs, a series of scores or a
tally. The class profile sheet can assist the
teacher in planning the grouping of students with
specific learning needs.

Organizing the faculty into teams facilitates
planning. With provisions made for a common
planning time, members of the team can discuss the
students' performances in all areas and develop
instructional units which meet the needs and
interests assigned to the team. The area of team
teaching is so crucial that a subsequent chapter
is devoted to this topic.

Although evaluation is also a separate chapter,
a few ideas concerning this topic will be presented
here. A teacher needs to have knowledge about the
status of the learner such as abilities, current
needs, and interests, all of which are derived from
the evaluative process.

If all phases of human growth are to be
considered in creating learning environments, evaluation will have to be carried on continuously, and
a variety of assessment settings and instruments
will need to be identified.

Use of The Mental Measurement Yearbook[14] and
Tests in Print[15] are a good beginning point in
searching for a variety of commercially prepared
assessment instruments. Specialists in various

---

[14]Oscar K. Buros, ed., The Mental Measurement
Yearbook (Highland Park, New Jersey: Gryphon Press,
1970).

[15]Oscar K. Buros, ed., Tests in Print (Highland
Park, New Jersey, Gryphon Press, 1970).

forms of evaluation can be contacted, such as the
reading specialist from the area university who can
suggest the most effective diagnostic instruments
for comprehension or work attack skills.

There are areas for which instruments are not
readily available. In such cases, other plans must
be made. Assessment of emotional maturity could be
an example. It is likely that the development of
questionnaires, interviews and observation check
lists would allow staff to infer emotional maturity.

Once the necessary tools and procedures have
been identified for the evaluation system, an in-
service program must be undertaken to assure that
the staff will be able to use the tools and procedures.

Because of the continuity of the evaluation task
in the continuous progress school, it is important
that as many self-assessing instructional materials
and instruments be purchased as possible. This
promotes implementation of the evaluation program
and self-reliance as well.

Given the tremendous variability among the
students of middle school age it should be obvious
that no one learning environment would be sufficient.
Seeking variations in learning environments is one
of the most important tasks of the school leader
and his staff. Several approaches can be used to
inject alternatives in the learning program.

1.  Manipulate the peer group through multiaging
    via creation of age ranges in instructional
    groups of two or three years. A talented
    twelve-year-old may not have sufficient
    challenge if he is placed only with other
    twelve-year-olds. Other approaches in
    alteration of the peer groups include
    placing the learner with a group of more
    socially mature learners, or less (or more)
    academically talented learners.

2. Alternate the modes of instruction.
   Instruction can be provided through use of
   machines, teachers, or use of independent
   study materials, and in a variety of
   groupings. Some learners need to have a
   teacher present; others learn best in peer
   groups which are allowed to interact. Some
   students prefer printed matter; others audio-
   visual materials.

3. Vary the expected performance levels for the
   learners. Given the fact that learners
   within themselves vary in their ability to
   perform in different curricular and extra
   curricular functions, it is clear that
   numerous levels of proficiency must be
   provided for. Some students will pursue a
   given academic area with vigor and to a
   sophisticated extent with highly specialized
   materials; others will not have such a
   capability, and will need middle or low-
   level demands on their capacities.

4. Organize the students into units which span
   several years and which represent a fairly
   wide range of instruction.[16] A learner
   could go outside the unit for special
   instruction if necessary. The units would
   operate on a continuous basis, and students
   would not move from unit to unit according
   to the calendar, but according to need.
   The change from one unit to the next would
   be based on needs for different peer groups,
   for a different teacher, for a change in
   instructional mode, or special academic
   subject need.

---

[16]Purdom, Exploring the Nongraded School, p. 35.

The middle school movement has been identified with many innovations in education. The common theme of these innovations has been to tailor instruction to the individual needs, interests, and abilities of pre-adolescents.

The implementation of a continuous progress program will be a difficult project to undertake. The suggestions in this chapter should be viewed as points of departure only. It is hoped that they will provide challenge, stimulate ideas, and lead to further study.

Chapter 3

FLEXIBLE SCHEDULING

## Introduction

Scheduling of any type is effective only to the degree that it facilitates accomplishment of organizational goals. In other words, scheduling is not an end in itself. Any contemplated change in scheduling should face the same rigorous examination given to the current schedule. Any schedule adopted will prove to have built-in frustrations, inconveniences and some undesireable side affects.

Considering all of the above, why should the administrative leader add to the complexities of his role by moving to flexible schedules? Simply because when done effectively, flexible scheduling can improve the educational experiences of boys and girls as well as provide a greater opportunity for teachers to effectively utilize available time, resources, facilities and staff.

## Elements of the Scheduling Process

A novice school administrator faced with a scheduling task is likely to initiate his or her efforts with an attempt to organize the time element. This common error leads to a great deal of wasted effort. The sequence is vital. In any scheduling process one whould consider the following sequence:

1. A list of each course to be offered needs to be made, including the number of inquiry and assembly groups called for each day of the week.

2. The number of students electing each course and assigned to each special section must be tabulated.

3. The number of sections of inquiry groups for each course is then determined, conforming to the specifications developed by

the teaching staff.

4. The number of rooms available and each specialized facility in each content area needs to be specified.

5. The sequential arrangement of meetings per week required for each size learning group must be identified.

6. The length of each learning group, determined by its purpose, needs to be stated.[1]

Organize data to include the background for each of the following:

1. Number and type of spaces available at any one time.

2. Staff available

3. Enrollment by type to be scheduled

   A. Sex
   B. Grade level
   C. Elective selection
   D. Special considerations

4. List of courses requiring special facilities:

   Physical Education   -   Gymnasium
   General Science      -   Laboratory
   Band                 -   Music Room

5. List all courses offered that will have only one section.  List those with only two sections per day and perhaps those with only three sections.

Armed with the above information, examine your planned flexible format by asking the following questions:

1.  Will the schedule provide teachers with an
    opportunity for varied use of time?  Can we
    schedule long films, field trips, guest
    speakers, extended sessions, group activi-
    ties.

2.  Will the existing facilities house the
    proposed schedule or will we need another
    gym, science room, art room, etc.?

3.  Do we have enough teachers to staff this
    schedule or has the planned schedule
    actually reduced teacher contact ratios.

4.  Can we actually schedule the student elec-
    tives or will we be forced to schedule stu-
    dents arbitrarily into enrichment classes?

Other similar questions could be asked, but by
now one is aware of the considerations that need to
be examined prior to any change in scheduling practices.  A degree of security for the administrator
and the teacher exists in the traditional six or
eight period schedule.  The repetitious nature of
this type schedule gives students a predictable
day.

These security factors coupled with a natural
anxiety toward an unknown frequently lead educators
to resist more flexible schedules.  They submerge in
their minds all those missed opportunities for
enrichment, interrupted learning sessions, deleted
audio visual experiences, unproductive time sessions,
rejected class plans due to unavailable time, facilities, and other equally discouraging factors.
Usually we hear the explanation for this avoidance
of scheduling changes expressed as a cry against
further meddling with the classroom experience.

Let's contrast some of the scheduling elements
between an effective traditional schedule and an
effective flexible schedule.

|                 | Traditional                                                              | Flexible                                                                          |
| --------------- | ------------------------------------------------------------------------ | -------------------------------------------------------------------------------- |
| **Time**        | Class meets 45 minutes daily.                                            | Class meets any part of 90 minutes or more as need for time exists.              |
|                 | Class ends when 45 minutes is up.                                       | Class ends when learning value of experience starts to drop.                    |
|                 | Class meets daily all semester or all year.                             | Class meets as planned by teaching team within broad guidelines.                |
| **Space**       | Science room is available 45 minutes daily.                             | Science room is scheduled for time needed to do activity planned.               |
|                 | Gym class is daily, 45 minutes per day minus two changing times.       | Gym is required as a part of a total learning team and can meet irregularly but for extended times if needed. |
|                 | Lunch is 45 minutes for everybody.                                      | Lunch fits a flexible schedule that only limits the total flow of students.     |
| **Staff**       | I teach science 6 periods a day.                                        | As a member of the science team I plan my time to be the most effective student helper. |
|                 | I teach my students and you teach yours. My classes vary from 36 to 14 students. | I am part of a team of teachers and we determine class size based upon the type of activity. |

The above examples indicate that an educational
experience can be provided by either schedule.  However, time becomes the master in the traditional
schedule.  All elements of the educational process
must become subservient to the time plan.  This will
lead relentlessly to reduced learning opportunities
for students and to less than professional existence
for teachers.  The master of any truly effective
schedule is the educational needs of the students
to be served.

This treatment of the problems of time utilization is by necessity brief, since time utilization
is not the major justification for flexible schedules.  Improved educational experiences for boys
and girls must result from the change in scheduling
or no change should be undertaken.  It serves no
purpose to spend time examining any of the many
"flops" resulting from supposedly well intended
scheduling gimmicks.  Your schedule will of necessity
be a living, changing, open ended document or it
will be only a control device.

Perhaps a brief explanation of support systems
and devices would serve to add clarity to the
positions that the schedule is a result of applied
human effort and that most if not all of these
wonder devices are wasted money.

Computers, Magnetic Boards and Silly Putty

Given a choice, one would choose silly putty
because it is at least fun to play with and to shape.
Silly putty will not help with scheduling but then
neither will a magnetic board, a sorting needle, a
card deck, or in most cases a computer.

A computer can be of assistance if you have "on
line" capacity.  "Batch type" schedules are totally
unacceptable.  Let's look at both types of computer
applications.  A batch operation exists when you
send material to a computer center, wait for a print
out, correct conflicts, send in another set of

materials, wait, etc., etc., etc. You can see that
any changes in the original "flexible" schedule
are very difficult to make and would be time con-
suming.

On line computer scheduling exists when you have
a terminal in your building and you can communicate
data to the computer via telephone and get immediate
return information on a monitor screen. This has
some possibilities for scheduling. It certainly
has value in rapidly determining conflicts in
schedules and testing possible alternative solutions
to conflicts.

Generally, these are needed for scheduling of a
middle school:

1. Good communication channels with the faculty
2. A chalkboard
3. Background data (listed earlier)
4. Pencils and paper
5. Duplicating machinery
6. Secretarial service

This doesn't sound too sophisticated or scientific but it will get the administrators' and the
teachers' parts of flexible scheduling accomplished.

## Myths That Must Be Eliminated

To administer a flexible schedule requires a
great deal of trust and confidence in a school
faculty. The administrator must have a willingness
to share decision making with the other professionals
on the team.

Prior to the move to flexible schedules, broadly
based acceptance of the following is needed:

1. It is not necessary for every class or any
   class to meet daily or at the same time
   every day.

2.  Other teachers could add to the value of
    my teaching if we worked together.

3.  There is no optimum pupil-teacher ratio
    that makes one class size ideal for all
    types of e ucational experiences.

4.  All subjects do not need approximately equal
    time to be effectively presented. Some sub-
    jects would benefit with longer sessions while
    others could best be presented in shorter
    sessions.

5.  Teachers are the very best people to decide
    the final time utilization schedule.

6.  Just because it didn't work in a neighboring
    school does not mean that it does not work.

7.  The State will not punish us for adopting a
    variable time schedule. Required minimum
    time exposures coming to schools from state
    agencies allow for teacher-principal judge-
    ment and are intended to be minimum rather
    than required daily time constraints.

If you have confidence in accepting the above
mentioned positions, it is time to address the rigid
part of the flexible schedule.

## Basic Cycles

All schedules are designed to repeat on some
regular cycle. The most rigid basic cycle would be
the daily cycle, where every day basically repeats
the schedule of the previous day. Illustration one
presents a daily cycle based upon a 45 minute time
module.

Illustration #1   -   Daily Cycle

| Time | Smith | Jones | Miller | South |
|------|-------|-------|--------|-------|
| 8:30- 9:15 | Art-8A | Math-7 | Science 7 | Pe-6 |
| 9:20-10:05 | Prep. | Math-7 | Science 6 | Pe-7 |
| 10:10-10:55 | Art-8B | Math-6 | Prep | Pe-8 |
| 11:00-11:45 | Art-7A | Math-8 | Lunch | Lunch |
| 11:50-12:35 | Lunch | Lunch | Science 6 | Pe-8 |
| 12:40- 1:25 | Art 6 | Math-6 | Science 7 | Pe-7 |
| 1:30- 2:15 | Art 6 | Math-8 | Science 8 | Pe-6 |
| 2:20- 3:05 | Art 7B | Prep | Science 8 | Prep |

Note:  A student schedule would replicate
daily and would regularly consist of 45
minute segments just as the teachers
schedule replicates daily on the 45
minute module.

A weekly cycle allows for some variation in the
daily routine and frequently in the time available.

Illustration two presents a possible weekly
schedule for a student based upon a 45 minute module
and a weekly cycle.

Illustration #2
The Weekly Cycle   -   Student Schedule

| Time | Mon. | Tues. | Wed. | Thur. | Fri. |
|------|------|-------|------|-------|------|
| 8:30- 9:15 | Math | Math | Math | Math | Math |
| 9:20-10:05 | Vocal Music | P.E. | Vocal Music | P.E. | Vocal Music |
| 10:10-10:55 | Art | P.E. | Art | P.E. | Art |
| 11:00-11:45 | Lunch | Lunch | Lunch | Lunch | Lunch |
| 11:50-12:35 | Soc. St. | Soc. St. | Soc. St. | Soc. St. | Lang. Arts |
| 12:40- 1:25 | Soc. St. | Lang. Arts | Lang. Arts | Lang. Arts | Lang. Arts |
| 1:30- 2:15 | Sci. | Sci. | Sci. | Sci. | Sci. |
| 2:20-3:05 | Speech | Study Hall | Speech | Study Hall | Speech |

The modifications included in illustration two
do not allow for flexible use of time. The added
time for social studies on Monday or for Language
Arts on Friday are manipulations intended to avoid
time constraints. Double physical education
sessions and alternating classes are similar, well
intended attempts to provide flexibility in the
basic schedules, but fall far short of this goal.

Utilizing the weekly cycle and the 45 minute
module let us take the next step. We can examine a
rather simple application of block time scheduling
with team teaching added to provided possible variations.

Illustration #3
Block Scheduling With Team Teaching

| Time | Mon. | Tues. | Wed. | Thurs. | Fri. |
|---|---|---|---|---|---|
| 8:30- 9:15<br>9:20-10:05 | L.A.<br>and<br>Soc. St. | L.A.<br>and<br>Soc. St. | L.A.<br>and<br>Soc. St. | L.A.<br>and<br>Soc. St. | L.A. &<br>Soc.<br>St. |
| 10:10-10:55 | P.E. | Vocal<br>Music | P.E. | Vocal<br>Music | P.E |
| 11:00-11:45 | Lunch | Lunch | Lunch | Lunch | Lunch |
| 11:50-12:35 | Math<br>and<br>Science | Math<br>and<br>Science | Math<br>and<br>Science | Math<br>and<br>Science | Math<br>and<br>Sci |
| 1:30- 2:15 | Unified<br>Art | Speech<br>Health | Unified<br>Art | Speech<br>Health | Unif.<br>Art |

This student schedule opens some opportunities
for teachers to plan daily time usage between two
subject areas. The principal has blocked out a 90
minute time and scheduled a group of students with
a team of teachers who are responsible for instruction in two areas. A similar circumstance could

exist in the art programs as scheduled in this example.

Flexible schedules are basically extensions of the changes reflected in illustration three. The choice of a basic time module is usually an arbitrary decision. It is difficult to realistically defend the merits of a 30 minute, 20 minute, 15 minute or similar module opposed to other options. The relationship of the time block to the flexibility sought is the key factor.

Selection of the cycle can be argued. The weekly cycle for scheduling may be preferred because it can be easily explained to students, teachers, parents and other interested parties.

The "float day" type of schedule is often more confusing to students than the worth of the additional benefits.

It seem appropriate for us to look at a truly flexible schedule at this time. This is a schedule that is simple to organize and to construct, that utilizes the abilities of all faculty members while providing great latitude for time utilization.

## Two-Phase Scheduling

The two phase schedule was successfully utilized for several years at Chippewa Middle School located in the Saginaw, Michigan area. The schedule was the result of collecting and combining teacher and administrator suggestions. Following is a step by step review of how to construct a two-phase schedule.

Step one: List all possible courses offerings for each grade level. Courses open to students in more than one grade level should be listed at each available level.

Step two: Following each course entry, write a description of the preferred delivery format for that course. Include special facilities,

Step four: Armed with all of the data generated
in the first three steps, schedule a series of
faculty sessions. Examine the student selections,
sections of classes needed, possible staffing
problems and any other considerations. After
you have resolved as many of the general concerns
as possible, address the topic of which courses
could benefit in content enrichment by being
scheduled in a block with other courses or even
with a single course correlation. Examine time
limits listed in the delivery format requests and
determine possible time blocks. Note that you
need to respect the basic interrelated nature of
any schedule so adjust your net time for any
block to a multiple of your basic time module.

Example

| | |
|---|---|
| Courses: | Basic Speech (Elective), Language Arts (Required), Social Studies (Required), Foreign Language (Elective), Reading Clinic (Arranged). Basic Time Module 45 Min. |
| Staffing: | 3 Full Staff (Language & Social Studies) 3 Resource Staff (Speech, Reading, Foreign Language) 120 Students. |
| Time Delivery: | Language Arts, 45 Min. Daily Avg. Social Studies, 45 Min. Daily Avg. Speech, 45 Min (Twice/Week) Foreign Language, 45 Min (Twice/Week) Reading Clinic, Variable Time Demands |
| Facilities: | Facilities offering large, medium and small group settings plus areas for independent study. |

Possible Phase One Arrays

| Time 135 Min or 3 Basic 45 Min Time Modules | Rooms: 101-102-103<br><br>Staff: 3 Lan. Arts & Soc. St.-Full Block<br>1 Foreign Lang. 2 Mod. Only<br>1 Speech 1 or 2 Mod.<br>Reading Specialist on Demand Basis |
|---|---|

| Time 120 Min or 6 Basic 20 Min Time Modules | Rooms: 101-102-103<br><br>Staff: 3 Full Time L.A. & Soc. Std.<br>1 Foreign Lang.-Modes 1-2-5-6<br>1 Speech-Modes 3-4-5-6<br>1 Reading - On Demand Basis |
|---|---|

After numerous block arrangements have been
examined by the staff a decision is made regarding
the basic time module, correlations of subject matter,
team compositions, facilities, student enrollments
available (available placements), other problem
areas to be discussed and resolved.

Step five: After all possible decisions listed
in step four have been made, reviewed, adjusted
and finalized, start the more clerical aspects of
Scheduling. Using the student elective selection
sheets generated in step 3, construct a conflict
matrix for all single, double and possible triple
section offerings. If you have computer assistance available you can obtain a conflict matrix
from the computer center. You can easily generate your own matrix as shown in the examples
below.

| Course | Creative Writing | Band (1) | Speech II (2) | French (2) |
|---|---|---|---|---|
| Creative Writing (1) | M | M | | |
| Band (1) | JF | | J | F |
| Speech II (2) | | | A | A |
| French (2) | | | | |

Mary elects:  Creative Writing and Band
John elects:  Band and Speech II
Alice elects: Speech II and French
Fred elects:  Band and French

Note initials rather than numbers have been entered in the chart as a method of helping you follow the process. Normally scores would be entered and then totaled.

Circled numbers behind course names indicate sections of a course to be offered.

A typical conflict matrix would look like the following example:

| Course | Creative Writing (1) | Band (1) | Speech II (2) | French (2) |
|---|---|---|---|---|
| Creative Writing (1) | ⁣TH̶L̶ (6) | ||| | | ||| |
| Band (1) | | TH̶L̶||| (11) | TH̶L̶ | ||| |
| Speech II (2) | | | ||| (8) | ||| |
| French (2) | | | | (9) |

Circled numbers included on the field of the matrix indicate possible conflicts for that offering. From our conflict matrix we can make several important scheduling decisions.

Examples:

a)  Six creative writing choices conflict with other single or double section offerings.

b)  Three creative writing students also selected band.

c)  If we schedule band and creative writing for the same period we will create three irreconcilable conflicts.

d)  The band group contains five students who also want Speech two and three who want French. Both Speech II and French are double offerings so no irreconcilable conflict exists.

e)  No conflicts exist between Creative Writing and Speech II.

As you study the conflicts you can begin to logically place your blocks on a schedule that eliminates or reduces conflicts. Please note that the conflict matrix lists single section offerings first, then double and finally triple section offerings. One could easily avoid placement of band students in a block time that offered Speech II and was scheduled at the same time as band. Further, if other sections of the block occur at other times, the five band students with conflicts shown in the matrix can be loaded first into the non conflicting block.[4]

Step six:  Continue to study the resolution of conflicts and move sections through various combinations until conflicts are eliminated. With patience it can be done. Use a chalk board to develop your master schedule grid based upon the basic time module. Simply block it off in neat

little squares that you can modify with an eraser.
Load one grade at a time beginning with the group
having the greatest array of electives available and working down to the group with the
fewest electives.  Do not load students at this
time, only sections to be taught.  Your master
grid could look something like the following
sections of a grid:

Example:

Language Arts - Social Studies Enrichment Block
135 Minute Block - Repeats Daily

| |
|---|
| Students = 80-90-Teachers 3 Full + Specialists |
| Rooms     = L.G.-2-M.G.-Comm. Space-Study Carrels |
| Subjects = Language Arts, Social Studies, Speech I & II, French I & II, Clinical Reading |

This block features a team of three teachers,
responsible for Language Arts and Social Studies, who
are supported by specialists part time on a flexible
schedule.

Example:

Unified Arts - Enrichment Cycle
90 Minute

| Team of 3 Teachers Teach up to 80 Students Unified Arts - Mon. Wed. & Fri. | |
|---|---|
| Vocal Music - 45 Min. Tues.-Thurs. | Vocal Music 45 Min. -T.-TH 40 students |
| Natural Resource 45 Min. Tues.-Thurs. | Natural Resources 45 Min. T.-TH 40 students |

This block features three 90 minute Unified Arts
sessions per week with two sessions each week of
90 minutes divided between Vocal Music and Natural
Resources. This arrangement provides longer work
sessions in art, flexible groupings in three subject
areas and opportunities for teachers to adjust time
allotments as needs arise.

Example:

General Science Team
45 Minute Period - Daily Cycle

> 3 Teachers provide General Science
> Instruction for up to 80 students.
> Large lab or adjoining small labs.

This offering provides opportunities for flexible grouping with a limited time frame. Added flexibility can be gained by mixing grade levels. To
mix grade levels the course content must be sequenced
and offered in a pattern to all involved grade levels.

Sub Example: In the above example students from
grades 7 and 8 would be mixed. All students
would spend the year in the physical sciences.
The following year would feature living sciences
for all students. By adjusting the variable of
curriculum content we have increased our ability
to put flexibility into our schedule and to
effectively utilize staff.

The above examples are only a few of the many
possible arrangements available when you are willing
to carefully study the variations available in any
one or more of the following:

> Time Modules
> Cycle Intervals
> Student Grade Groups
> Staff Teaming
> Curriculum Sequencing & Correlation
> Course Time Allotments

Once you have loaded your master grid with the
blocks and sections, you are ready to add total
spaces per module available for students. Be sure
each module has enough enrollments to accommodate each
grade level enrollment.

Step seven: Using your conflict matrix, double
check your master grid for conflicts and then
load students one at a time into the master grid.
Schedule those students first who have potential
schedule conflicts. Mix students as often as
possible and avoid scheduling students in
batches. In other words, do not develop class
sections of students that have identical
schedules. Your discipline concerns will be
reduced by thoroughly mixing students during a
typical day.

Once you have loaded students onto the master
grid you can send their individual schedules to the
secretary for processing.

Example:    Individual Student Schedule 45 Min.
            Mod. Weekly Cycle Features Correla-
            tion Block Schedule-Team Teaching

| Time | Subject | Room | Day |
|------|---------|------|-----|
| 8:30- 9:15<br>9:20-10:05<br>10:10-10:55 | Block-L.A.-S.S.<br>French II | 116 | Daily |
| 11:00-11:45 | Lunch | Cafe. | Daily |
| 11:50-12:35<br>12:40- 1:25 | Math-Science<br>Block | Lab<br>#1 | Daily |
| 1:30- 2:15<br>2:20- 3:05 | Phys. Ed.<br>Unified Arts | Gym<br>Art | Daily<br>Daily |

Example:    Individual Student Schedule 45 Min.
            Modified Weekly Cycle-Team Teaching-
            Block Design

| Time | Subject | | Room | Day |
|------|---------|---|------|-----|
| 8:30- 9:15 | Phys. Ed. | | Gym | Daily |
| 9:20-10:15 | U.A. | Nat. Res. | Art 106 | A-M.W.F. V.M.-T.TH |
| 10:10-10:55 | | V.M. | Music | N.R.-T.TH |
| 11:50-12:35 | Math & Science | | 124 & Lab II | Daily |
| 12:40- 1:25 1:30- 2:15 2:20- 3:05 | Lang. Arts- Social Studies- French I | | 127 | Daily |

As you finish phase one of your scheduling, you
have prepared class lists, room utilization schedules and other needed forms you feel would be helpful.
Copies of the master grid should be made and dupli-
cated for all staff members, custodians, etc.

Phase Two of Two Phase Scheduling

Prior to this point most of the steps listed
could be applied to all scheduling tasks. At this
point our earlier decisions now allow teams of
teachers to schedule time as they feel student needs
warrant. A Math-Science block team of three teachers
dealing with 75 students can easily schedule small
lab oriented sessions, large group audio visual
sessions, independent study, and other similar
experiences for students.

Team planning is the key to phase two success
and the principal should be active in and supportive
of team planning. Early trials and frustrations
should not be discouraging. As time passes, the
construction of daily block time utilization

schedules becomes less difficult and easily understood by students.

Planned time allotments should be based upon student need, enrichment, opportunities, nature of
activity planned and certainly not on such ill
advised conditions as equal time for unequal needs.

## Advantages of Two Phase Scheduling

Two phase scheduling offers a number of potential
advantages, some of which are listed below:

1. Everything needed is found within one
   building.

2. Teachers are involved continuously in the
   scheduling process.

3. Student needs can be accommodated.

4. No two days need to be identical but the
   master grid remains constant.

5. Laboratory courses can be scheduled into
   longer sessions as can physical education.

6. Team teaching enriches the educational experience for students.

7. Movement between separated areas of the
   school is reduced and less time is lost
   passing between classes.

8. Large group instruction is easily accomplished as are other size groupings.

9. Field trips become easier to accommodate.

10. Materials can be clustered for intensive
    usage.

These benefits are but a few that could be included. Interesting and challenging is the aspect that two phase scheduling can be advanced after a period of adjustment. Most other flexible scheduling concepts can be utilized in conjunction with this basic approach. For example, a float day plan can be included or the odd and even day alternating schedule can be added.

At this point you probably are tempted to replicate last year's schedule rather than get into this complicated plan. The first year or two will be learning experiences but if you continue to sharpen your procedure you can arrive at a position where scheduling involves very little frustration and where the time spent upon the task is minimal.

With this scheduling pattern, a principal and two assistants loaded the master grid with sections and scheduled six hundred students in just over two hours. There were zero conflicts and excellent faculty support for the process. This experience can be equalled by carefully preparing data step by step, involving teachers through the entire preparation stage and with support for teacher efforts in phase two scheduling.

Sample schedules are available in quantity from the National Middle School Resources Center and from various state middle school associations. Studying master grids does not provide much insight into the basic decisions that were needed to create the final compromise. Frequently master grids appear very complicated and often may discourage teachers and administrators from trying flexible schedules. For these reasons as well as for space considerations the master grids have been displayed in the appendix materials of this book.

Study these examples but avoid blanket adoption of any schedule. It probably won't work without serious modification and the modifications will create problems far more complex than those created by systematic development of your own schedule.

## Final Considerations

Flexible scheduling requires teacher team planning time. Flexible scheduling cannot be productive unless the administrators are secure individuals who openly share information, problems and concerns with the entire teaching staff.

In reality flexible scheduling becomes truly flexible only when final planning is in the hands of the teachers and students. Irregular schedules are not necessarily flexible.

Strange as it may seem it is advantageous to schedule in-service training sessions for teachers as a method of building their scheduling skills. Don't expect teachers to have had training in the area of scheduling. Often, even administrators have not had training other than those valuable lessons learned through experience. This experience and the shared experiences of other colleagues, such as those contained in this chapter, can help to overcome the training deficiency.

| TIME | M | MON., WED., FRIDAY | TUESDAY, THURSDAY |
|---|---|---|---|
| 8:15 A.M. | 1 | Homeroom | Homeroom |
| 8:20-9:00 | 2-6 | BAND elective or SPECIAL UNITS with cluster teachers | BAND elective or SPECIAL UNITS with cluster teachers |
| 9:10-10:20 | 7-14 | ACADEMIC UNITS with cluster teachers | ACADEMIC UNITS with cluster teachers |
| 10:30-11:10 | 15-19 | LUNCH | LUNCH |
| 11:20-11:50 | 20-23 | ACADEMIC UNITS | ACADEMIC UNITS |
| 12:00 P.M.-1:10 | 24-31 | PHYSICAL EDUCATION or STUDY SKILLS with cluster teachers (Specific Time Scheduled With P.E. Teachers) | PHYSICAL EDUCATION or STUDY SKILLS with cluster teachers |
| 1:20-2:40 | 32-40 | ACADEMIC UNITS with cluster teachers | EXPLORATORY ELECTIVES (one each semester) TEAM PLANNING TIME for cluster teachers |

FIGURE 2

POSSIBLE SCHEDULE - SIXTH GRADERS

18-MINUTE MODULES

| Module | Monday | Tuesday | Wednesday | Thursday | Friday |
|--------|--------|---------|-----------|----------|--------|
| 1<br>2<br>3<br>4<br>5 | INTERDISCIPLINARY BLOCK<br>(HUMANITIES)<br>Language     Social<br>Arts        Studies | | | | Indep. |
| 6<br><br>7<br><br>8 | Music | Art | Music | Art | Study<br>Reading<br>Skills<br>Develop.<br>Group<br>Guid. |
| 9<br>10<br>11 | SEQUENTIAL BLOCK<br>Math | | | | |
| 12 | LUNCH | | | | |
| 13<br>14<br>15<br>16<br>17 | SEQUENTIAL BLOCK<br>Science     Foreign Language | | | | |
| 18<br>19<br>20 | Phys.<br>Ed. | Shop<br><br>Home<br>Economics | Phys.<br>Ed. | Shop<br><br>Home<br>Economics | Phys.<br>Ed. |

## QUAD 7 - 6TH GRADE

| TIME (10 min. mods) | M | MONDAY WEDNESDAY TUESDAY THURSDAY FRIDAY | | |
|---|---|---|---|---|
| 8:35-9:45 | 1-7 | Unified Arts | Physical Education | Unified Arts<br>P.E. |
| 9:45-11:25 | 8-17 | Academics With The Team | | |
| 11:25-11:55 | 18-20 | Lunch | | |
| 11:55-12:55 | 21-26 | 6A Gen | Quad 7 Band<br>6B Gen | 6A Gen<br>6B Gen |
| 12:55-3:00 | 27-39 | Academics With The Team | | |

EFFECTIVE MIDDLE SCHOOL

## MASTER SCHEDULE

| Mod | Time | Grade 6 | Grade 7 | Grade 8 |
|-----|------|---------|---------|---------|
| HR | 8:00-8:10 | HOMEROOM | HOMEROOM | HOMEROOM |
| 1 | 8:10-8:40 | Problems | ↑ | Lang U.A. Mus |
| 2 | 8:40-9:10 | (E/SS/M/SC) | | Lang U.A. Mus / U.A. Mus PE |
| 3 | 9:10-9:40 | | Problems | U.A. Mus PE |
| 4 | 9:40-10:10 | ↓ | (E/SS/M/SC) | Lang   PE |
| 5 | 10:10-10:40 | Lang   PE | | Problems |
| 6 | 10:40-11:10 | U.A. Mus PE | | Problems |
| 7 | 11:10-11:40 | U.A. Mus PE / Lang U.A. Mus PE | ↓ | (E/SS/M/SC) |
| 8 | 11:40-12:10 | Lang U.A. Mus | Lunch | Lunch |
| 9 | 12:10-12:40 | Lunch | Lang   PE | Problems |
| 10 | 12:40-1:10 | Problems | U.A. Mus PE | Problems |
| 11 | 1:10-1:40 | Problems | U.A. Mus PE / Lang U.A. Mus PE | (E/SS/M/SC) |
| 12 | 1:40-2:10 | (E/SS/M/SC) | Lang U.S. Mus | |

TEAM TEACHING - AN OPPORTUNITY FOR CREATIVITY


The 1960's marked the beginning of significant
development in the current middle school movement.
A prolific growth of the middle school idea and a
simultaneous increase in the practice of team
teaching have come about primarily due to the
dependence of the two concepts upon one another.
These two educational concepts do belong together
because in each there is a commonality of basic
purposes. Each of these educational movements
includes a strong dedication to the individual
student's growth and well being. Both are attempting
to make it possible for teachers to bring a more
meaningful program to middle school students.

Many innovative and creative educational
practices are being utilized by today's active
middle schools. These approaches are designed to
specifically meet the requirements of the ten to
fourteen year old student. Team teaching has been
labeled as one of these creative techniques of
instruction. The modern and conscientious middle
school will find it difficult, if not impossible,
to neglect the incorporation of the team teaching
process in the courses of study designed for this
age group. Along with the other characteristics
of the middle school, team teaching has grown to
represent a new frontier for the utilization of the
varied talents and strengths of school personnel

Recently, eighteen basic characteristics were
developed by Georgiady, Riegle, and Romano relative
to the identification of a true middle school.[1]
Team teaching comprises one of these eighteen basic
characteristics. Thus, according to these researched
characteristics, the practice of team teaching

---

[1]Romano, Louis G., Nicholas P. Georgiady, and
James E. Heald, The Middle School: Selected Readings
on an Emerging School Program. (Chicago, Illinois:
Nelson-Hall Co., 1973), pp. 73-84.

becomes a significant factor in determining a good
middle school program. The incorporation of this
particular and basic characteristic provides students
in the middle school grades a needed chance to
interact with several adult persons. If properly
executed, team teaching will provide for the students
a selective group of resource persons.

Various definitions of team teaching have been
developed over the past several years. Throughout
these many definitions, an effective team is identified as a combination of teachers that is able
cooperatively better than individually to meet the
needs of their students. However, the basic philosophy of the middle school requires that team
teaching be more than merely a cooperative gesture
among the teaching staff. Its very existence is
designed to provide opportunities for a new utilization of the varied talents and strengths of the
teaching staff. Team teaching represents a cooperative opportunity for teachers to professionally
demonstrate their united strengths to the direct
benefit of their students.

The concept of team teaching seems to mean
different things to different people. Agreement
appears strong on the premise that it is not just an
opportunity to group kids together for a lecture.
The process must be planned by the teachers involved.
Thus, this initial cooperative effort must develop
into a type of unity among the team members.

There exists a traditional teaching exercise
called "turn teaching." The team approach and turn
teaching are not to be considered synonymous terms.
Turn teaching is simply a teaching convenience method
of instruction. It occurs when two teachers decide
to bring their students together and conveniently
take turns teaching. An arrangement of this nature
is generally considered ineffective. This ineffectiveness is created because of the convenience
motive of the parties involved. Additionally, there
exists a lack of team planning for the presentation
and evaluation and team planning must be recognized

as the heart of team effort. Team teaching must
not be considered as just an occasional combining
or swapping of classes by teachers as the mood
strikes them. This type of convenience exchange
or bringing together of students for large group
purposes does not constitute team teaching.

Teams may be comprised of two or more teachers.
These teachers practice team planning, collaborate
constantly, and have no major problems in being
able to communicate with one another. They express
sincere interest in the team concept and the many
things it allows them to do for their students in
classroom-sized groups, small groups, or when providing instruction on an individual basis. Whatever
the form or grouping or presentation being used, it
must be cooperatively planned and evaluated.

Dean and Witherspoon bring this cooperative concept of team teaching into perspective by stating:

> "The heart of the concept of team teaching
> lies not in details of structure and organ-
> ization, but more in the essential spirit
> of cooperative planning, constant collabo-
> ration, close unity, unrestrained communi-
> cation, and sincere sharing. It is reflected
> not in a group of individuals articulating
> together, but rather in a group which is a
> single, unified team. Inherent in the plan
> is an increased degree of flexibility for
> teacher responsibility, grouping policies
> and practices, and size of the groups, and
> an invigorating spirit of freedom and oppor-
> tunity to revamp programs to meet the educa-
> tional needs of children."[2]

------

[2] Dean, Stuart E. and Clinnette F. Witherspoon, "Team
Teaching in the Elementary School", Education Briefs
No. 38, (Washington, D. C.: U. S. Department of
Health, Education, and Welfare, Office of Education,
January 1962), p. 4.

Perhaps a true definition of team teaching is not
possible, nor even desirable. Team teaching is not a
fixed style of instruction. Through a cooperative
effort of all concerned parties, rigidity will take
a back seat to creativeness. Growth of team members
is assured when the team relaxes with one another
and lets the professional process of planning and
evaluation naturally evolve.

Three significant and positive reasons appear
for incorporating a team teaching approach in the
middle school. All three reasons are intended to
make a more efficient use of staff, facility, and
equipment. They are:

1.  There is a desire for improved utilization
    of the building, equipment and school-
    community resources.

2.  There is a desire for a more effective use
    of the skills and talents of the teaching
    staff.

3.  There is an interest in placing a greater
    emphasis on individual student instruction.

Members functioning ideally under the team
concept will no longer desire to isolate themselves
in a classroom or departmental setting. A real
stimulus for a team member's personal growth as a
professional is developed when there is a cooperative
team experience available. Individual staff competencies will appear and compliment one another as a
better and more flexible teaming arrangement continues to develop. There is an increased personal
excitement for teaching when there is a sharing of
ideas and experiences with team members. Personal
benefits can be derived when professional interaction
with various members becomes a reality. Above all
else, there is a rededication to improved instruction
and learning for the individual students.

However, all does not come up on the positive
side of the personality ledger. Some team members

may find it difficult to function openly in front of their colleagues. Personality problems, even clashes may develop. There is the possibility that only a minimum amount of support for individual colleagues toward one another will present itself. Planning sessions may become unproductive at times. Fear of peer scrutiny and the dread of the unfamiliar turf can be a definite obstacle to the proper functioning of a group of teachers attempting to team. The traditional style of professional evaluation has served to produce on the part of some teachers and administrators an insecurity and dread of the innovative process and evaluation.

The increased length of the work day may be considered by some as a handicap to the team's possibility for success. Few teaching styles provide an easy way of teaching or planning. All methods require time and energy. However, team teaching will require additional time and effort for preparation compared to the traditional and conventional approach. It will necessitate more time to become familiar with the increased number of students and their particular characteristics. When problems arise, there will be a tendency to regress into departmentalization or the self-contained classroom situation.

Organization for team teaching in the middle school can assume various forms. They are essentially methods of organizing an instructional program to better reach the needs of the middle school students. In designing an arrangement for teaming, it is necessary to recognize the following points:

1. The arrangement must provide for a more efficient utilization of time in the daily program.

2. The arrangement must capitalize on the special talents and abilities of the staff.

3. The arrangements must directly involve the staff in the grouping of students and time.

4. Time and grouping arrangements must be fluid
   and easily adaptable to change and need.

Likewise, the arrangement for teaming must consider the ten to fourteen year old middle school
students.  Such considerations will provide for:

1. Continuous progress for students in all significant areas of academic and personal
   development.

2. The opportunity for students to develop
   those skills and talents which will prepare
   them for the maximum use of their abilities.

3. A challenge for students regardless of their
   abilities.

4. A program that gives priority to the special
   needs of the middle school students.

5. An opportunity for students to develop an
   inquiring mind seasoned with creativity and
   a sense of responsibility for eventual
   self-education.

Generally, there are two basic forms of teams
practiced in the middle school, the interdisciplinary
team and the single-discipline team.  From these two
types many alternatives may emerge.

The interdisciplinary approach to teaming permits
team members from the different disciplines to use
their teaching time was they deem necessary for the
purpose of instructing their students.  Such a team
arrangement is usually organized on a block time
basis.  Regardless of the type of punctuation given
to the school day, it is essential that the arrangement provide for the various transitional requirements of the middle school students.

A single discipline team works in one academic
subject area with each team member responsible for
certain topics in that subject area.

To facilitate the learning process and use of
teacher talents, a form of flexibility must exist in
the time arrangement.  The procedure should serve to
organize the school day into varied lengths of time
for different classes and other activities.  Academic
time must not be abused by punctuating the day into
periods or fixed amounts of time.  In other words, if
a team member requires thirty-five minutes to accomplish a given goal, the time arrangement should be
flexible enough to accommodate that.  The traditional
arrangement of sixty minute periods frequently only
serves as an administrative and teacher convenience
and often has a tendency to waste valuable teaching
time.

Teaming is not intended to be only a method to
permit longer or shorter periods for a given subject.
Team teaching and flexible scheduling should be designed to increase the possibility of student
learning.  A productive team combined with a flexible
arrangement of time will be able to give greater
recognition to individual differences.  After all, a
team that is responsible for a given group of students
should be provided the opportunity for organizing
their own time.

One approach to developing a flexible time
arrangement is to consider the middle school as a
continuation of the time arrangement begun in the
elementary school.  Students advancing from the
elementary school are certain to be familiar with the
elementary approach to a greater degree than the
secondary.  This transitional concept implies a need
to look closely at the familiar flexibility of the
elementary time arrangement.  The following diagram
depicts graphically the transitional position of the
middle school in relationship to the elementary and
senior high school.

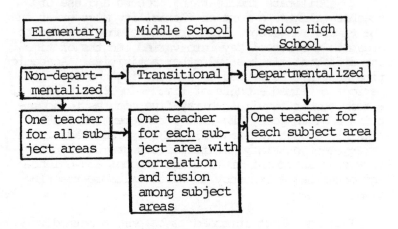

This transitional position of the middle school lends itself to a time arrangement like that conventionally utilized in the elementary school. Generally the elementary day is divided into a type of time blocks. Therefore, it appears desirable that the middle school develop a similar day.

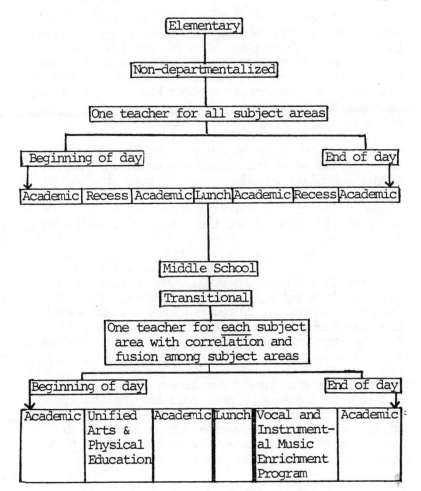

In this elementary setting, the principal usually assigns one teacher and approximately thirty students to a given block of time. The teacher, for the most part, plans the various activities and academic time. The teacher also groups students as deemed necessary. Basically, the elementary teacher has the opportunity to treat the arrangement of time and grouping of the students in a very flexible manner.

The middle school arrangement of time discussed here is related to the elementary approach. Conventional secondary school periods of time give way to time segments or blocks. Teaching teams then become directly involved in the arrangement of time, grouping of students, and the planning of each school day.

There is no single pattern for organizing team teaching in the middle school. One is able to find various sizes and arrangements of teams. But they should all have this in common: the setting whereby the team members can best exercise and further develop their talents to reach the personal needs of their students.

One method of interdisciplinary teaming in the middle school creates a dual role for the individual teacher within the team. When teaching in an area of direct responsibility, a team member takes on the role of directing teacher. In other areas, a team member is referred to as a supporting teacher.

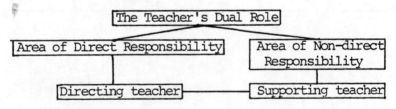

From this dual role pattern of organizational teaming, strategy can take on many forms. Team teaching organization does not have to be complicated to be effective. A new idea or approach does not have to be difficult to produce something of

educational significance. When creating new patterns
of organization, teachers and administrators should
not hesitate to use the less complicated and clear
approach toward obtaining their goal. Often the
simple and less complicated accomplishes much more
than believed possible--at any grade level.

A basic model of team formation can begin very
simply as demonstrated below:

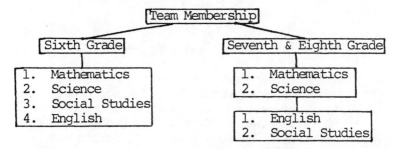

Many styles of interdisciplinary teaming can be
developed from this initial arrangement. For
example:

1.  The Thematic or Unit Approach

    This arrangement utilizes four teachers and
    approximately 120 students. Usually team
    membership is organized to include a teacher
    from each subject area (mathematics, science,
    social studies, and language arts). The team
    concentrates its efforts around broad themes
    or units such as ecology, communication, or
    transportation. A prerequisite is that the
    team develop and plan the units of study.
    The individual team teachers will be respon-
    sible for teaching and evaluating in their
    disciplines.

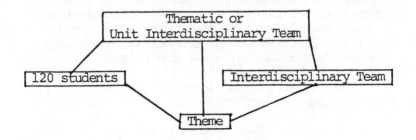

2.   The Pre and Post Testing Approach

This approach may involve two to four
teachers representing each subject area.
Like the unit of study approach, the team
works together to develop the needed course
of study. However, a basic difference is
that all team members teach in each instructional area. Once again, approximately 120
students are involved but each is pre-
tested. In order to meet the individual
needs of the students, the team must determine what the students require. Students
are then grouped according to their
instructional needs.

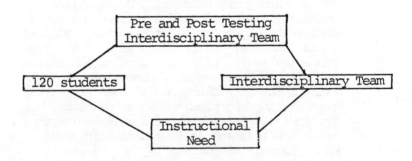

3.  The Block Time Approach

This arrangement utilizes the instructional
skills of four teachers but teams them into
two blocks of English, social studies and
mathematics, science. Both teachers of each
team involve themselves in teaching each of
the two subjects. Each team member is
responsible for developing plans for one of
the instructional areas. The two teams
instruct four teams of students.

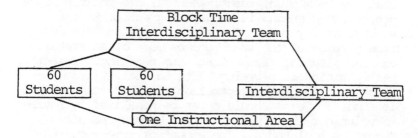

4.  The Single Discipline Teaming Approach

This arrangement for teaming utilizes two or
more teachers who are given the responsibility
for a particular subject. They will then
share the teaching responsibility required by
the subject to meet the needs of their students. Usually this approach involves all
the students assigned to the team. In other
words, two or more teachers team to provide
instruction in a single discipline for the
needs of several groups of students.

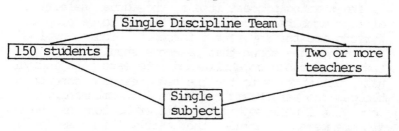

Team teaching and the middle school provide the
opportunity for educators to utilize a fresh approach
toward an improved instructional program for students
between childhood and adolescence. They both are
vitally interested in the individualization of instruction and a balanced program of experience. Each
concept is seeking an alternative to the conventional
classroom approach. Both offer teachers and students
opportunities unlimited.

The interdisciplinary approach to teaming demands
that the team plan, teach, and evaluate their endeavors. Team planning is a basic ingredient to the
success of any team. Therefore, the structure and
true purpose of the team becomes more of an emphasis
on team planning rather than team teaching. Effective
team planning is a prerequisite to quality team
teaching. Adequate preparation time for team members
is a must. Teams should never be penalized by having
to volunteer their planning time before and after
regular school hours. The amount of time required
for team planning will depend upon the number of team
members and what they desire to implement. To be
successful, a team will require at least one common
planning period during the day.

A successful team of teachers is balanced with
regard to experience and teacher attitude. To have
all members identical would not be professionally
beneficial. Members of teams must be flexible and be
encouraged to openly express enthusiasm for what
they are doing.

One of the most important steps in team teaching
is the teaming process itself, the actual selection
of team members. Problems are likely to develop if
persons are for any reason forced to become involved.
Experience has shown that teachers should choose their
team-mates based on skills and interests. An individual's willingness to try the team teaching concept
becomes the very basic criterion for membership.
Educational philosophies can differ as long as the
team membership includes the basic willingness factor
and, of course, the academic competencies necessary

to develop a balanced program. If a willing and
capable team member begins to really team teach,
there is only a slight chance of that member ever
desiring to regress back into a former setting. Thus,
the imperative ingredient for a successful team is
that the members be willingly committed to the team
style of teaching.

The middle school team concept requires that
teachers experience success and have academic
independence. Likewise, students require a degree
of independence and a sense of accomplishing their
own thinking. Such student freedom could pose a
rather delicate situation for a team if not understood. Therefore, the development of a type of
teacher directed, student choice concept becomes
desirable.

The words "teacher directed" and "student choice"
imply in themselves the definition of this concept.
A primary premise and concern is that the total
educational program must be team directed. On the
other hand, it is believed that students must be
treated as individuals. The teacher directed,
student choice concept is intended to provide a student with careful training in making decisions as an
individual. Proper and tactful team and teacher
guidance will provide the student with needed direction in making the choices best suited to individual
needs, interests, and abilities.

An imperative of the teacher directed concept
is that the students be involved in such a manner
that they become significant factors in the planning
process or decisions that are made. A teacher must
carefully participate in the consideration being
discussed to such a degree that students will be so
involved that they believe they are making the
choice. This is not to be considered deception or a
manipulation of students. It is simply an attempt
to emphasize the students using their own abilities
to determine a plan of action, but with the professional guidance of an adult who is genuinely concerned about them.

The creation of additional teacher-student
planning sessions should involve students in many
decisions concerning what will be studied and
especially the learning activities to be used.  In
this setting, students should be encouraged to
exercise considerable initiative in selecting and
planning studies during specific segments of the
time arrangement.

However, even though team teaching is advocated
herein, one must keep in mind that some good teachers
rightly belong in a self-contained classroom situation where they work as  students. The teacher's
role in the self-contained classroom is important to
the education of some students.  Teachers who are
self-contained oriented should not be forced into
teaming but should be permitted to teach in the
situation of their strength.  Only those teachers
who sincerely desire to make the necessary adjust-
ments and devote the required time should be included
as members of a teaching team.

Team leadership may exhibit itself in many forms.
Like teaming, there is no standardized approach.  Few
team teaching groups larger than two can function
well without some type of leadership.  A review of
the various teaming arrangements suggests three basic
types of team leadership.  Each of these arrangements
can produce success in a given situation.

However, in the opinion of this writer, the
"shared leadership" role is considered to be the most
effective method of providing for this facet of
teaming.  The shared leadership method requires a
team member in an area of direct responsibility to
assume the leadership role of the team and literally
become the team leader for a given assignment.

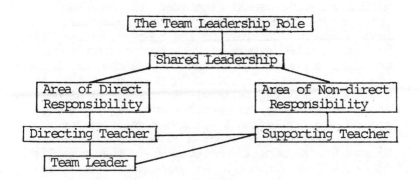

The remainder of the team members are responsible
for providing the directing teacher, or team leader,
with their assistance whenever required.  During this
time of assisting, they become supportive personnel
to the team leader.  When the area of responsibility
of the supportive teacher appears in the team process
there is an assumed changing of roles and they then
become the directing teacher or team leader.  This
simple and functional approach to team leadership
insures that the role is shared and that all members
of the team become periodically obligated to participate.

The shared leadership concept promotes a continual discovery and reinvestment of team resources.
All team members keep out front and benefit from one
another without the permanent and formal team leader.
By making everyone important, this approach to team
leadership serves to encourage the shy and reluctant
team member who may possess latent leadership capabilities.  It provides for continual professional
growth of the total team by requiring all members to
take an active part in the leadership function.
With the incorporation of the shared leadership concept, education is spared the establishment of
another hierarchical level and the communication
process is simplified.

Apart from the benefits provided for students by
the academic function of the team, there are

additional supplemental benefits. The team can
arrange time to become involved in student enrichment programs. The role of the teacher during this
enrichment time is primarily that of a consultant
or resource person. A student enters the enrichment
time segment with a specific interest upon which the
teacher quickly capitalizes. In brief, the student
brings an interest; the teacher supplies the encouragement and professional guidance; and together they
cooperatively plan the course of action to be
followed to accomplish whatever goals they establish.

The enrichment program provides time for an
administrator, counselor, social worker, or team
member to work with the student's everyday type
problems. In this opportunity for dealing with
student behavior problems, the involved teacher
discusses the student concern they are experiencing
with the entire team. During this discussion time,
the team will respond and the reporting teacher will
find out if other teachers are having similar
difficulty with this particular student. This is the
time for the affected teacher to fully discuss with
the team membership their dealings with the student
who is causing the behavior problem. The most
desirable conclusion is that a plan for corrective
action be formulated by the team.

Not only can a student's program be enriched
through teaming, the development of a creative
opportunity for teacher centered enrichment can also
be arranged by the team. This individual team
member process of self-evaluation recognizes the
need for teachers to have the opportunity to objectively observe their own teaching skills and techniques. One method used in this self-evaluation is
video tape recordings of teacher-student interaction.
After video tape recording the interaction, teachers
make use of the video tape to review and observe
teaching performances and skills and conduct their
own self-evaluation for improvement purposes.

The teaching team can apply a team approach to
substitute teaching situations that may possibly be

known in advance. That is, when there is going to be a known teacher absence, the remaining team members are given the opportunity to modify the schedule and to instruct the missing teacher's students instead of hiring a regular substitute. The truly functional teaching team works together daily to plan and direct the learning of the students assigned to them. Therefore, it becomes a very natural thing for the team to be aware of the teaching plans of the individuals on their team. Generally, only planned absences (teachers attending conferences, etc.), are considered as applicable to the team teaching concept of substitution.

This team-substitute arrangement provides the team with the opportunity to search for a better educational solution to teacher absences. In the past, there has been little effort toward improving or enhancing the learning situation for students when teachers are absent. Usually, the substitute teacher only supervises a class and the students' advancement of learning is held in limbo until the regular teacher returns.

The financial consideration given to a substitute teacher also represents funds that could be directed to the team's instructional program. Thus, the team not only has the possibility of a better solution to teacher absences, it also can even provide additional funds for the always tight instructional budget.

Possibilities for the implementation of this substitute teacher concept include the skills enrichment experience approach; the absorbing of students approach; and the unit approach.

1.   Skills Enrichment Experience Team Approach

     Objective:  To give needed practice of a
     specific skill in each of the four academic
     areas.

Each academic area is to determine a skill in which reinforcement or enrichment is needed by the students. Lessons are to be prepared at three levels: remedial, average, enrichment. According to past achievement, students may be divided into groups and practice skills accordingly.

2. Absorbing of Students Team Approach

Objective: To continue the flow of learning without the interruption of a substitute teacher.

One academic class of students can be absorbed by the remaining team members. The team would then proceed to maintain all four academic areas for the students.

3. The Unit Approach

Objective: One team member establishes the objectives and the means of achieving the objectives in a particular subject area.

This arrangement involves the use of time and grouping of students to achieve the daily objective. The student will have a time arrangement schedule for the unit, know what is expected during each time period, and evaluate the unit upon completion. The amount of time in a particular area may vary from day to day depending upon the objective to be achieved, but time is to be equal when the unit is completed. The absence of a team member is incidental to the objective achieved. Each team member has a directing function for his subject area and a supporting function in the other subject areas.

The strength of a teaching team can be greatly increased when clerical aides, teaching assistants, and other supportive personnel are used. These paraprofessional aides serve to relieve the team

members of the traditional and non-professional
teaching tasks. An aide's time must be arranged so
that it can be shared with each of the team members.
It is necessary to include these paraprofessionals
in certain planning and preparation sessions. Wise
use of the paraprofessional staff serves to free the
regular team members for planning, parental and
student conferences, and will greatly beef-up the
possibility for improved instruction. The non-
teaching duties of the team members are to be eliminated whenever possible. Paraprofessional utilization provides certified personnel more precious time
to spend in preparation and in meeting the needs of
their students.

There is no place on the team for poor esprit de
corps. Effective teams do not develop by chance;
they are the result of individual members really
trying to make the team function smoothly. Conflicts
among team members can destroy the team and create
great strain on everyone. Problems of conflict must
be recognized without delay and then quickly solved
by the parties involved or by the team as a whole.
Honest discussions of the team's doubts and fears
must be a regular part of the planning process. To
ever be successful, the team has to develop the
ability to freely ask questions and speak frankly
about reactions to each other.

As part of the communication function of the
team, members cannot spend valuable time, time that
could be devoted to students, guessing how a team
member feels regarding a certain item or topic.
Nor, can the fellow team member spend his time
wondering if he was really informed of the total situation. The person who does not speak to a colleague
regarding a difficult matter fails to meet his
professional obligations. He has grossly erred
against himself as well as his colleague. Unlike a
friendship matter, to remain silent in a professional
team matter does more harm than telling all. Neither
the informer, nor his team colleague, is able to
grow without total professional honesty toward one
another.

In other words, a dual professional injustice results when colleagues fail to fully discuss a concern. The first is a personal injustice. This is caused by the individual who is not willing to state his opinion or position to his associates. As a second injustice, his associates have lost because they lost the value of the opinion or position of a colleague.

The possibility of anger or temper being exhibited must not serve to deter the communication process. Silence is a greater detriment to professionalism than the problems which could arise as a result of certain expressions deemed necessary and fitting of professionals. Without a doubt, more harm is created on a team by not stating the case than by the mode of discussion. The silent team member or administrator helps no one—especially students!

The middle school administrator plays an important, if not crucial, role in the degree of success of team teaching in his school. Educators agree that the role of the student and his teachers has changed drastically over the past few years. Likewise, the principal must be of a flexible and creative nature to make his teams succeed; and must make every effort to provide teachers with facilities, materials, a workable time arrangement, along with suitable evidence of his blessings on what the team is attempting to accomplish. In brief, he assists the teams in whatever way necessary to enable teachers to best work with their students. He is compelled to remember that his school is not organized for teachers or his own administrative convenience, but for students. There must be every evidence that the building administrator supports his teachers even when they fail. Above all else, he keeps up to date on what happens with the teams and their students. A strong professional reply to the inquirer exhibits the hope and faith that the administrator has in his teams. The atmosphere rings with the assurance that he supports and can justify team teaching and its benefits to the

students of his school.  Without the full support
of the building administrator, team teaching will
never approach its real potential.

In conclusion, whatever the blueprint of
organization, team teaching in the middle school must
provide teachers with the opportunity to make a
greater contribution toward meeting the needs of
the students.  The availability of a variety of
techniques of teaching and learning are necessary.
Good education takes place when it is implemented
according to the personal needs of the students.
A secure and professional atmosphere is required to
cultivate the necessary freedom for the teams of
teachers to innovate and create.  When administrators
and teachers work together in a happy and secure
middle school program the same satisfaction and
security is passed on to the most important team
member, the student.

## MULTI-MEDIA MATERIALS APPROACH

The teacher is sitting behind his desk which is
located in the front of the classroom while he is
conducting a "discussion". The sixth graders are at
their seats which are in neat rows with their textbooks apparently open at the right page. Two of the
youngsters are fast asleep, three are doodling, two
on paper, and one on the desk, four seem to have
their eyes glued to the clock which was on a 15
degree angle, and as for the rest of the group they
are apparently "listening".

The teacher was saying in a booming voice,
"Jefferson was not interested in what happened in
Europe. Yes, he wanted to stay out of their hair.
In the meantime, Spain had a secret treaty with
France...they were returning Lousiana to France.
All that land would be France's. Jefferson didn't
want the French here. He was afraid that they would
close New Orleans. We needed New Orleans..." This
monologue continued for eleven minutes, and the bell
rang. The students jumped to their feet and
scurried out of the door except for one boy who was
still asleep. His buddy shook him and said, "Let's
go, man!"

In another classroom, the seventh grade teacher
was standing before the class reading out loud a
story in the literature textbook. The pacing was
much too fast to follow, but the reading continued
for almost twenty minutes. No discussion was held
or questions asked concerning the content of the
story. "Now", said the teacher, "John will pass out
the literature books, and you will read silently the
remainder of the story starting on page 115.
Tomorrow I will have a mimeographed list of questions
for you to answer."

In another classroom, all of the students were
answering questions on a three page mimeographed
item in science. Some of the questions were as
follows: Name the nine planets. Which planet does

man live on?  Which is the largest planet?  Which
planet has rings on it? etc.  This activity continued for twenty-five minutes followed by fifteen
minutes of group correction of these tests.

Are these typical classrooms?  Obviously, the
sampling is far too small to draw any conclusions.
In another report[1] in which shadow studies were
completed, it was found that the most prominent
classroom strategy was one dominated by the teacher
in full direction of the learning.  Lectures were
common in classes ranging from English to art.  In
other classrooms, the collecting of homework papers,
going over homework, making the next assignment,
introducing new work, and allocating time for starting the homework in class was common.  Other
instructional practices included (a) lecture-demon-
stration, (b) read-recitation and (c) correct-
explain-practice.  In these classrooms there was the
need to "cover" the material, and workbooks were
quite evident.  Although these activities were found
in junior highs at that time, they also seem to
represent what is being practiced in many of our
middle schools today.


### These are Middle School Youngsters

The classrooms observed were conducted as though
all students were identical mentally and therefore
performing at the same level.  Data on the development of preadolescents show they are as different
as their fingerprints yet we treat these unequal
youngsters as though they are equal.  As one person
aptly stated, "There is nothing so unequal as the
equal treatment of unequals."

Wattenburg points out that in a class of 40 sixth
graders made up of twenty girls and twenty boys,

there are two fully adolescent girls, eight pre-adolescent girls, ten childish girls. As to the boys, there are no adolescent boys, four pre-adolescent boys, and sixteen childish boys. This same wide range is found when we examine the intellectual development of these youngsters. Furthermore, a study of five sixth graders shows that there often are sharp differences within each student in each instructional area as shown in the graph below.

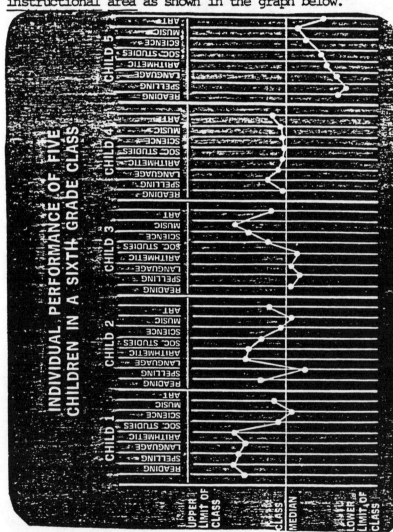

In Figure 2 the graph shows greatly accelerated growth between grades 6 and 8. In the basic skill areas we find a range of at least six years in reading, math and spelling at the sixth grade level while at the eighth grade level, the same class shows an even greater disparity of performances. One could truly call the middle school youngster a juvenile hodgepodge.

What are the implications of these wide variances in the growth characteristics in the middle school students? Frankly, it means that we are going to have to eliminate some of our traditional practices and to implement those practices which are consistent with what we know about the variances we find in the classrooms. It is unfortunate that we tend to hang on to the old practice in education. It is very much like the Rhesus monkey. Trappers of these monkeys would take a coconut and cut out a hole large enough for the monkey to put his hand in and then place some delicious food inside the coconut. The trappers would hang this coconut from a tree. The monkey would then examine the coconut and seeing the delicious food would place his hand in and grab the food. He would try to get his hand out, but with the food in his hand he was trapped. He would not release the food. He would scream and the trapper would know that he had caught another monkey. We are often very much like the monkey...if we would only change, we could be free too!

## What Is The Multi-Media Approach?

With the wide range of abilities within the middle school, an approach to teaching and learning is needed to meet the various learning styles of the students. The multi-media approach recognizes that learning which is always complicated, is further complicated when one examines the diversity of talents and interests within a middle school class. Specifically, multi-media refers to the use of various materials of instruction, both hardware and software, which reinforce one another to insure that we provide the most effective teaching-learning for the mastery of the objectives to be learned.

For example, if the objective to be learned in a unit on meteorology is "Students should be able to show how the processes of evaporation, condensation and precipitation are related to weather and the water cycle", the suggested activities to help the student to assign this objective are as follows:

1.  Draw and label the water cycle and its various pathways.

2.  Observe the film: What Makes Clouds? See list of questions for discussion purposes.

3.  Read pages 103-118 in Investigating the Earth. Be able to describe, in some detail, the processes of evaporation, condensation and precipitation.

4.  Experiment: Follow the directions on how to experience the process of evaporation, condensation and precipitation. All materials are on the experiment table.

5.  Take black and white photos of at least seven different cloud formations. Classify them according to a U.S. Weather Bureau cloud chart. Find out what these various cloud types tell you about the condition of the atmosphere.

These activities take into consideration the abilities and the learning styles of the students. In the first activity the student can draw the concept of the water cycle. He may be especially talented in art and could present a most interesting chart which can be useful to others in the class. The second activity calls for viewing a film on the topic. A small group or the whole class could very well see this film. For some students, it would be an activity for learning this objective while others would use it to reinforce the learnings gained from another acitvity. The fourth point calls for a hands on activity. An experiment to show evaporation,

condensation and even precipitation can be conducted
at the science table. A guide sheet asks the student
to record what happens in each of the experiments.
The fifth activity enables any student with a camera
to take a series of pictures on cloud formations.
These can be carefully labeled and mounted on the
bulletin board to be shared with others in the class.
Each of these activities are directed toward meeting
the objective, and in most instances, insure that all
students master this particular objective. It should
be pointed out that the choice of learning activity
is left up to the student. Students will usually
choose an activity which they feel they will be
successful in accomplishing. Teachers can then ask
them to choose a second activity to reinforce the
learning and to insure mastery.


## What Media To Use?

Dale  talks about his "cone of experience" as a
model for media selection. This model serves as a
reminder to teachers of the various kinds of experiences that are available to learners.

The model may be envisioned as an up-side-down ice
cream cone, broad at the base and coming to a narrow
point at the top. Thr purpose of this model is to
show the degree of abstraction of the message presented to the learner. At the lowest level we see
"direct purposeful experiences". These experiences
involve "doing" and are the least abstract types of
instruction possible. For example, a class may be
studying ecology and would be on the topic of farming
practices such as strip farming. Plans would be made
by the group to visit a model farm where various conservation practices could be observed on the farm.
Besides viewing, the students don old clothes and
actually take part in various conservation practices--
including spreading manure with the farmer and his
manure spreader. This experience would constitute
direct purpose experience (Level 1). At the other
extreme, or the top of the cone the messages are
highly abstract and consist of spoken or printed

Figure 3

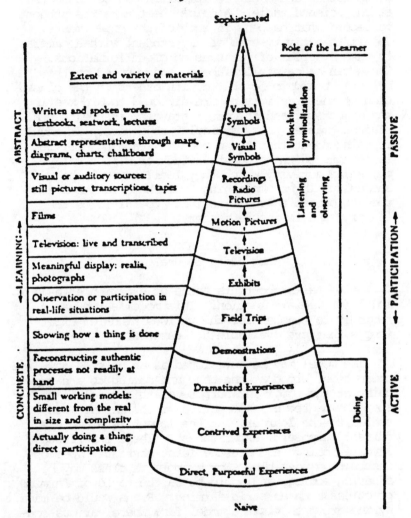

symbols (words). Between the lowest and the highest
level represented on the cone are a number of intermediate levels as shown in Figure 3. Each level
becomes more abstract than the one below it; that is,
there is less active involvement of the student so
it loses elements of reality found in direct, purposeful experiences. These intermediate levels are
represented by some media that carry messages, and
in many cases it is the attributes of these media
that determine the degree of abstractness of the
message.

Visiting the farm and observing the various conservation practices is reality itself (Level V),
but certain elements of reality are lost when these
conservation practices are seen in a motion picture (Level VIII) and further loss takes place when
still pictures (Level IX) are observed. Another
example might be moving from the level of direct
purposeful experience which contains all the elements
of the "real world" to contrived experiences, where
the environment of the learner is simulated, and
lacks some of the atmosphere of the direct experience. Dale further states that one cannot arbitrarily attach a "good or bad" label to the media
at any level. Whether the media (or degree of
abstraction of the message) are good or bad will
depend on many things, including variables related
to the learner and the task.

Too often the teaching-learning situation centers
on verbal and visual symbols rather than experiences
enumerated in the base of the cone. School principals list textbooks as the resource most useful
and influential in the teaching program.[2] This is
unfortunate when there is a plethora of resources
available to teachers to meet the various learning
styles of students. This is not to suggest the
abandonment of the textbook. The textbook can be a

---

[2]The Princpals Look at the Schools, 23-25. Prepared for the Project on the Instructional Program of
the Public Schools. Washington: National Education
Association, 1962.

valuable resource if employed for the needs of the
students, but it must be questioned if it is the only
instructional tool used in the teaching-learning
situation.  Other stimuli which can be used in conjunction with the textbook are films, filmstrips,
records, tapes, transparencies, television, charts,
games, field trips, etc.  With the use of many
stimuli, the classroom does not become a limited
learning environment.  It can be greatly expanded
through various multi-media materials.  Learning
environments such as parks, businesses, museums,
homes, factories can be invaluable learning resources,
too.


## Is Multi-Media Approach Effective?

Do students learn more of the vocabulary of
science units when motion picture films and project still pictures are added to the use of other
audio-visual materials?  This question was examined
by Romano[3] in a study which included students from
two fifth, sixth and seventh grade groups in the
public schools of Shorewood and Whitefish Bay, Wisconsin.  These groups were rotated so that each
served in turn as an experimental and a control group.
Blackboards, bulletin boards, charts, models, flat
pictures, and field trips were used both in the
control and experimental situations, but motion
pictures and projected still pictures (filmstrips,
2x2, and 3½x4 slides, and pictures used with the
opaque projector) were used only in the experimental
situations and served as the experimental factors.
Both groups also used a wealth of printed materials.
This study according to Wittich and Schuller was
unique in that he chose as his subjects students who
were already used to a learning environment that

---

[3]Louis Romano, "The Role of 16 mm. Motion Pic-
tures and Projected Still Pictures in Science Unit
Vocabulary Learning at Grades 5, 6 and 7", unpublished
Ph.D. thesis, University of Wisconsin, 1955.

their teachers considered unusually enriched.[4]

Greater vocabulary gains were made by the film-using group (Fig. 4 )

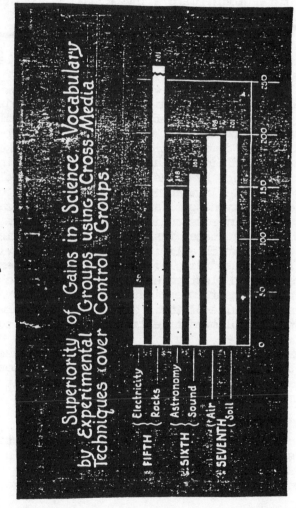

Figure 4

The fifth grade students learned up to 300 per-cent more science vocabulary, the sixth grade groups twice the vocabulary, and the seventh grade groups 200 percent more than the control groups learned.

Four years after the completion of this study, Georgiady[5] studied the effect of the 16 mm. sound motion picture film and the use of related projected still pictures on vocabulary development and growth among students in grades 6, 7 and 8. This study closely paralleled Romano's investigation and the results almost matched those of the earlier study. Thus, two careful investigations of using films with related audio-visual materials substantiate the value of the multi-media utilization in the teaching-learning situation.

These studies are significant because they did not attempt to determine the effectiveness of a single audio-visual material over other visual materials such as slides, demonstrations, maps and the like, or the more traditional classroom procedures using verbal instruction by means of textbooks or supplementary reading. Instead, they attempted to determine the effectiveness of an audio-visual utilization in which numerous audio-visual materials were employed in coordinated fashion over an audio-visual utilization in which a limited number of audio-visual materials were used singly. Dale[6] states that experimenters often neglect to establish normal schoolroom procedures in their investigation which may result in lessening the value of their data. The procedures in these studies followed a realistic classroom situation.

These studies have added significance because they showed that an important basic skill, acquisition of vocabulary, can be achieved in a multi-media situation in the middle school.

---

[5]Nicholas Georgiady, "The Role of 16 mm. Motion Pictures and Related Projected Still Pictures in Social Studies Unit Vocabulary Learning, Grades 6 to 8", Unpublished Ph.D. thesis, University of Wisconsin, 1959.

[6]Edgar Dale, F. W. Dunn, C. F. Hoban Jr., and E. Schneider, Motion Pictures in Education, The H. W. Wilson Co., New York, 1938, p. 319.

The reaction of students following the Romano study indicate the inherent value of the multi-media approach to learning.

"We learned more because we could see what was meant instead of reading about it or hearing it alone."

"Astronomy filmstrips are more interesting. They help me to get a better idea of what the book said."

"I'll never forget how the layers of earth folded over. I just couldn't understand that when we talked about it in class, but I get it right away from the film."

## How To Implement the Multi-Media Approach

One of the best techniques to insure that teachers will use the multi-media approach in the classroom is to develop units of study or modules. The basic idea of a unit is very simple and all teachers can use it effectively. More importantly, all teachers should have these units available for pre-planning purposes prior to teaching. More importantly, all teachers should have these units available for pre-planning purposes prior to teaching. Simply, a unit of study is a collection of suggested learning activities and materials organized around a given topic to be used as a basis for a teacher's advanced planning.[7]

In the development of units of study, a body of research as related to pupils at this level presents some guidelines for the grade placement of social

---

[7]Lavonne A. Hanna, Gladys L. Potter and Neva Hagaman, Unit Teaching in the Elementary School (adapted from), Holt, Rinehardt and Winston, 1963, pp. 51-52.

studies units and for activities within the units.
Although these statements are related to social
studies they obviously have implications for other
instructional areas.

Keeping in mind the growth characteristics of
the middle school students the selection of topics
for units should (1) be cultural rather than chronological in nature and emphasize how people have adjusted to and adapted their environment to meet their
needs, (2) deal with man's technical control over
his environment and his use of natural resources
because of interest in mechanics, science and
natural phenomena, (3) help students understand
themselves, adjust to their immediate physical and
social environment, and establish satisfactory personal relationships, (4) help students understand the
likenesses and differences in people and the desire-
ableness of cultural plurality in American life and
the world community, (5) include great personages
in order to satisfy the inclination toward hero
worship, and (6) satisfy their basic drives to be
active, to dramatize, to construct and manipulate, to
satisfy curiosity, to communicate; as well as to satisfy their ego-integrative needs.


## Examples of Units

Hopefully in the determination of units of study
in social studies, science, English, etc. care will
be taken that there is a sequential development of
learnings from the elementary grades to the middle
school grades.  For example a sequential development
in social studies would eliminate unnecessary duplication and insure to a certain extent that important
topics are not omitted from the instructional program.
Once a sequence of topics is determined, then the next
steps include writing the units of study.

Although there are several models to choose from,
the following has been used over a period of several
years in a number of middle schools and found to be
simple to write and most appropriate to pre-planning.

| Format for a Unit of Study |

<u>Title Page</u>:     Title of Unit
                Grade level/s
                Purpose of the unit

<u>Pre-Test</u>

| Behavioral Objective | Suggested Activities | Suggested Materials |
|---|---|---|
| | | |

The title page includes the title of the unit, grade level or levels, and the purpose of the unit. For example:

TITLE:  English Colonization in the New World

GRADE LEVEL:  8

PURPOSE:  To give the students an understanding of how the English settled thirteen colonies along the Atlantic coast of North America to become prosperous and progressive, and why they revolted and won their independence to form a new nation, the United States of America.

The pre-test should be developed which coincides with the behavioral objectives to be learned in the unit of study.  The pre-test itself should be short answer type, matching, etc. rather than essay type

at this point. The purpose of this pre-test is to
assess the student's knowledge of this topic, and then
to plan and individualize the instructional program
to include only those behavior objectives which the
student does not understand. Other students with the
same learning needs can be formed into a small group
and can work together. In other words, the teacher
has arranged for learning activities which teach what
the student does not know rather than what he already
knows.

## Pre-Test

Mark each of the following either true or false.

_____ 1.  Religious freedom was one reason why people
            left England and migrated to America.

_____ 2.  The "Lost Colony" in Virginia was a group of
            people who disappeared.

_____ 3.  Government by laws was one democratic ideal
            reflected by the Mayflower Compact.

_____ 4.  An indentured servant could be sold to a
            new owner.

_____ 5.  The Indians taught the colonists to grow corn.

_____ 6.  Puritans wanted to break away from the Church
            of England.

_____ 7.  A charter was required before a group could
            settle a region in America.

_____ 8.  Learning to grow cotton was one reason why
            Virginia colony grew and prospered.

_____ 9.  The Jamestown colony was started by Sir
            Walter Raleigh.

Pre-Test (Continued)


Match each of the following people with a role in the
early colonies.

_____(a)   John Smith                  1.   Governor of Massa-
                                             chusetts Bay Colony
_____(b)   Roger Williams
                                        2.   Started village of
_____(c)   Sir Walter Raleigh               Hartford

_____(d)   John Rolfe                   3.   Leader of Jamestown

_____(e)   John Winthrop               4.   King of England
                                             when Jamestown was
_____(f)   King James I                     founded

                                        5.   Learned how to
                                             grow tobacco from
                                             the Indians

                                        6.   Founded colony at
                                             Roanoke Island

                                        7.   Founded colony of
                                             Rhode Island

On the map locate the following places;

a.  Jamestown                    c.  Roanoke Island

b.  Plymouth                     d.  Massachusetts Bay
                                     Colony


The above pre-test can also be used for the post-test which is given at the termination of the unit of study to determine mastery of the behavioral objectives.  The writers recommend that the post-test may include some objective type questions, but should also include essay type questions.  Students should be given an opportunity to learn how to pull together key ideas of the unit of study into coherent essay type questions.

## Behavioral Objectives

The writers of units of study should keep in mind that the behavioral objectives should be written first before writing the pre-test. In other words, the pre-test should be closely geared to the behavioral objectives because these are to be achieved by the students. Specifically, what are behavioral objectives? They are clearly worded instructional statements which can be measured. Mager[8] states that the most meaningful stated objectives attempt to exclude the greatest number of possible alternatives. Since many words are "loaded" and open to interpretation, he suggests the following which are open to fewer interpretations: to recite, to identify, to differentiate, to solve, to construct, to list, etc. Note that these words describe what the learner will be doing. On the other hand, other words are open to many interpretations: for example, to understand, to appreciate, to enjoy, to believe, etc. He further states that to make each objective more specific, one might include the following:

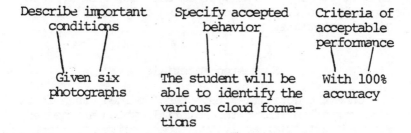

| Describe important conditions | Specify accepted behavior | Criteria of acceptable performance |
|---|---|---|
| Given six photographs | The student will be able to identify the various cloud formations | With 100% accuracy |

## Suggested Activities

An important part of the unit which deals specifically with the multi-media approach are the suggested activities. In this section, the writer

---

[8]Robert F. Mager, Preparing Instructional Objectives, Fearon Pub., Palo Alto, CA, 1962.

must have at least five different activities for students to achieve the particular activity. If the writer only includes activities which call for reading and writing, then we have limited the options for the students. What about the student who has difficulty reading, or lacks an understanding of the printed page? What about the student who learns best through an audio-visual presentation or one who can reinforce the learnings of the printed paper through the film or filmstrip? Or the student who has art talent, and pull together all of the key ideas of the unit into a pictoral presentation or the construction of a papier-mache item? Activities should be included which give the student opportunities to achieve the objectives through problem solving techniques, through skills of inquiry and research, through the use of the basic skills, through dramatic plays, through construction, through art and music, through audio-visual materials, etc. Throughout the unit every effort would be made to include examples of the various types of activities, that is, art experiences, research experiences, construction experiences, etc. Care should be taken that certain students don't limit themselves to just one type of activity such as reading only the textbook, or viewing only certain audio-visual materials.

## Suggested Materials

Once the activities have been defined, then it is a matter of including the materials which are needed for the particular activity. Specificity is important, such as listing the pages in the textbook, the name of the filmstrip and source, the materials and directions for making a papier-mache model, etc. This procedure would eliminate the teachers or the students having to hunt for these materials during the teaching-learning situation.

Let's examine the unit: "English Colonization in the New World" to see what it looks like with the behavior objective, suggested activities and suggested materials.

| BEHAVIORAL OBJECTIVE | SUGGESTED ACTIVITIES | SUGGESTED MATERIALS |
|---|---|---|
| The students will be able to explain the role of the Indians in the growth of the colonies | 1. Read textbook-pages 77-89 looking for information on how the Indians helped the early colonists to survive. | 2. Textbook-Liberty & Union, pages 77-89. |
| | 2. Discuss the role of the Indians in the growth of the colonies. List of a chart of their efforts. (3 students) | 2. Colored chart paper in art cabinet. |
| | 3. Film-"The Pilgrims", look for the role of the Indians in the survival of the Plymouth Colony. | 3. Film-"The Pilgrims" (in Resource Center). |
| | 4. Role-Playing, have the students play the parts of the Indians and the early colonists, making sure to bring out how the Indians could help the early colonists. Six students will write and present their role-playing to | |
| | 5. Have the students write reports on one of the following: Squanto, | 5. See list of books these Indians on the |

|  |  |
|---|---|
| Massasoit or Po-cahantas, and the role each played in assisting the colonists. | bulletin board. |
| 6. Draw a picture showing how the Indians helped the colonists. | 6. Art materials are in the art cabinet. |
| 7. Construct a table top scene of the Indians and colonists working together. | 7. Plasticene and other art materials are in the art cabinet. |

## Summary

The Multi-media approach is a technique which enables the teacher to coordinate the use of a variety of media, including the text book, to enable students of various abilities and interests to learn the behavioral objectives in any instructional area.  Studies in both science and social studies have shown the effectiveness in the acquisition of vocabulary learnings in these two areas.  Being effective, then the multi-media approach should be included in the teaching-learning.

One of the best instructional tools which provide for the range of learners is the unit of study.  The unit of study includes behavioral objectives, suggested activities, and suggested materials.  It is primarily a pre-planning tool for the teachers and enables them to provide learning activities which are consistent with the needs and interests of the middle school student.

BASIC SKILL REPAIR AND EXTENSION

Purpose and Objectives

Some people insist that the middle school is probably the most challenging yet exasperating professional assignment in the teaching field.  The very
nature of pre-adolescent children offers a challenge
to every person who relates to them.  We consider
here the actions of the teacher, an authority figure
who attempts to transmit in a meaningful, understanding manner academic and social-cultural concepts.
At the same time these children represent a wide
variety of individuals who are themselves on a roller-
coaster in their cognitive, affective and psychomotor
development.

The topic to be discussed here represents the
very essence of the middle school years, an outline
of the academic opportunities to meet these children
at their peaks and valleys.  The middle school
program should provide opportunities for students to
receive clinical help needed for learning and extending the basic skills.  These skills fostered
by the elementary school program(s) should be built
upon to further both the self concept and the academic development of each student.  Morever, because
of the vast individual differences among the youngsters in basic skill development, a careful program
must be undertaken at this level.  These students
should be provided with organized experiences to
improve their basic skills as well as their personal
development.

This chapter primarily focuses on basic skills
assessment and development.  Three areas of study
are reviewed with respect to the middle school
level.  These areas are (1) reading, (2) language
arts, and (3) study skills.  Each section has components that review the basic objectives for middle
school programs.  The second component of each area

focuses on teaching, diagnostic ideas and suggestions that aid the teacher(s) in deciding where to start with their students. This chapter concludes with a summary. However, before the specific areas of study are considered, a brief discussion is offered to demonstrate the need for such programs. This discussion of need revolves around two recent studies in Illinois. It is further suggested that perhaps Illinois is typical of the "state of the middle school"--undeveloped.

## Recent Studies

Humm[1] conducted a study of junior high schools in Illinois and stated the following:

1. The junior high school is the most compromised area of the common school....It gets confused organizationally and philosophically with the middle school.

2. The junior high school has a mission. It tends to be a transition to high school. Its small size, limited grade span, preparatory nature and constraints in budgeting...cause it to be a "no-personsland" of public K-12 schooling.

3. The use of uniform class periods each week was the predominate schedule reported. Only about 10 percent of the schools tend to have a structure different from the uniform class period schedule.

4. Schools in suburbs were most likely to report alternative learning programs; rural schools were least likely to report these programs.

---

[1]Humm, William M. "The Junior High School: "No-Person's Land of Compromise", Thresholds, College of Education, Northern Illinois University, DeKalb, Illinois, July, 1979, Vol. V, No. 2, p. 8-12.

5. Over two-thirds (69%) of all courses were
   one school year in length, and about one-eighth
   (13%) were a half year in length.

6. Typical were courses which were:  52 percent
   academic, 16 percent arts (music and art),
   13 percent vocational related and 13 percent
   health related.

Even more crushing, according to Humm was that...
"detailed analysis indicated how compromised the
program of studies is in schools which must provide
students opportunities for preparation, remediation,
and exploration in an "in-between school" setting.

The current Study[2] was interested in the perception of reading, language arts and study skills
programs in middle schools in Illinois.  A discussion of this study is outlined in the following
paragraphs.

A questionnaire was sent to 110 middle and junior
high schools in Northern Illinois.  Of these, 28
were completed and returned.  The questionnaires,
aimed at collecting information concerning developmental skills programs in reading and math at the
junior high and middle school level, included the
following questions:

1. Do you have a developmental skills program
   to help remedial students in math or reading?

2. What levels of reading and math may be
   covered in this program/

3. How much time is devoted to each student for
   each area?  How are student schedules
   organized to accommodate these programs?

---

[2]Sloan, Charles A., "A Survey of 110 Northern
Illinois Middle/Junior High Schools", An unpublished
paper, 1979, Also see Sloan and Walker, Association
for Perception, Winter 1980.

4. Does the program utilize special resource
   rooms, in-class teaching, or some other
   arrangement?

5. Do you use an interdisciplinary approach,
   or is each subject completely independent?

6. Do you have any further comments, information
   and/or descriptions which you would like to
   add about your program?

The findings of this study were as follows:
Most of the schools did have some type of program
involving remedial help in both math and reading
(25 of 28). One school had a developmental skills
program for reading only, and another (1) had a
program for math only. One school had no program
for either area. The remaining schools (25) had
implemented a reading program aimed at developing
reading comprehension skills. In addition, skills
in the application of math, social studies, literature, science, and critical thinking were also reported.

There was a wide range of skill levels covered
by the various programs. Ten out of the 28 schools
simply reported individualized levels, according to
the students' needs. Four of the schools worked
with students who were approximately two years
below the grade norm: 7th grade programs covered
5th and 6th grade level skills, and 8th grade programs involved 6th and 7th grade levels.

A variety of settings are used for developmental
skills programs. Some schools combine different
types of groupings and settings, depending upon the
individual student's needs, while others utilize
single settings or forms of classes. Special resource rooms are the most commonly-used setting for
developmental skills programs; 11 out of 28 schools
used resource rooms. Next, in-class teaching, with
individualized student goals was reported by 10 of
the 28 schools. Four schools reported using Title I
reading classes, one of which was TAP (tutorial

assistance program) funded by Title I.  "Bilingual
students, who were weak in reading also receive
special TAP classes."  Some schools (6) have
developed special LD, BD, EMH, or EH classes for
their remedial students.  Team-teaching was another
approach reported.  Also listed were study periods,
study halls, homeroom periods, utilizing an in-
class LD teacher, after-school tutorial programs,
reading centers, E.S.E.A. teacher in the classroom,
ungraded remedial math classes, and a labs program
in math for "special education" students.  Finally
a "Reduced Ratio Room" based on PPS and IEP's was
reported.

The amount of time devoted to each student was
about the same in both the reading and mathematics
area.  (approximately 40-45 minutes per day)

The reading center at one middle school has
daily classes for 6th grade remedial reading students; "each month the Reading Center tries to provide some type of motivating project dealing with a
holiday or theme of the month... 6th graders also
make a monthly calendar... and write one creative
story dealing with the holiday or theme of the
month..."

In summary, this chapter was developed to
assist regular classroom teachers because of the
large number of teachers who deal with general teaching responsibilities in contrast to the few special
programs currently available.


Reading Instruction

Back to the Basics!  Competency testing!  Copperman[3] in the Literacy Hoax suggests that American education has a nationwide deterioration in the basic
skills...and the post-Sputnik  gains have quickly

---

[3] Copperman, Paul, The Literacy Hoax, New York:
Williams, Morrow and Co., 1978, pp. 185-186

disappeared.

Critics and criticism pervade society and haunt
the educationsl community. The thrust here was to
review objectives and effective practices in middle
school reading programs in order to improve instruction.

In order to grasp the totality of reading and
reading instruction at the middle school level,
(1) present statements about the nature of reading
in middle school reading programs are examined and
(2) suggested diagnostic teaching procedures are
offered to the reader. Moreover, reading has always
been at the center of attention. Once again the
perceptions of ideal versus real were considered. The
goal here was to concisely review suggested purposes
of reading instruction at the middle school level.

In general, initial and fundamental reading
instruction occurs in the primary grades in most
school districts. Barrett and Smith[4] suggest that...
After Grade three, however, this emphasis should
shift, and students should receive less instruction
in how to read with materials and exercises designed
primarily to teach reading skills and more help with
reading materials designed primarily to transmit
information or provide leisure time activity. Moreover, they suggest reading at this level is "to
learn to read by reading."

Otto and Smith[5] have suggested that reading programs consist of three phases.

---

[4] Smith, Richard J., and Barrett, Thomas C.,
Teaching Reading In The Middle Grades. Addison-
Wesley Publishing Co., Reading, Mass. 1974, p. 106.

[5] Otto, Wayne and Smith, Richard, Administering
the School Reading Program, Boston: Houghton Mifflin
Co., 1970, pp. 72-74.

    (1) Developmental--developing reading skills with
        materials designed for that purpose

    (2) Functional--getting information for a specific
        purpose

    (3) Recreational--enjoying reading and self-selec-
        ted materials

The above typology offers an excellent framework for
consideration of reading.  However, there is a need
to identify specific principles for middle school
reading.

Heilman[6] has suggested twelve (12) specific
principles for reading instruction at the middle
school level.  They are:

1. Evaluation of individual students is necessary
to determine each one's capacity and level of instruction in relation to

    a. sight vocabulary
    b. work recognition
    c. silent reading level
    d. vocabulary and conceptual level
    e. level of listening comprehension
    f. oral reading level
    g. ability to use reference materials and
       study skills
    h. habits of work and attitudes toward reading
    i. rate of reading

2. Diagnose and devise a reading program designed
   to give all students a successful reading
   experience.

3. Develop a systematic and specific reading
   instructional program.

---

[6]Heilman, Arthur W., Principles and Practices of
Teaching Reading, Charles E. Merrill, Columbus, Ohio,
1972.

4. Incorporate reading instruction into all content area subjects

5. Help children expend their stock of concepts

6. Give opportunity for practice in functional reading

7. Guide students in recreational and leisure reading

8. Broaden students' reading interests

9. Make available a wide selection of reading materials

10. Develop appreciation for good literature, poetry, drama

11. Develop reading programs for the gifted

12. Help children increase their rate of reading and to vary this rate to suit the material and purpose for reading

These principles were formulated to be representative of a theory and direction for reading instruction in the middle schools. Moreover, the principles of instruction suggested by Heilman seem to be utilized in a number of middle schools today. The primary objectives of diagnosis and prescription of instruction, the use of materials at or near the instructional level of the students, the development of skills and abilities as needed, the development of appreciation of literature, interests, and recreational reading, and the integration of the reading program into all aspects of the school curriculum when put into practice, all help middle school teachers to become effective reading instructors.

It appears that a definite reading program needs to be implemented at the middle school level. The basics seem to be that:

(1) All upper grade students need some help in
    developing specific reading skills.

(2) General reading abilities profit from direct
    instruction.

(3) Only through a broad based program of diagno-
    sis and sound instruction can reading be
    improved.

With the foregoing in mind, the section which
follows focuses on specific suggestions for middle
school teachers.


Instructional Suggestions for Reading

First it is very important to place in perspective the teachers role and the importance of reading.
Bond and Tinker  clarified these aspects as well as
a general guideline for a schoolwide philosophy of
reading.  These four guidelines are described in the
following paragraphs.

Bond and Tinker[7] estimate that seventy-five percent of the children who become remedial reading cases
could be helped successfully by the classroom teacher
before they reach that stage.  The necessary conditions are as follows:

1. All pressure from the teacher for every child
   to complete the same work in the same amount
   of time with the same amount of practice be
   eliminated;

2. Each child be accepted as an individual and
   permitted to work at his or her instructional
   level of reading, moving only as fast as the
   child is able to learn;

---

[7]Bond, Guy L. and Tinker, Miles A., Reading Difficulties:  Their Diagnosis and Correction, New York:
Appleton-Century-Crofts, 1967, p. 245.

3. The teacher's effort be bent toward providing many learning activities at many levels of difficulty so that each child would be challenged at his or her growing edge of learning:

4. The philosophy of the school be that other personnel are also concerned about each child's learning so that no teacher need operate alone.

Bond and Tinker's argument motivated this author to reiterate and display a few well known and established teaching procedures. Many of these ideas are long standing ideas suggested by many specialists and teachers. An effort was made to classify and categorize these ideas. Four major categories selected were: (1) General objectives, (2) Factors affecting motivation in reading, (3) In class reading ideas, and (4) Suggestions for working with poor readers.

1. General Objectives (Duffy[8])
   The teacher might consider:

   a. individual evaluation in order to determine the capacity and level of each student.
   b. a flexible reading program based on this diagnosis
   c. reading instruction should be deliberate and systematic
   d. in addition to specific reading instruction, reading skills must be incorporated with all subject matter.
   e. the child should be helped to expand his stock of concepts.
   f. basic texts should be supplemented in all areas with various types of functional reading: newspapers, magazines, and books, etc.

---

[8]Duffy, Gerald G., Reading In The Middle Schools, Perspectives In Reading, #18, International Reading Assoc., 800 Barksdale Rd., Newark, Delaware, 1971. p. 20.

     g. guidance is given in reading for recreation,
        pleasure, and personal growth.
     h. appreciation is developed for good litera-
        ture, poetry, and drama.
     i. children should be helped to increase the
        rate at which they can comprehend printed
        word symbols in combination.
     j. critical reading skills are improved by:
        1) coping with figurative or picturesque
           language
        2) drawing inferences
        3) classifying ideas
        4) evaluating ideas and arriving at the
           author's purpose or intent.
        5) detecting bias and differentiating
           between fact and opinion
     k. developing the following reading-study
        skills:
        1) using books effectively (index, table of
           contents, appendix)
        2) acquiring facility in the use of diction-
           aries
        3) using reference books effectively
        4) using library resources, card catalogues,
           and periodical indexes
        5) note-taking and outlining materials

2. Factors affecting motivation for reading--(Roe,
   Stoodt, and Burns[9]).  Teachers are reminded
   that the use of the following are important:
   a. Teacher enthusiasm:  setting an example or
      model is very important.
   b. Booklists, librarians, and reading special-
      ists to suggest books and supplementary ma-
      terials of various levels and interests.
   c. Motivational devices such as: classroom
      atmosphere--surround students with a wide
      variety of interesting books.  Set up a

---

[9]Roe, Betty D., Stoodt, Barbara D., and Burns,
Paul C., Reading Instruction In The Secondary School.
Rand McNally College Publishing Co., 1978. pp. 5,
10-15, 35.

   browsing area.
d. Magazines and newspapers:  providing a variety of topics and current subjects for the
   classroom.
e. Uninterrupted, sustained reading periods where
   students may select their own reading for
   pleasure.
f. Effects of instruction:
   showed "promising results" when suggesting
   that "teachers of English emulate strategies
   of thinking by explicitly teaching young
   people to understand and apply methods of
   mathematics, such as creating a structure of
   relations among ideas, abstracting, general-
   izing, and interpreting."
   1. Discussion with peers is important; group
      discussion raises the level of thinking.
   2. Types of teacher directed questions
      affect thinking:  "Analytical questions
      tend to stimulate analytical thinking." [11]
g. Consider the use of the laboratory approach:
   It is characterized by:
   1. Wide variety of reading goals.
   2. Self direction and responsibility where
      'every pupil may plan an individual pro-
      gram with the teacher'.
   3. Used by all the students, but is flexible
      and appropriate for all individual levels.
h. Developing and using interests in and related
   to reading:
   1. Oral reading by the teacher:  expose the
      students to good literature.  Read

---

[10] Henry and Brown found in Roe, Stoodt and Burns.

[11] Duffy, Gerald G., Reading In The Middle
Schools, Perspectives In Reading, #18, International
Reading Assoc., 800 Barksdale Rd., Newark, Delaware,
1971. p. 20.

[12] Smith, Richard J., and Barrett, Thomas C.,
Teaching Reading In The Middle Grades. Addison-
Wesley Publishing Co., Reading, Mass. 1974., p. 106.

'selectively and widely...from a broad
variety of readings...and carefully selected exerpts.'

2. Using tapes, records, filmstrips, and
other 'nonbook' media:  Expose the students to what is available in printed form:
stimulate interest.  Give poorer students
practice in reading along with the tapes,
etc.

3. Oral reading by the students to one
another; grouped by interest or cross
interest, and across grade levels.

4. Sharing literature through reading,
writing, speaking, dramatization, and
visual arts.

3. Regular Classroom "In Class" Reading Ideas:
The following suggestions are offered for
regular classroom teachers, they are:

a. Out of class special instruction is
necessary, but it must be coordinated with
the classroom program.

b. Realistic, individualized goals must be
set.

c. 'Total Programs' have been implemented,
where the regular classes (social studies,
mathematics, science, etc.) also emphasize good reading and study skills.[13]
Also, extra developmental classes
supplement these integrated programs.

d. Content teachers can also help in the
classrooms.[14]  In setting individualized
teaching and learning methods, it is
important to 'distinguish between inability

---

[13]Gunn, M. Agnella, What We Know About High
School Reading:  National Conference on Research in
English, 1969.

[14]Op cit. Duffy, p. 20.

to understand the concepts and inability
to read the concepts in the first place.'

e. Better readers may read aloud to others,
or poor readers could read silently along
with a tape recording. Learning concepts
may be presented through some avenue other
than reading.

f. The teacher may emphasize the transfer of
information from reading to thought.

g. Reading materials need to be varied, with
different levels and interest.

h. Reading assignments need to be adjusted
to fit all the students.[15]

The teacher may utilize:

1. Study guides to help students
focus on particular information.

2. Structural overviews, which involve using a graphic arrangement
of terms that apply to the important concepts in the passage.

3. Directed reading approaches, including:

a) motivation and building background

b) guided reading of the story,
(silent and/or oral)

c) skill development activities

d) follow-up activities

4. Suggestions to use with poor readers:[16]

a. Discover each poor reader's reading
strengths and weaknesses. Using a combination of assessment procedures including
standardized tests, and informal diagnosis from a conference with the reader,

---

[15]Op cit. Roe, Stoodt and Burns, p. 5, 10-15, 35.

[16]Op cit. Smith and Barrett, p. 158-166.

using basal readers, multilevel kits, etc.

b. Give poor readers encouragement and opportunities to read materials of their own
own choosing, with no comprehension checks
or other penalties to pay after reading.

c. Teach poor readers to rely heavily on
context clues to get the meaning of unfamiliar words. Allowing the child to concentrate on contextual cues instead of phonetic
analysis and 'sounding out' words will give
him the success of understanding what he
is reading and will eventually learn to use
both contextual clues and phonetic-analysis
skills.

d. Before poor readers begin reading a selection, alert them to specific linguistic
structures and devices likely to use interpretation difficulties (e.g., figurative
language, unusual or long sentence structures, specialized vocabulary, punctuation).
Note: The teacher should read the assigned
material in advance to be able to
prepare poor readers for potential
'trouble spots' in the linguistic
structure of the material.

e. Provide poor readers with information that
relates to the ideational content of their
reading material.
"Poor readers frequently possess meager
experiential backgrounds....Time spent
discussing concepts, viewing a film,
or looking at pictures...can provide a
cognitive framework into which the
ideas in a reading selection can fit..."

f. Teach poor readers to pause periodically in
their reading to reflect on what they have
just read and make some predictions about
what they will read next.

g. Do not require poor readers to read orally
in front of their classmates.
"Many students with reading problems
are better silent readers than they are
oral readers, and an embarrassing display of their greatest weakness is a

degrading experience of no instructional
value."

h. Give poor readers opportunities to be
successful with tasks or projects that do
not require reading.  This is to preserve
the poor reader's self-concept, and give
him a useful place in the classroom.

i. Assemble a library of audio tapes, filmstrips, phonograph records, and films to
help poor readers get the information
they need without reading.

j. Poor readers should, whenever possible, be
provided with content area-related reading
materials at easy readability levels instead of the materials good readers use.
Besides giving the poor reader successful
reading experiences at his own level, class
discussions are often more interesting
and meaningful when they bring out the
student's different reading experiences
relative to a broad, common topic.

k. Give poor readers many opportunities to
discuss reading experiences with better
readers in small groups.  This will provide
the poorer reader with the model he needs
if he is to learn what a good reader does
when he reads and what he gets from his
reading experiences.

l. Refer seriously disabled readers to remedial instruction and coordinate classroom programs with remedial programs.

### Language Arts

The thesis of this text and chapter hinge on the
notion that formal specialized instruction in basic
skills may be necessary and made available to middle
school age students.  The language arts are related
and an integral aspect of all teaching; therefore,
deserve attention herein even though taught
as a separate subject.  It is not the author's intent
to review the whole of language arts, but to present
basic tenets that all teachers can utilize in their

teaching. In addition, a few selected ideas and references are put forward for consideration for the reader's use.

Burns[17] proposes that the following are aspects that are more or less unique to language instruction. Other notes and ideas supplement these ideas in the remaining passages.

1. Oral language development is fundamental to other language arts. Children who express themselves effectively in speech tend to succeed in other areas of language arts. However, oral language development depends in a great measure on the various aspects of a student's environment. It is especially noteworthy for teachers at the middle school level to be cognizant of the "gang" and other social pressures...[18]

   Polley suggests that teachers who recognize the influence of social pressure will avoid an "only-one-way-is-right attitude..." Further he suggests that the teacher's task is to...
   a. Make the...student...an observer of the languages spoken about him,
   b. Instruct the...student...in standard usage patterns, and
   c. Lead the...student...to establish goals which are realistic...
2. Pupils should work with content in practical situations before the ideas are analyzed...In this way...pupils would be encouraged to see a pattern for themselves, forming their own

---

[17]Burns, Paul C., Diagnostic Teaching of the Language Arts, F.W. Peacock, Publishers, Inc., Itasca, Illinoism 1974, p. 2-9.

[18]Polley, Robert C., The Teaching of English Usage, The National Council of Teachers of English, Rubana, Illinois, 1974, p. 187.

conclusions or generalization about the accepted use of words.
3. For fuller language development, the child
   must participate actively in the process of
   learning. Growth in any curriculum requires
   action; growth in language skills requires
   greater action.
4. Because of the creative, intimate nature of the
   relationship between language and the child, a
   feeling of abiding regard and respect for the
   worth of each child must be maintained.

Many language arts teachers subscribe to...The
Diagnostic Point of View as a tenet of teaching.
Burns relates that....the word "diagnostic" is
derived from two Greek roots which means "to know
thoroughly." As related earlier, knowing the child
thoroughly and their progress was essential to preparation for teaching. Here too in the language arts,
this concept is essential...

DIAGNOSTIC CHECKLIST     D. Triplett[19]

Developmental Evaluation Scale:

1. Shows awareness — is conscious of                                     ) can do it sometimes
2. Undertakes         — is introduced to a skill           ) with teacher guidance
3. Recognizes         — identifies, discriminates       )
4. Knows               — understands, comprehends    ) can do it independently
5. Uses                — listens, speaks, reads, writes )
                                  effectively

ORAL LANGUAGE

1. Listens for the following purposes:

   a. to follow directions

   b. to identify main ideas

   c. to remember sequence

[19]Triplett, DeWayne, A Developmental Checklist (for Language Arts), 1980. (Permission given) Unpublished. Northern Illinois University, DeKalb, Illinois.

---

    d. to remember details

    e. to distinguish relevant and
       irrelevant information

    f. to predict outcomes, make inferences,
       and draw conclusions

    g. to sense sounds, rhyme, rhythm,
       images, moods, prejudices

    h. to detect speaker's purpose—inform,
       persuade, entertain

    i. to detect fact from opinion

    j. to judge the validity of information

2. Uses language creatively

    a. to express needs, concerns, thoughts

    b. to make individual presentations—
       dictating, recording, reading, reporting

    c. to share ideas interactively—dramatic
       play, discussion, debate, conversation

    d. to entertain—puppets, plays, poems,
       literature, readers' theatre, story
       telling, choral reading, singing

1. Writes for the following purposes:

   a. to label: pictures, titles, descriptions, forms, directions

   b. to request or inform: letters, notes, telegrams, announcements, advertisements

   c. to react: editorials, reviews

   d. to record: messages, outlines, logs, minutes, diaries, notes, reports

   e. to entertain: stories, poetry, music, plays, essays

2. Uses writing techniques and devices:

   a. to employ rhyme, rhythm, alliteration

   b. to express feelings: humor, nonsense, amusement, pathos, distress, lament, sadness

   c. to generate figurative language: idioms, similes, metaphors, imagery, onomatopoeia

   d. to influence word choice: pronouns, tense forms, meanings, usage

   e. to interpret relationships: cause-effect, general-specific, time-place, part-whole

   f. to differentiate fact and opinion: news stories, advertising

   g. to employ a literary genre: realism, fantasy, fable, folktale, mystery

   h. to achieve time and tone: flashbacks, foreshadowing, irony, suspense.

   i. to establish an interpretation: mood, point-of-view, characterization

3. Writes words:

   a. to express ideas: accuracy, vividness, specificity, appropriateness, variety

    b. to communicate effectively:  tense forms, plurals, possessives, spelling

4. Writes sentences:

    a. to express intent:  declarative, imperative, interrogative, exclamatory

    b. to offer variety:  simple, compound, complex

    c. to lend interest:  varied patterns, lengths, contrasts

    d. to achieve coherence:  meaning, sequence, transition, coordination, subordination

5. Writes paragraphs

    a. to develop unity of thought:  introductory, supporting, concluding sentences

    b. to express a unifying theme:  logical progression, supporitng data, consistency of viewpoint, sense of audience

    c. to indicate transitions:  conversations, change in time, place, setting, or topic

6. Uses knowledge of mechanics:

    a. to punctuate:  periods, commas, question marks, apostrophes, hyphens, colons

    b. to capitalize:  I, first word in sentence, proper nouns, proper adjectives, important words in titles, words and letters in outline

    c. to execute form:  margins, paragraph indentations, handwriting, spelling, usage

Triplett[20] has developed a diagnostic checklist as an aid to regular and language arts teachers. This checklist is offered as a means to assist teachers.  Finally, Burns text, Diagnostic Teaching of

---

[20]Ibid.

the Language Arts is suggested as a practical guide
for further assistance in each of the areas in
language arts for all teachers. This text has a
wealth of excellent teaching ideas.


### Study Skills/Content Areas

The point of view taken in this section is that
all teachers, regardless of discipline can assist
middle school age students in their development.
Friedman and Rowls[21] suggest commonalities among
content areas exist and should be utilized. Their
observations are as follows:

Current thinking and trends in each of the
content areas emphasize a number of common concerns.
The curriculum in English (including literature and
grammar), science, social studies, and mathematics
has, according to current thinking, the following
general factors in common:

1. That each content area is concerned with the
   language and thinking abilities required to
   understand the content, and that communication is of central concern.

2. That each content area should emphasize the
   relationship between the knowledge in that
   area and people, that is, how knowledge of the
   content helps one to understand individuals,
   societies, and whole cultures.

3. That each content area possesses structure
   and that this structure can be utilized in
   enhancing the learning that goes on in each
   content area.

4. That each content area is related to other
   disciplines and areas of knowledge and that

---

[21] Friedman, Myles I., and Rowls, Michael D.,
Teaching Reading & Thinking Skills, Longman Inc. New
York, 1980, p. 389-390, 425.

the content should be presented, studied,
and learned in the context of other
disciplines.

5. That the knowledge in each content area has
practical utility for improving students'
abilities to live effectively in a complex
society.

These common factors certainly crystallize how
middle school teachers can relate to the overall
program at this level.  In addition, there is always
a concern of how study skills relate to the several
areas of study.  A comprehensive analysis was
conducted by Van Dongen.  This summary is included
to further integrate the use of the study skills and
content areas.

Van Dongen[22] surveyed several graded series of
readers to find out which study skills are commonly
taught.  From this research he synthesized the
following outline.

I. Ability to locate information
  A. Ability to locate information by using
     the aid of book parts
     1. Cover, title page, title, author,
        publisher, location of publisher,
        editor's name, name of series, and
        edition
     2. copyright page and date of publication
     3. preface, introduction, foreward
     4. table of contents and locating topics
        by pages

---

[22]
    Van Dongen, Richard D., "An Analysis of Study
Skills Taught by Intermediate Grade Basal Readers,"
M.A. Thesis, University of New Mexico, August, 1967,
(pp. 47-54).  Found in Zintz, Miles V. The Reading
Process, Wm. Brown, Dubuque, Iowa, 1980. (3rd
edition), pp. 281-286.

     5. table of contents to locate topical
       organization of book or determine impor-
       tance of topic by number of pages
       devoted to it
     6. locating specific pages rapidly
     7. lists of illustrations, maps, figures
     8. chapter headings, main headings, sec-
       tion titles, subtitles
     9. footnotes and references at end of chap-
       ters
   10. glossary
   11. indexes, select and use key word, cross-
       references
   12. locate and use the appendix
   13. locate and use the bibliography

B. Ability to locate information by using
   knowledge of alphabetizing
     1. ability to locate any given letter
       quickly
     2. knowing sections; beginning, middle, end
     3. arranging words by initial letter
     4. arranging words by second letter
     5. arranging words by third or following
       letters
     6. alphabetizing any given list of words
     7. locating words or titles with Mc or Mac
     8. use of articles a, an, and the in
       locating words or titles
     9. alphabetizing people's names when first
       and last names are given

C. Ability to locate information by using
   references
     1. locate information by using references
       a. finding words quickly
         using the guide words
         using a thumb index
       b. locate the pronunciation key
       c. use of special sections of dictionary-
         geographical terms, biographical
         dictionary, foreign words and phrases
       d. ability to use the dictionary as an
         aid in pronunciation; ability to

interpret phonetic spelling and
diacritical marks determining
pronunciation of words spelled alike;
determining preferred pronunciation
e. use of dictionary to determine
   meanings
   select meaning from context
   pictorial or verbal illustrations
   determine what part of speech a
   word is
f. use of dictionary as an aid in checking spelling
g. locate base word as an entry
h. derivations of the base word
i. noting syllabic divisions of a word
j. origin of words
k. synonyms or antonyms
2. locating information in the encyclopedia
   a. locating volume from information on
      the spine of the book
   b. using initial letters and guide words
   c. using the index in the last volume
   d. using specialized encyclopedias
3. ability to use and locate other
   references
   a. selecting appropriate references for
      locating information
   b. locate and use various guides and
      sources:
      (1) almanac
      (2) atlas
      (3) city directory
      (4) government publications
      (5) junior book of authors
      (6) newspapers and periodicals
      (7) posters
      (8) radio or television schedules
      (9) telephone directory
      (10) time schedules
      (11) yearbooks
4. ability to use text books and trade
   books for locating information

  D. Ability to use the library and its aids for
   locating information
   1. card catalog
    a. desired topic, author, or title
    b. alphabetical arrangement in card
     catalog
   2. organization of the library for locating
    material
    a. shelf plans, labels, and floor plans
    b. Dewey-decimal system, Library of
     Congress, or other methods
    c. locate reference books
    d. locate and use the magazine file
    e. locate and use appropriate indexes
     (1) Readers' Guide to Periodical
      Literature
     (2) Who's Who
     (3) Biographical dictionaries
     (4) Thesaurus
     (5) Unabridged dictionary
     (6) Subject Index to Poetry for Chil-
      dren and Young People

  E. Locate information by using maps, graphs,
   charts, pictorial material


II. Ability to organize information

  A. Use knowledge of alphabetizing or organizing information

  B. Construct an outline
   1. ability to put material in sequence
    a. arrange steps of a process in order
    b. construct a time line
   2. classify information on two-way charts,
    tables
   3. construct an outline
    a. find main headings
    b. give main and subordinate topics
    c. provide subordinates when given
     main heading or provide main
     heading when subordinates

        d. outline single paragraphs
        e. outline short selections
        f. outline more complex selections
        g. put ideas together from various
           sources in outline form
        h. outline what has been read and use
           outline in a presentation--either
           written or oral

   C. Ability to summarize material
     1. summary statement for a paragraph
     2. write summary statements for a short
       selection
     3. write summary statements for more com-
       plex selections
     4. use a summary as data for oral or written
       reports
     5. bring together information from several
       sources
     6. write a summary using an outline
     7. construct maps, graphs, charts, or
       pictorial material as a summary of
       information

   D. Ability to take notes
     1. take notes in brief--they may be
       grammatically incorrect and abbreviated
     2. in outline form--formal or informal
     3. in precise writing (spaced intervals of
       listening or reading)
     4. take notes in fact-inferences charts
     5. note origin of information for footnotes
       and bibliography


III. Ability to use and interpret maps, graphs,
    charts, and other pictorial material

   A. Use and interpret maps and globes
     1. ability to locate desired information
       a. interpret key and map symbols
       b. use map scales
       c. interpret directions

      2. ability to demonstrate understanding of
         map distortions or type of projection

  B. Use and interpret graphs, tables, diagrams,
    and other pictorial matter
     1. interpret graphs
       a. bar graphs
       b. circle graphs
       c. line graphs
     2. interpret tables
     3. interpret diagrams
     4. interpret time lines
     5. interpret other pictorial material

  C. Read and use charts

The knowledge of this information can appraise
teachers of the interrelationships of content areas.
The above guide can also be used as a checklist to
determine the competency level of students. This
process is applicable as a pre-test or simply as
information necessary to the teaching in the various
content areas.

## Competencies/Mastery Learning

Because competency based education continues to
face educators, a review of basic strategies on the
part of the teacher are in order. A resume of these
concepts were outlined by Friedman and Rowls[23] which
fit nicely in the scheme of this review. They review
the work of Block and Anderson appropriately for
exhibit and use.

There has been sufficient research evidence
supporting Carroll's and Bloom's positions for
us to advocate the use of mastery learning
strategies in the classroom. Block (1971)
described the application of mastery

---

[23]Op cit. Friedman and Rowls, pp. 389-390, 425.

learning strategy to classroom learning.
Block and Anderson (1975) have published
a booklet which summarizes the procedure.

To apply the mastery learning strategy,
the teacher defines instructional goals,
prepares a final exam to test the achievement of the goals, and establishes a score
on the final exam that indicates mastery
of the goals much as we have described.
In addition, the teacher prepares instructional activities to facilitate the
achievement of the goals and a short diag-
nostic-process test to be administered at
the end of each instructional activity to
assess progress toward the goal and to
diagnose impediments to student progress.
The instructional activities are used
initially to produce the desired learning
and as corrective activities for students
who do not show adequate progress on the
diagnostic-progress tests.

The implications of the mastery learning
strategy for instructional planning require
the teacher to prepare a variety of instructional activities to facilitate the achievement of a desired learning outcome.  Some
activities are used in initial instruction,
and some are used as correctives.  The
corrective activities are to be different
from the initial activities so that a student
who does not make acceptable progress as a
result of the initial instruction may choose
an alternative mode as a corrective.  In
addition, the teacher prepares short tests for
administration at the end of each instructional activity.  She uses the tests to
provide feedback for herself and the student
concerning student progress and reasons for
lack of progress.  She prescribes corrective-
ness for students who need to be directed back
on the track that leads to the desired
learning outcome.  Students are given all the

opportunities they need to achieve the
desired outcome.

Further, they outline the structure for planning
teaching.  For more information, the basic outline
in seven steps is as follows:

Step 1:  Orienting the Students. To orient
the student he is informed of what he is
going to learn and how he is going to be
taught.
To orient the student to the total instructional program the teacher can distribute to
and discuss with the student the table of
specifications.  It shows what the student
has mastered so far and what he is to learn.
The teacher can discuss the mastery learning
strategy to acquaint the student with how
he will be taught.
As the teacher prepares to move students
from a readiness state to a particular
desired learning outcome, she can distribute and discuss the relevant goal statement.
This acquaints the students with what they
will learn next.  To acquaint the students
with how they will be taught, the teacher
can describe the sequence of instructional
activities she has planned as well as the
diagnostic-progress tests she will use and
when they will be administered.

Step 2:  Administering Instructional Activities.  The isntructional activities are
administered according to plan.

Step 3:  Administering Diagnostic-progress
Tests.  The diagnostic-progress tests are
administered on completion of each activity.

Step 4:  Relating Feedback to Students.  The
students are given feedback.  The results of
the test are discussed with the students
privately and their strengths and weaknesses
are described.  They are also given

encouragement.

Step 5:  Moving to the Next Learning Activity.  Students who have made satisfactory progress move on to the next learning activity.  Correctives are administered to students who do not make satisfactory progress.  If the teacher desires to keep students moving at the same pace, he can have the students who made satisfactory progress tutor the others.  Or he can involve students who make satisfactory progress in enrichment activities.

Step 6:  Monitoring Corrective Activities. The teacher monitors the corrective activities to make certain that the students who need correctives get as much guidance as they require in order to get back on the track.

Step 7:  Administering the Final Examination. The final exam is administered.  The teacher certifies mastery for those who score above the mastery cut-off score on the test.  If the feedback corrective procedures have been thoughtfully planned and carried out, most of the students will achieve mastery.  The few who do not are recycled to an earlier stage of instruction and given more correctives so that they may achieve mastery.

The general review up to this point was to focus on basic notions of teaching at the middle school level for most teachers.  Included in these areas of concern is the common concern for reading and reading materials.  The following paragraphs consider these ideas and concerns.

Reading in the Control Areas:  It is clear from the literature and this author's recent studies that a need exists for instruction at the middle school level in all subject areas.  Teachers in content areas must be drawn into active reading instruction.  If content area teachers accept the responsibility and opportunity to increase reading ability, the independence of the

student and mastery of the subject matter will
occur. It is especially necessary to help students
develop requisite comprehension skills in content
areas. Bush and Huebner[24] suggest that these
student skills are:

1. Setting his own purposes
2. Acquiring the special or technical vocabulary of the subject matter
3. Understanding the concepts specific to the
   content area
4. Noting main points and supporting details
5. Noting sequence and interrelationships in the
   presentation of ideas
6. Being alert to ways of making the new
   learnings functional in his own life.

These are excellent student oriented objectives.
In addition, other authors suggest guidelines for
teachers. Otto and Smith[25] suggest five additional
guidelines for the teacher who wants to help middle
grade students read content area materials successfully.
They are:

1. Whenever possible have materials relative to
   the topic being studied available at different
   levels of reading difficulty to accommodate the
   differing reading abilities of students in the
   class.

2. Make reading assignments short when the
   ideational content is difficult to understand
   or the writing style is difficult for young

---

[24]Bush, Clifford L., Huebner, Mildred H., Strategies for Reading in the Elementary School, (second
edition), New York, Mac Millan Publishing Co., 1979,
P. 167.

[25]Op cit. Otto and Smith, pp. 72-74.

readers.
3. Know the reading strengths and weaknesses of the students well enough to
   anticipate difficulties with certain
   materials.
4. Read the material to be assigned carefully beforehand to become aware of
   ideational content, words, sentences,
   figurative language, or other aspects
   likely to present obstacles to comprehension.
5. Prepare students for the ideas they
   will encounter and for linguistic
   elements which are likely to give them
   trouble.

In addition to the above basic skills suggestions,
teachers in the various content areas need to be
mindful of their special content and requisite
specialized knowledge and reading skills (i.e. reading in science may be very different than english
literature). Careful analysis of the reading task
can help students to become successful both in reading
and the special topic.

In summary, the following passage is offered
regarding the content areas. This was developed by
Harold Herber[26] in his book Teaching Reading in Content Areas:

Students' lack understanding of when to
apply the skills they apparently know. It is,
for example, easier to underline a sentence
that appears to be important than it is to
recognize how the sentence fits into the
total organizational pattern of the content
that is being studied. Such indiscriminate
practices may prove to be more confusing than
helpful. Most study skills courses are based

---

[26]Herber, Harold L., Teaching Reading In
Content Areas, Prentice-Hall, Inc. Englewood
Cliffs, N.J., 2nd Ed., p. 70-72.

upon the premise that students will benefit
more from an orderly plan of learning than
they will from a hit-or-miss approach. Some
courses place heavy emphasis on improving
students' attitudes, motivations, and
interests while others emphasize a particular
technique or plan. Experience indicates
that overemphasis on either the psychological aspects of learning or the skills is
not the most fruitful approach. A successful
study skills program is one in which a
competent teacher has time to meet with students, provide extrinsic motivation when it
is needed, supply students with numerous
interesting materials at their own reading
levels, and teach them the skills they need
for learning.

To consider study skills primarily as
a set of mechanical procedures is to limit
one's view of study, and to oversimplify;
study skills, when properly taught, include
a systematic, sequential approach to learning.

Because mathematics is included in the basic
3 R's and a few schools are providing special
instruction, a brief section is offered here. The
subsection focuses on reading mathematics and also
included a brief statement about general objectives
and concerns in this content area.

General and Reading Concerns in Mathematics: The
concerns in mathematics over the past few years have
revolved around "new math." Most educators, not to
speak of the general public, do not understand where
mathematics educators stand today with respect to
their discipline. In order to bring some understanding to the regular classroom teacher and other educators, information on this topic was sought.

Bell[27] has offered his view. He has stated that:

> Essentially, curricular concerns in mathematics currently revolve around a host of substantive issues. These issues will, in turn, influence both the teaching of mathematics and the content of the mathematics curriculum to be taught. In part, these issues might be summarized as follows:
>
> 1. Making the content of mathematics more purposeful and showing students how math content can be applied to other areas of knowledge as well as the practical problems students encounter daily.
> 2. Teaching mathematics in a topical sequence that will optimize students' mathematics achievement by emphasizing the structure of the content.
> 3. Emphasizing the relation of mathematics to other areas of interest, knowledge, and pursuit.
> 4. Showing how mathematics has influenced civilization and culture.
> 5. Teaching both deductive and inductive logic using mathematics as the vehicle.

The importance of Bell's statement here is that mathematics teachers too hold a concern for interrelationships. The concern is fundamental to the thrust of basic education. In addition, it was a concern of this section to explore reading in content areas.

---

[27]Bell, Frederick H., _Teaching Elementary School Mathematics: Methods and Content for Grades K-8_, Wm. C. Brown Publishers, Dubuque, Iowa, 1980, p. 566-568.

It is generally held that students who have difficulties in reading will also have difficulties in content areas.  Bell has said that "An erroneous assumption about teaching mathematics is that reading mathematics isn't a very important activity in learning
the subject."  Moreover, Earle[28] states that... "Most
professionals agree that reading in any subject matter
field can not and should not be separated from concept
development in that area."  Because of this concern a
few suggestions about the teaching of reading in
mathematics are offered as reminders to teachers.  They
are:

1. Most people agree that teaching reading of
   mathematics materials will result in improved
   attitudes and achievement results.
2. Carefully prepared directions and study guides
   assist students in reading and gaining concepts in mathematics.
3. "Middle school mathematic teachers should not
   assume that students have learned how to read
   textbooks and study mathematics."  Practice in
   these skills need continued review and
   emphasis.
4. Bell states emphatically, that, "Mathematical
   reading requires precision, orderliness, flexibility and concentration."  He describes this
   as follows:
   a. When reading a section of a mathematics
      textbook, the reader must know the
      precise meaning of each mathematical
      term and each mathematical symbol.
      There is little room for connotation,
      conjecture, and speculation.  When a
      student attempts to understand a con-
      cept or principle, he or she cannot
      afford to ignore or skim over a word
      that is not understood.  Each mathemat-
      ical concept has a precise meaning and
      plays a definite part in comprehending

---

[28]Earle, Richard A., Teaching Reading and Mathematics, Newark, Delaware:  International Reading
Association, 1979.  An 88 page monograph.

a principle or solving a problem.

b. When reading mathematics, each word and each sentence should be read carefully. Charts, tables, diagrams, and examples should be studied thoughtfully. Steps in the solution of an exercise or problem and each sentence of an explanation should be read and thought about until they are fully understood.

c. Flexibility is required in mathematical reading. At times it may be useful to stop and look up the meanings of terms in the glossary. It may be necessary to read a passage several times before the author's intention becomes clear.

d. If a student becomes disinterested in the material or if his or her mind begins to wander, the sequence, structure, and organization of the material will quickly be lost.[29]

These suggestions make excellent guidelines for all teachers in the content areas! Finally, these ideas must be utilized in daily teaching preparation.

## Summary

This chapter focused on basic skill repair and extension. The overall thesis was on basic concepts required in the middle school instructional programs. Specifically, attention was given to basic concepts and instructional strategies for the general classroom teacher. All teachers in middle schools need to be teachers of reading and study skills regardless of their discipline or assignment.

At the outset, two recent studies were quoted to develop the overall rationale and urgent need for

---

[29] Herber, Harold L., Teaching Reading In Content Areas, Prentice-Hall, Inc. Englewood Cliffs, N.J., 2nd Ed., p. 70-72.

general instructional improvement in the middle schools.
The remainder of the chapter provided ideas and concepts in reading, reading the content fields, language arts, and study skills.  Teachers who are
serious about improvement of their instruction may
wish to follow these basic ideas and/or turn to
additional study by seeking the references used
herein.  These materials appear to possess many
excellent concepts and teaching ideas.

### EXPLORATORY AND ENRICHMENT STUDIES

Transescents love to explore, investigate, inquire and test many things and ideas with which they come in contact. This is their nature at this time in their development and middle school educators need to know this, to understand this characteristic and to make plans that fit the situation.

The methods used by students to find out about things that attract their curiosity range widely and perhaps wildly, too. They may take something apart to see how it works. Whether or not they ever put it back together is another matter. They may pursue a minor detail through persistent reading just to see if it is, indeed, so. They may question a teacher, sometimes challenging the teacher to the point of exasperation on the adult's part. Though easily frustrating to teacher and parents, this is merely the means that curious transescents use to find out more about themselves, their environment and their roles in that environment.

Knowledge of this important character trait is not enough alone. The challenge for middle school teachers is to use this innate exploratory drive of transescents to enhance the social, intellectual, emotional and physical development of these students while in school. The program of the middle school/ junior high school should reflect this knowledge. This chapter will present some practical ideas and methods and make other general suggestions which may be of help to teachers as they seek to cope with this strong student drive in their classrooms. Many of the best ideas, however, will come as teachers apply some of the more general guidelines to their own unique school settings.

Exploratory programs in the middle/junior high school can be divided into two major categories:

1.  Classroom exploratory programs, which refers to ideas, methods and materials that can be

used in the instructional classroom setting.
These can generally be used in all the disciplines or subject areas and in any school
staff organizational pattern.

2.  Special exploratory programs refers to the
multitude of grade-wide or school-wide activities designed to be exploratory in nature.
They may be of short duration or may take a
considerable length of time to reach full
implementation.

## Getting Started

Getting started properly is greatly helped when
there is a well-defined and generally accepted reason
for changing to a more exploratory program. The
absence of a well-defined reason for such a change
or reliance on a poorly defined reason can cause
serious problems including ultimate failure. If
teachers do not understand why changes are being made,
they are certainly not going to be ready to move into
implementation of any program. This is particularly
true of exploratory programs which may often be
markedly different kinds of activities than the ones
teachers have been accustomed to.

Often, in education, when new concepts or ideas
are to be implemented in a curricular program,
planners simply tack on another course designed to
deal with the new idea. While this approach to
curriculum change may be direct and easily implemented,
the results are often less than desired. The curriculum soon becomes an accumulation of added-on
courses without any real threads running through all
of them. Teachers may then be heard to complain
about the results of such accretions. They may say,
"I just don't have enough time in the day to do all
these things," or "I'm already grading and planning
until midnight, how can I possibly do else?" or "How
important is this new stuff, anyhow?" It is not hard
to see that a curriculum can get out of hand without
some attention to its overall aspects. So, change
of any kind and certainly change to the use of more

exploratory activities and opportunities for students
calls for careful planning and preparation on the
part of teachers and students in the middle/junior
high school.

Early in such planning, it is necessary to find
out how well, if at all, the present instructional
program is providing attention to this exploratory
need on the part of the students. Analyze the present program to identify those activities that are
exploratory in nature or at least seem to be exploratory. Look carefully at teaching strategies used,
instructional materials on hand, instructional goals
and objectives as these reflect exploration by
students and whether evaluation procedures take into
account the exploratory drive of students and how
this is being met in the school.

Specifically, one might begin the task by examining a weekly lesson plan based on the planning
format found in this chapter in Table I, page 4.
Future or past lesson plans may be used to examine
the extent to which exploratory opportunities and
activities are being implemented in the classrooms.
To get a true evaluation of the lesson plans, it is
imperative that "honesty be the best policy." Do
not "stretch" or exaggerate what really happened or
what will happen when students do what the lesson
plans suggest. Be factual and "tell it like it is."

Examine the planning sheet on page 4. You will
note the objective area at the top left corner of
the page. In the proper space, write the major
objective set for the students to accomplish. If the
objective defines anticipated affective growth on the
part of students, then more general terms can be used.
It could be possible for one objective to seek both
cognitive and affective growth. Often, instructional
objectives are already identified for the teacher in
the school curriculum guide or in some commercial
materials. If these instructional objectives are
available, they may be used for this planning format.
Be sure that the objectives are the ones desired for
the activity.

Table 1

PLANNING SHEET

Objective _____     Teacher _____

                            Date _____

| Student Learning Opportunities & Activities | Major Skill Development | Teaching Strategy |
|---|---|---|
| SLOA 1 | | |
| SLOA 2 | | |
| SLOA 3 | | |
| SLOA 4 | | |

Resources Needed                Evaluation

SLOA 1                          SLOA 1
SLOA 2                          SLOA 2
SLOA 3                          SLOA 3
SLOA 4                          SLOA 4

It must be remembered that objectives are important organizing elements of any educational program. Poorly stated objectives may lead to ill-defined student outcomes. Well-stated objectives describe clearly those student outcomes that are desired.

Examples

1. Poorly stated objective--The students will learn spelling words.

   Clearly stated objective--The students will spell and define with 80% accuracy a list of 20 spelling words selected from Science, Social Studies, Math or Literature texts.

2. Poorly stated objective--The students will know how our country is different from the country of Brazil.

   Clearly stated objective--The students will list three ways in which the government of the United States differs from the government of Brazil.

After the objectives have been stated on the planning sheet, the next step is to define the student learning opportunities, (SLO) and student learning opportunities activities, (SLOA) that will be used for students to accomplish each stated objective. In the SLOA, describe what the student will be doing in order to meet the objective, not what the teacher will be doing. What the students do or are exposed to will determine if the objective will be met or not rather than what the teacher does or teaches. It is very possible for teachers to teach and students not to learn. It is also possible for the students to learn even though the teacher doesn't teach.

This statement is even more appropriate when examining and designating exploratory and enrichment activities. Students should play the active role in exploratory and enrichment while the teacher usually

becomes a passive but concerned and observant
facilitator. The following are examples of Student
Learning Opportunities and Activities (SLOA).

Objective: "The student will verbally or in
written form explain and/or demonstrate how
simple crystals are formed."

Under the SLOA column will be listed a number
of different activities designed to help the
students meet the objective.

"The student will plan and demonstrate how
crystals are formed." Under the SLOA column will be
listed a number of different activities from which
the student can choose, each designed to meet the
objective.

SLOA 1.   Read and discuss a chapter in the
          science book dealing with crystal forma-
          tion.

SLOA 2.   Follow the instructions for making rock
          candy to show simple crystal formation.

SLOA 3.   Plan a visit to a nearby cavern or cave
          to study the crystal formation.

SLOA 4.   Invite a guest speaker to talk on the
          subject of crystal formation.

SLOA 5.   View a film on crystal formation.

Further appropriate activities may be listed--
the more, the better.

The next step in this procedure is to show the
major skill development for each SLOA. The first
called for the student to read about crystal formation as contained in the science text. One skill
development involved here is the ability to secure
information about crystals through reading. Another
skill could be the improvement of the reading process,
particularly those with reading problems. The SLOA

involving a laboratory demonstration by student of
how crystals are formed has an advantage for some
students who learn best when dealing with concrete
operations. Here, they would actually do, as well as
see, the process they were learning. For each SLOA,
the desired major skill development that is desired
should be stated.

In Table 1, under the heading "Resources Needed,"
there would be information about the materials needed
for each SLOA and suggestions for its use. These
materials should be placed in the classroom so that
they are accessible to students. For the SLOA
involving reading about crystal formation in the
textbook, the text and possible other reading materials would be available. If the activity involved
taping, as suggested earlier, then the tape recorder
and player would be found there, too. For the
laboratory demonstration of the crystal formation
process, the equipment, supplies and instructions for
doing this would also be placed there.

Table 2 suggests numerous possible instructional
techniques that could be used under the heading of
"Teacher Strategies." It is not an exhaustive list,
and there are other possible teaching strategies or
instructional methods that can be added to the list.
For each stated SLOA, a decision must be made on the
teaching strategy or strategies that will be employed
for the lessons.

The evaluation section of the lesson plan is based
on the assumption that if something is worth doing,
it's worth evaluating. Each learning opportunity
should have an appropriate kind of evaluation to see
if the major skill areas have been attained by the
students. Table 3 shows examples of possible evaluation techniques to be used under the evaluation
heading. Suggested are a variety of different
summative and formative techniques for evaluation.
Under the first SLOA of reading a text, a possible
evaluation technique might be a pen and paper formal
written assignment. This might take the form of
questions dealing with the important aspects of the

Table 2
INSTRUCTIONAL METHODS

Definition of Terms

a. lecture . . . . . . . . . . teacher centered processing of information: students taking notes.

b. inquiry . . . . . . . . . . teacher as a facilitator presenting a concept needing investigation: students actively participating.

c. demonstrations. . . . . . . teacher presenting a model, chart and/or graph illustrating an idea: students observing, note taking or demonstrating to other students.

d. questions and answers . . . teacher asking probing questions: students answering and discussing.

e. homework assignments . . . . work assigned by teacher: due dates given, tasks defined and quality expected.

f. small group . . . . . . . . student groups of between 2-10

g. large group . . . . . . . . student groups of between 10-25

h. discussion. . . . . . . . . small and large groups of students discussing a given task.

i. mutual goal setting . . . . teacher and students establishing the necessary skills to meet an individual learner's needs.

j. debates . . . . . . . . . . students presenting both sides of a critical issue.

k. audio-visual presentations. teachers and/or students presenting a concept through audio-visuals such as films, filmstrips, slides, records, prints and tapes.

The following are evaluative procedures that could be used to judge the outcomes of instruction

Table 3

| EVALUATION PROCEDURES | DEFINITIONS |
|---|---|
| 1. FORMATIVE | Formative: on going evaluation used to continually assess a child's progress to determine if a student is meeting objectives. |
| a. paper and pencil . . . . . . | formal written assignments |
| b. oral . . . . . . . . . | verbal assessment |
| c. pretest . . . . . . . | test before a lesson begins to establish student needs |
| d. post-tests . . . . . . | test at the close of a unit to establish student gains |
| e. conferences . . . . . | discussions between teacher and student to establish goals of a learner or to assess progress |
| f. self-evaluation . . . . | student assesses his own motivation and learning outcomes |
| g. homework . . . . . . . | work completed outside of school |
| h. group participation . . . | assessment based on work in a group |
| i. class participation . . . | student's involvement in a class |
| j. observations . . . . . | teacher watching students in groups and as individuals |
| 2. SUMMATIVE | Summative: final evaluation used at the close of a unit to plan for the next unit of objectives. |
| a. standardized . . . . . | norm referenced assessment |
| b. post-test . . . . . . | test at the close of a unit to establish student gains |
| c. projects . . . . . . | classroom, group, outside, inside, assignment for extra credit or a requirement of the unit. |
| d. conferences . . . . . | discussions between teacher and student to establish goals of a learner or to assess progress. |

process of crystal formation. An alternative to the
written test would be an oral assessment, possible
asking questions about the process. The learning
style of the student and other instructional details
would help in selecting the form of evaluation best
used. As to the laboratory demonstration of the
process, observation of the student at work, including discussion with the student, might provide enough
evidence for an evaluation decision.

After completing the appropriate number of SLOA's
on which students have worked, it is advisable to
analyze these lesson plans to see how the lessons are
reflective of exploratory learning. Each area should
be examined for evidence of exploratory and enriching
learning. Look for indications that students have
been involved in a variety of roles in accomplishing
the lessons rather than limiting themselves to just
one technique. It is difficult to have truly
exploratory or enriching experiences in a program
when using a limited approach. Involvement is the key
here. Students need to have hands-on manipulation as
well as more verbal-oriented experiences. Another
question to be asked is whether or not students are
using a variety of materials for learning or are the
same materials used for one lesson after another? Is
there small group activity and discussion? Are audio-
visual techniques used? Do the students debate about
different viewpoints and interpretations? Reliance on
pen and paper tests is common, but it provides only
some of the evidence needed for effective evaluation.
Observation can supplement this with more information
of a different kind and is very useful.

The analysis of student learning activities and
results so that they are truly reflective of the
exploratory and enrichment characteristics can be
used in any subject or discipline. Middle and junior
high school educators are concerned with the social,
physical, emotional and intellectual development of
students. Therefore, student learning opportunities
should reflect the emphasis on all of these areas.

In summation, evaluation using the learning

opportunities plan will assist in showing the extent
to which exploratory and enrichment experiences are
being implemented in the curriculum and in classrooms.
Gaps in a program may be revealed through such evaluation.  By changing teaching strategies and hence
learning opportunities, studies in science, math,
social studies, or literature can become more truly
exploratory in nature.  A teacher can ask if these
lessons really fit and reflect the exploratory drive
of transescent students in the middle or junior high
school.  If the answer arrived at is uncertain in any
way, a new lesson planning format sheet can be used
to begin the process of planning with the stated
objectives listed at the top of the page.  Following
this, a new listing of SLOA can be completed in
relation to the stated objective keeping in mind the
students' exploratory traits and interests.

Another middle/junior high school program that
belongs under the exploratory and enrichment heading
is the Unified Arts program.  This program, properly
designed and implemented, can do much to increase the
student's exploratory and enrichment experiences in
the middle/junior high school.

## What is the Unified Arts Program?

Unified Arts is defined as a joint effort of the
Industrial Arts, Home Economics and Art staff to create a single  Unified Arts discipline.  In some instances, Unified Arts programs may include Music,
Physical Education and Drama.  This involves a total
revamping of the philosophy, methodology and curriculum previously practiced by the three separate departments.  The result is a comprehensive, co-educational,
exploratory curriculum which allows maximum utilization
of personnel, facilities and funding.

## Philosophy

The Unified Arts program follows an experimental-
ist framework.  It is student centered, with the main

emphasis on the students' interaction with divergent technological and artistic media. The course content does not place a high emphasis on the development of skills, but focuses on the student's exploration of as many different tools, materials and concepts as possible within the middle school years. The exposure to and the exploration of a multitude of different technological and artistic activities provides the middle school student with a positive avenue for self-expression and emotional release. The Unified Arts program strives to improve the self-image of the student through positive and successful experiences within the disciplines. Concurrently this exposure is guided by educational goals which are reflected in the program curriculum and are integrally related to the goals of the overall middle school program.

## Rationale

The rationale for the Unified Arts program will be discussed under three different categories to facilitate the explanation of the benefits of the program in a middle school. The material will be divided into the following categories: Middle school characteristics, co-educational programming, and improved use of staff, funds and facilities.

## Middle School Characteristics

Characteristics already established that need to be considered in the development of curricula at the middle school level have been identified in earlier studies.[1] The Unified Arts program is representative of many of these characteristics, particu-

---

[1] Georgiady, Nicholas P., Riegle, Jack D., Romano, Louis G., "What Are the Characteristics of the Middle School?" The Middle School, Nelson-Hall Company, Chicago, 1973, pp. 73-84.

larly: exploratory and enrichment studies, as well
as multi-material approach, creative experiences,
flexible scheduling, team-teaching and community
relations. Students are offered laboratory based,
exploratory courses within a wide range of subject
areas. Projects and course offerings can utilize
labs and materials from any or all of the three
disciplines, allowing a creative and flexible
approach by students and teachers. Stress is on
exposure to and involvement with materials and
methods rather than pressuring for conformity in
projects. This allows the students to act upon
materials creatively within the framework of the
course. The block scheduling arrangement easily
accommodates team-teaching, interdisciplinary teaching,
and allows for a variety of flexible patterns for
class size and structure.

The Unified Arts program has, perhaps, the most
potential of all middle school programs for fostering
positive community relations. First, it allows
community members to enter the school as resource
persons, demonstrators, and aides. Secondly, it can
offer programs, such as art fairs, craft demonstrations, fashion shows, and bake-offs for the communities' information and enjoyment. Also the students
learn skills and knowledge that can be used in the
home and for personal interests. In meeting the
characteristics listed above, the Unified Arts program has demonstrated theoretically and in practice
that it can be an appropriate and successful middle
school program.

## Co-Educational Programming

Another factor for a middle school to consider
is adopting a Unified Arts program is due to the
existence of Title IX of the 1972 Federal Education
Amendment. It states:

"No person in the United States shall, on the
basis of sex be excluded from participation in,

be denied the benefits of, or be subjected
to discrimination under any educational program or activity receiving federal financial
assistance."

This statement concerns almost every school system in
the country, public or private.

The educational offerings within the Unified Art
program can be of great assistance to a school
system in efforts to meet Title IX's regulations.
Industrial Arts and Home Economics programs that have
traditionally excluded students from participation
because of sex, or have offered sex-segregated classes
of each, may fall under non-compliance of the law.
On the other hand, course enrollment in a Unified
Arts program depends on the student's educational
needs and interests, not on the sex of the individual.
The co-educational nature of the Unified Arts program
allows for equal distribution of information and
experiences to both sexes. A properly designed Unified Arts program fosters compliance with Title IX.


## Improved Use of Staff, Facilities and Funds

Art, Industrial Arts and Home Economics programs
within many, if not most middle schools and junior
highs, function with little knowledge of each others'
curriculum. This lack of communication has led to
many duplications and the needless misuse of instructional time. Because of its interdisciplinary
approach, a Unified Arts program can eliminate much
of its repetition and allow more time for program
expansion. Not only does unifying the departments
remove curriculum duplication, it also combines the
staff members' knowledge, teaching styles, methods
and philosophies, to multiply the human resources and
potentials available for educating the students. As
a unified group, new ideas for course offerings,
student evaluation systems, classroom management techniques, teaching aids and organizational procedures
can be developed and implemented for the benefit of
all students and teachers.

As separate departments, Industrial Arts, Art, and Home Economics programs can be a costly item in the middle school budget. A Unified Arts program can help reduce some of this cost by eliminating duplicate purchases of supplies and expensive equipment as well as by utilizing volume purchasing. A single system for budget accounting and ordering can be used to reduce the time taken by school personnel in keeping accounts and budgets.

## Differences in Program

There are basic differences between a middle school Unified Arts program and the traditional separate programs. The major and most important differences are in the areas of scheduling, course content and length, utilization of staff and resources and stereotyping of sexes (see listing below.) It should be noted that the items listed under the Unified Arts program describe a more student-centered, exploratory curriculum than that of the traditional approach.

| Stereotyped previous jr. high program | New attitudes and expectations created by reorganization into Unified Arts |
|---|---|
| sex-segregated classes | co-educational classes |
| Three separate departments | One unified department |
| Each separate department is too small to justify a chairperson | A large department is able to finance a chairperson |
| Teachers of the arts working separately | Teachers of the arts working together |
| Facilities in each lab used by only one teacher | Facilities are available to all Unified Arts teachers |

| Stereotyped (cont.) | New attitudes... (cont.) |
|---|---|
| Duplication in purchasing equipment and supplies | Sharing equipment provides funds for expansion into new areas |
| Courses are limited to a few areas | Courses are offered in a multitude of areas |
| Teachers can become stagnant working in one area | Teachers continuously learning new areas and their interrelationships |
| semester courses | many mini-courses of less than semester length |
| teachers decide course offerings | students have input as to course offerings |
| courses offered to students determined by grade level | courses taken determined by interests of students |
| Administrator places student in course | student chooses own course |
| Three separate art areas must be considered in the master schedule | one large block provided in the master schedule. |
| Emphasis on the development of semi-skills | Exposure and exploratory orientation—meeting a major need of this age group |

## Implementation Needs

The forming of a Unified Arts Program from the three previously separate departments of Art, Industrial Arts and Home Economics can be a fairly simple process. The author has identified five major factors that should be present before implementation of the program begins, namely,

1) Supportive backing of administration for Unified Arts concept.

2) Willingness of Art, Home Economic and Industrial Arts teachers to move to the Unified Arts approach.

3) Willingness of Arts staff to participate in active learning experiences in the new areas of the program (team-teaching).

4) Willingness of Unified Arts teachers to give more time to planning and organization.

5) A student-teacher ratio  at a workable level.

If the above five factors are not present before implementation, varying degrees of difficulty may occur.

Indicated below are some operational forms used where staff were working on developing an expanded program of exploratory and enrichment studies for students.

MEMO:   (Date)

   To:  Morgan Middle School Staff

From:  Ron

Subject:  Curriculum preparation

As you know we have a great need for workable curriculum.  In this memo are presented suggestions and a time line for completion of curriculum writing tasks.

I. Each Curriculum will have the following parts.

A. Table of Contents
B. Introduction
C. Philosophy
D. Board Goals

E. Board Instructional Objectives of each subject area. (sub goals)
F. Scope and Sequence of content
G. Instructional Methods
H. Evaluation Procedures

*(A-H are the items necessary to meet the board's and state's requirements.)

II. A - H are not enough to have a workable curriculum. The following items also will be necessary for this to become a usable plan.

I. After each sub-goal, have a series of instructional objectives.

II. Each instructional objective will suggest several student learning opportunities to use to accomplish the instructional objective.

III. Each Student Learning Opportunity (S.L.O.) will have an identified Teaching Strategy.

IV. There will also be a method of evaluation for each S.L.O. using the stated evaluation procedures.

The following is an explanation of the outlined points under I above.

A. Table of Contents
        Self Explanatory
B. Introduction
        Statement specifying the purpose of the course of study. It should also state how it will be used and its limitations.
            Example: This curriculum (course of study) is a document designed to meet state and local requirements, while also securing a system for sequential educational planning. This document should be evaluated each year.

The purpose of this document is to provide:

1. Content organization for the total social studies program;

2. Grade levels for the introduction, reinforcement or mastery of social studies skills;

3. A working document for instructional planning;

4. An administrative guide for accountability for the instructional program of the schools;

5. Information to parents about the approved curriculum.

C.  Philosophy

We have one, but it may need to be changed. Within the philosophy section, it is usually good to have an overview of your program. This overview should cover some of the affective domain items, as well as items that are part of the hidden curriculum.

D.  Broad Goals

Statements of major educational goals.  Do not be too specific.  The Broad Instructional Objectives and specific instructional objectives have to be organized under these broad goal statements.

    Example:  Students will acquire the Knowledge and Skills appropriate to their level of maturity and development, for dealing with their changing world.

*Three to five broad goals are usually enough.

E. <u>Sub-Goals on Broad Instructional Objectives</u>.

Each statement should be identified under one
of the Broad Goals. (One way to do this is to
write all sub-goals and then note if they all
fit under a broad goal. If some do not you
may need more broad goals.)
Sub-Goals should reflect the scope of your
total instructional program. You might want
to break them down into school years or in
some other manner.

Sub-goals should consist of several statements
of what students will learn.

> Example: Student will learn about the
> early days of Ohio Statehood.

F. <u>Scope and Sequence of Content</u>.

Write down the major skills, attitudes and
motor development you are trying to develop
in each learner. (This will need to be a
K-12 effort eventually.)

Organize this section under headings as
Cognitive, Affective, and Psychomotor. Then
decide where and if each skill is to be
introduced, reinforced, and/or mastered.
Use your best judgment.

G. <u>Instructional Methods</u>

This should be a list of instructional methods
used in your program. (Look at the social
studies list.)

H. <u>Evaluating Procedures</u>

Evaluative Procedures used in your program.

## CREATIVE EXPERIENCES

### Creativity - A Precious Commodity

Creativity, particularly scientific creativity, has become the focus of a great deal of attention in recent years. In the 1950's, it became increasingly apparent to those who were concerned about such matters, that in order to survive international competition, our nation would have to encourage the development of highly creative persons. Nonetheless, Toynbee in 1964 charged that America was neglecting her creative minority. He felt that in the attempt to abide with the ideal of equality for all and adjust to the syndrome of preserving the status-quo, the creative child was being stifled before he had time to fully develop. Perhaps with the resurgence of interest in creativity that has developed in the last three decades, the crisis that Toynbee and others feel that America is facing will soon be met. But with this interest in creativity had also come the realization that no one knows for sure just what creativity is.

One conclusion on creativity regarding ultimate criteria was that the products rather than the individuals must be judged. The rationale for this approach was that biases due to personality factors must be eliminated, and that only products could be evaluated objectively.

In recent years there seems to be a welcomed movement away from studying creativity as a product. But the essential remains: creativity is by its very nature confounded with productivity, whereas the two may be utterly different. The creative-productive individual is very visible; his products continue to revolutionize the world. His traits have been studied, and we have been able to point to certain personality and motivational traits that are common to this type of individual. The difficulty comes in the attempt to distinguish between those traits which

contribute to creativity and those which contribute
to productivity.  If this could be done it might be
possible to help the creative person become more
productive and the productive person more creative.
But because of the emphasis on products it seems that
productivity has often been touted at the expense of
creativity.

Trying to find a definition that would place
creativity in perspective for the educator resulted
in many different definitions being considered.
Carl Rogers and E. Paul Torrance certainly help
bring things into focus.

Rogers contended that the creative process
"...is the emergence in action of a novel relational
product, growing out of the uniqueness of the individual on the one hand, and the materials, events,
people, or circumstances of his life on the other."[1]
Regarding his definition, Rogers concluded that there
are three important, yet unmentioned variables --- a
status of positive or negative value assigned to the
creativity, an approval of the creativity at some time
by a group, and an approximation of the degree of
the creativity.[2]

Although this particular definition may be quite
appealing in terms of the emphasis placed upon
creativity as a process, it becomes unwieldy and
even more abstract when the additional three variables
are considered.

In contrast, Torrance has proposed a definition
that appears succinct and has major implications for
education.  He also defines creativity as a

---

[1]Carl C. Rogers, "Toward a Theory of Creativity,"
Creativity and Its Cultivation, Ed. by Harold H.
Anderson, New York and Evanston: Harper and Row,
1959, p. 71.

[2]Ibid., pp. 71-72.

process —— "...the process of sensing problems or
gaps in information, forming ideas or hypotheses,
testing and modifying these hypotheses, and communicating the results."[3]

One of the advantages of accepting such a definition is that it removes creativity from the realms
of the mysterious and absolute.  It can readily be
seen that anyone not seriously handicapped in mental
ability can, at least to some degree, participate
in the process.  Thus, creativity need not be viewed
as a magical quality or a prescribed set of environmental conditions that an individual either possesses
or finds within his immediate range.

The question, "Do our schools and educational
institutions currently focus on development of
creative endeavors?" might be logically pursued once
acceptance of an adequate definition has been confirmed.  Numerous research projects have been carried
out with respect to the relationship between creativity and intelligence which allow for a general-
ized response to the proposed inquiry.

It is common knowledge that intelligence tests
have been overemphasized in education as the most
powerful indicator of learning.  As stated by Taba,
"Several researchers have pointed out that intelligence tests are composed on the pattern of convergent
thinking, do not accommodate divergence in cognitive
functioning or cultural experience, and penalize the
tendency to detect relationships other than common-
place or to follow an unconventional association
pattern."[4]

---

[3]Paul Torrance, Creativity, Washington National
Education Association, 1963, p. 4.

[4]Hilda Taba, "Opportunities for Creativity in
Education for Exceptional Children," Exceptional
Children XXIX, February, 1963, 254.

The stress on testing measures, as mentioned, is believed by many to have been increasing to the point where curriculum planners design curricula for the seemingly sole purpose of improving the learners' scores on such tests. Klausmeier and Goodwin agreed that, "The typical school curriculum, filled primarily with assignments and other activities through which the students are to learn and reproduce what mankind already knows, does not in itself encourage original expression."[5]

Thus, on the basis of the research performed and the interpretations of the findings by reputable educational theorists, generally speaking, creative experiences leading to the enhancement of creative ability have not constituted an acceptable portion of current curricula.

Adamant in his opposition to the time spent on non-creative thinking activities, Torrance listed four reasons why this trend has not been in the best interests of all concerned. These arguments are:

First, creativity is important from the standpoint of personality development and mental health. Second, creative thinking contributes importantly to the acquisition of information. Third, creative thinking is essential in the application of knowledge and in the achievement of vocational success. Fourth, it is tremendously important to society for our creative talent to be identified, developed, and utilized.[6]

---

[5] Herbert I. Klausmeier and William Goodwin, Learning and Human Abilities, New York: Harper and Row, Publishers, Inc., 1965, p. 289.

[6] E. Paul Torrance, "Explorations in Creative Thinking," Education LXXXI, December, 1960, p. 216.

One last position, DeVito and Krockover's,
stressed yet another valuable aspect of creativity,
namely the joy associated with the creative-thinking
process. Although they have expressed the value of
creativity in relation to their own discipline, their
rationales can easily be ascribed to education in a
much broader sense. DeVito and Krockover maintained
that, "Science is creative."[7] Furthermore, they
stated, "There is joy and excitement in having confidence in oneself, posing questions and problems,
seeking answers and solutions, and making conclusions
based on one's own confidence in one's investigation
and quality of work."[8]


Creativity in the Middle Grades

Much has been written about creativity at the
elementary level. Much research and many inventories
have been centered around grades 1 through 6, although grade 5 is placed in some middle schools and
grade 6 is common to many more. Still, little can
be found about the 7th and 8th grades. Many of the
principles that apply to the elementary studies and
research can be adapted to the middle school level.

This writer was intrigued by the most recent
research that is being done on brain growth periodi-
zation by Dr. Herman Epstein at Brandeis University,
and the subsequent research that is being done on its
possible impact for the curricula of the transescent
learner. The research on curriculum implications is
being done jointly with Dr. Conrad Toepfer, Jr. and
Dr. Bambii Abelson. Brain growth spurts are facts.
Dr. Epstein has demonstrated that brain growth spurts
at three to ten months, and during approximate two
year periods centered at ages 2-4, 6-8, 10-12, and
14-16 years. The study of these periods of brain

-----

[7] Alfred DeVito and Gerald H. Krockover, Creative
Sciencing, Boston: Little, Brown and Company,
1976, p. 7.

[8] Ibid., p. 7.

growth spurts in humans has shown them to be correlated with spurts in various aspects of developing intelligence.[9]

Thus the proposition arises that children can develop novel thinking complexities during spurts and this development is much less successful between spurts. The implication for curriculum development is that children in a between-spurt phase should have an altered set of inputs to maximize the effectiveness of their learning, both during that period and also during the spurt period which will follow the phase of low brain growth.

Although most students at the middle school level will fall in the fallow brain growth period, some students will just be completing a brain growth spurt while others will be at the onset of a new brain growth period. Since the middle school will more than likely have students at these three different states, it is then the challenge of the middle school program to provide for students at these three stages. Since the majority of the students will experience a hiatus in brain growth and development between the ages of 12 and 14, this writer feels that the use of enrichment activities and creative teaching can consolidate the gains that have taken place through the brain growth spurts. This reinforcement is certainly necessary to prevent the loss of gains that have been made and may very well be the only hope for increasing intellectual understanding during the fallow brain growth period.

Fostering Creativity in the Teacher

If those who value creativity are accepted as correct in their postures, there remains a solid,

---

[9] Herman T. Epstein. "Brain Growth Spurts During Brain Development: Implications for Educational Policy and Practice," 1978 Yearbook of the National Society for the Study of Education, University of Chicago Press, 1978.

rational base upon which schemes for promoting
creativity in education can be explored and implemented. Once this last assumption is deemed pal-
atable, the most likely questions to follow are,
Can creativity actually be developed through formal
classroom education; and if so, how can this be
achieved? Smith, in his book, Setting Conditions
For Creative Teaching, says:[10]

"The role of the teacher in the creative process
is consistently clear as the various aspects of
creativity are explored. The teachers to
develop creativity must:

1. Set conditions for creativity to
   develop. This means to provide a
   desirable physical, emotional, social
   and intellectual environment.

2. Teach several skills simultaneously,
   preferably through demonstration and
   in meaningful situations so children
   may bring these skills into play in
   the creative process.

3. Teach facts in meaningful situations and
   whenever necessary but also create
   situations in which this knowledge
   may be put to use in problem solving.

4. Provide rich experiences in every
   curriculum area. This means teacher
   dominated problem solving and conventional methods of problem solving are
   minimized for more challenging ways of
   creative problem solving. Learning is
   more divergent and open ended than convergent and closed."

---

[10] James A. Smith, Setting Conditions for Creative
Teaching, New York: Allyn and Bacon, Inc., 1966,
p. 190-191.

Torrance, in his book, Guiding Creative Talent, states the following behavior is necessary in teachers to establish creative relationships:

"Genuine joy and pride in creative powers of pupils; the sort of relationship which does not build self-esteem in individuals; genuine empathy; a creative acceptance of limitations and assets rather than the use of them as vulnerable areas by which to gain control of the individual; a search for truth about a situation rather than an attempt to impose group concensus or individual opinion; permissiveness; a friendly environment.[11]

Many of the above-mentioned qualities are possible to attain if we believe that people can be educated but they must accept the premise that they can learn to be creative. Creative teachers are not necessarily the most talented ones. They have educated certain skills and aspects of their personality which others have not. Teaching is a science and an art. Some people feel that the teacher becomes more and more limited in their fields of operation as the new theories are tested and researched and one method is discovered to be better than the other. The creative teacher then is the one who takes the new knowledge applied by the science of education and finds the new and practical ways to put it to use in the classroom. They operate on a frontier of educational knowledge, thinking up new ways to implement the knowledge and in doing so they suggest new ideas that need to be scientifically tested. They create the optimum conditions for learning in their own ways with their own resources and materials and for their own children making their work an art.[12]

---

[11] E.P. Torrance, Guiding Creative Talent, Englewood Cliffs, New Jersey: Prentice Hall, Inc., pp. 167-168.

[12] Smith, op. cit., p. 192.

Miel, says in her book, Creativity in Teaching:

". . .that the products of the teacher's creativity are opportunities for individuals and groups
to experience and learn. To create these opportunities, the creative teacher uses ideas of
others discreetly and thinks up ideas of their
own. They realize that the potential for
solving their teaching problems lies within
themselves and not by a book written by some
person who knows neither them nor the children
they teach."[13]

Zirbes, in her book, Spurs to Creative Teaching,
says:

"Creativity is the sensitive, insightful developmental guidance which makes learning experiences
optimally educative and conducive to the development and fulfillment of creative potentialities
of individuals and groups."[14]

How often we hear teachers say, "Well, that
might be alright for some, but I just can't teach
that way; I'm not creative," or "I just believe that
not all teachers can be creative." Such statements
are more indicative of personality problems than a
teaching skill. A teacher who recognizes her
limited ability to teach creatively can do something
about it. To say one can't teach creativity is to
admit that one cannot teach. As knowledge increases
in any profession, untruths are discarded and truths
take their place. Teaching must be no exception.
The curriculum content of the teacher is often fuzzy
and unsure but the future need for creative people
is clearly cut out as an algebraic formula. By

---

[13]Alice Miel, Creativity in Teaching: Invitations and Instances, Belmont, Calif.; Wadsworth
Publishing Co., Inc., 1961, p. 8.

[14]Laura Zirbes, Spurs to Creative Teaching, New
York: G. P. Putnam's Sons, p. 36.

entering the profession, teachers commit themselves to develop the creative potential of every
child and to support the political ideology of the
democratic society which needs this potential.  If
they cannot do this, they had best turn their jobs
over to those who can.[15]

In the closing lines of the poem by Robert Frost
in his book, You Come Too, we will see what must be
said about the self-actualized creative person and
it is fitting that they challenge us.  "Two roads
diverged in a wood and I took the one less travelled
by and that has made all of the difference."[16]

Creativeness cannot be taught; it can only be
released and guided.  This in essence is the job
of the teacher - to release inner power into
productive outer challenges.

Creativity as such cannot be taught.  It is not
a subject or a skill which can be learned like
history or demonstrated like baseball.  It is an
inborn developmental quality, like love and can only
be developed.  Various aspects of creative thinking
and doing can be modified through learning to the
degree that all learning can be modified, but because creativity is a quality already present in
every individual, it needs to be coddled to help
develop it.  The uncreative children in our schools
today are living testimonies to the degree to which
it can be killed off easily.  Once it appears on the
surface, its reappearance can be assured by the use
of all those techniques which can cause behavior to
reappear but it does not appear unless certain conditions are present which cause it to come forth.
The problem then seems to be to get it to appear so
the teacher can work with it and by reinforcement

---

[15]Smith, op. cit., p. 193.

[16]Robert Frost, You Come Too, New York:  Holt,
Rinehart and Winston, 1959, p. 84.

stimulate its reappearance. In other words, set
conditions for creativity.[17]

Creativity seems to be discouraged in an environment wherever one is assigned enough activity to fill
each working period. It might be helpful to consider
a pacing plan proposed by Dr. Alfred Arth from the
University of Wyoming in which he contends that each
teaching period should provide for a time for the
teacher to present materials, a time for the students to ask questions about the materials, a time
when the students are left alone to sit and think,
read, write about the materials, but communicate with
no one, and a time for the students to discuss the
materials among themselves. The quiet, reflective
time may just be the one thing that will spark some
creativity. James A. Smith contends that there are
two basic kinds of conditions or experiences used in
provoking creative behavior. There is the natural
type and the contrived type. Natural conditions
are those which happen naturally in any classroom
when the teacher is quick enough and sharp enough
to utilize the situation for the development of
creative work. Contrived experience is one where the
teacher plans a lesson with the specific intent of
plunging the children into a problem where creative
thinking and creative production results.

The class needs to be organized where children
learn to make their individual contributions and
learn to make group decisions by practicing these
skills in the classroom. They need to respect
others, to share ideas when they have the opportunity to listen to other ideas and enjoy the
experience of solving the problem in a group. In a
permissive, creative and democratic classroom, children and teachers plan the day's work together. Students have the experience of working in small groups,

---

[17]James A. Smith, Setting Conditions for Creative Teaching in the Elementary School, Boston,
Mass.: Allyn & Bacon, 1966, p. 117.

large groups and individuals. Children learn from
each other as well as from the teacher. Children are motivated to the degree that they can carry
on when the teacher must leave the room on an
errand. Individual differences are honored and encouraged for creativity means individuality and the
class must be organized so that the teacher can
capitalize on the different talents each child
brings into the classroom. The "formal" school
room quickly destroys the job of creating individuality because it is wrong to be different according
to the standards set by the teacher. For although
the drive to create is as strong within children
as the drive for status, the drive to be loved is
stronger and is a more basic need. Students seeking
emotional and psychological security will quickly
conform to the teacher's wishes in order not to pro-
voke her disfavor or ridicule. It is the same social
pressure from other influential individuals in the
child's life and later his society itself that
makes for a nation of conformists. New patterns of
organization such as departmentalized middle schools
and the homogeneous grouping of children in nongraded reading groups is causing great concern among
people who see them as detriments to the development of creativity. The short periods of time each
child spends with many teachers does not provide for
the ongoing development of the creative process such
as the self-contained classroom does. The development of creativity can take place in these organizational plans to some degree, depending as it does
in all cases on the teachers involved. But the
chances are less because of the number of teachers
involved. Team planning and flexible time by the
teachers tend to encourage creativity in the students.

## Educational Conditions

Educational conditions are those which develop
the reality that creative teaching is a method of
teaching different from ordinary methods of teaching.
Although all children are born with creative drives
and creative powers, just as all children are born

with creative drives and creative powers, just as all
children are born with potential to love, the lack
of practice of psychological time of readiness may
impair the function of love and the function of
creativity. Therefore, there must be a readiness
for creativity just as there is a readiness for
reading. Erich Fromm suggests the following individual conditions necessary for creative development:

1. The capacity to be puzzled.

2. The ability to concentrate.

3. The ability to experience self.

4. The ability to accept conflict and
   tension resulting from polarity rather
   than avoid them.

5. The willingness to be born every day. [18]

Each human being is a creation and as he grows and
develops he continues to be creative in the process.
His personality is emergent in the formulation
of a personality that is creative and depends upon
the experiences that he has during his formative
period of that personality. [19]

Creativity as such cannot be taught. We can only
set conditions for it to happen. The task at the
middle school level is to set these conditions which
include: intellectual conditions, proper physical
conditions, certain social and emotional conditions,
selected psychological conditions and some particular educational conditions.

Creativity differs from close ended, convergent
learning in that the outcome is unpredictable. In
the creative learning process there comes a time

_____

[18] Ibid., p. 140.

[19] Ibid., p. 141.

when the teacher must withdraw from the teaching act
and the child must face the unknown by himself.    To
encourage discovery, to develop capacity of the child
to wonder and be puzzled and to stimulate sensitivity
are all creative teaching acts.    James A. Smith
suggests that   there are 18 principles of creative
teaching.    They are as follows:

1. In creative teaching something new, different
   different or unique results.

2. In creative teaching, divergent thinking
   processes are stressed.

3. In creative teaching, motivational tensions
   are prerequisites to the creative process.
   The process serves as a tension relieving
   agent.

4. In creative teaching, open minded situations
   are utilized.

5. In creative teaching comes a time when the
   the teacher withdraws and the children face
   the unknown themselves.

6. In creative teaching the outcomes are unpredictable.

7. In creative teaching, conditions are set
   which make possible preconscious thinking.

8. Creative thinking means that students are
   encouraged to generate and develop their
   own ideas.

9. In creative teaching, differences, uniqueness,
   individuality, and originality are stressed
   and rewarded.

10. In creative teaching, the process is as
    important as the product.

11. In creative teaching, certain conditions must
    be set to permit creativity to appear.

12. In creative teaching, teaching is success
    rather than failure oriented.

13. In creative teaching, provision is made to
    learn knowledge and skills, but provision is
    also made to apply these in new problem
    solving situations.

14. In creative teaching, self-initiated learning
    is encouraged.

15. In creative teaching, skills of constructive
    criticism and evaluation skills are
    developed.

16. In creative teaching, ideas and objects are
    manipulated and explored.

17. Creative teaching employs democratic
    processes.

18. In creative teaching, methods are used
    which are unique to the development of
    creativity.

Creativity could be defined as the ability to
tap one's experiences and to come up with something
new. The new product need not be new to the world,
but it must be new to the individual. This simple
definition explains the kind of creativity most
commonly shown by children. Because there are
degrees of creativity, a higher degree of it would
mean the creator would produce something new to the
world. (Example: a new math formula, a new technique for painting, a new way to reach the moon.)
Because creativity is a process and a product,
attention must be paid to the process if it is to
be developed in children. A spring of fresh water
is a nuisance if it first issues from the ground,
producing only mire and mud. It cannot be stopped

by cement or earth fill. Its flow will continue to
seep around the edges, but when the spring is given a
protective and deliminating margin, a channel is provided for its stream. It becomes a source of joy.
The same is true of creativity. Bronowski distin-
guishes among discovery, invention and creation by
pointing out that Columbus discovered the West,
Bell invented the telephone and Shakespeare created
Othello. A fact is discovered, a theory is invented, but only a masterpiece is created, for creation
must engage the whole mind.

As a middle school teacher, supervisor or principal, you may have some misgivings about development
of creative abilities through formal
educational experiences. You may even have doubts
that creative abilities actually can be developed
through school experiences. You may doubt that
teachers who have been taught and have taught in
traditional authority oriented ways can encourage
their pupils to behave creatively and to learn crea
tive ways. You may be afraid that such teachers
would feel psychologically uncomfortable if they did
encourage their pupils to behave creatively. If
you are willing to examine the evidence available
today, presented by Calvin W. Taylor in Developing
Creative Characteristics, and Paul Torrance in Guiding Creative Talent and Gifted Children in the Classroom, you could not have much doubt that it is possible to develop creative talents through educational
experiences. Of course, you could agree that even if
a child developed these abilities to a high degree it
does not guarantee that we have creativity, or that
he will make important creative contributions.
These may be partly true because creative achievement requires commitment, courage, hard work, honesty
and the like. The development of creative abilities
certainly increases the chances that a person will
behave creatively. Paul Torrance in his book,
Rewarding Creative Behavior and Creative Process and
Potential, edited by Calvin Taylor, cited a great
deal of evidence that he believes shows that it is
possible to provide educational experiences that will
enhance the development of creative abilities in

school children. Again a number of experiments have
shown that these abilities can be developed in
children, classified as mentally retarded and that
growth can take place during the fourth grade period
when a decrement in creative functioning usually
occurs in schools in the United States. Torrence
must admit that we do not yet have any massive amounts
of evidence to assure that teachers who have been
taught and have taught in traditional or authority
oriented ways can encourage children to behave creatively and to learn creative ways. To make such a
change requires considerable change in orientation
and development of a number of skills that have not
heretofore been developed. Such changes require
that the teacher be concerned by effectiveness of his
teaching and willingness to expand some expensive
energies in practicing and mastering these skills. He
has to be prepared for some failures, discouragement,
criticism and hard work. To a teacher who has been
taught and taught in traditional or authority oriented
ways these are non-habitual ways of behaving and non-
habitual behavior takes deliberate efforts and practice. Such a teacher has to give his creative abilities a workout and develop them. One way of getting
started in achieving some success in creative ways of
teaching is to use some of the already prepared guided
planned experiences in creative teaching in the form
of recordings, teachers' guides, idea books and
the like. Success will not continue to come, however,
unless you start using these to get new ideas and new
experiences yourself to develop creativity. Torrence
suggests to individual teachers and faculty groups to
undertake a year-long program of deliberate and systematic efforts to workshops to develop some of the
skills needed for this kind of teaching. He, Paul
Torrance, in a series of ten articles entitled,
"Creativity in the Classroom," which appeared in the
1964-65 issue of The Instructor, outlines a series
of experiences that he has developed on the basis of
the best that he has been able to find out about
creative ways of teaching or the kinds of teaching
most likely to draw from the development of creative
abilities. A suggested workshop program is as
follows:

1. Being respective of questions and ideas.

2. Asking provocative questions.

3. Recognizing and valuing originality

4. Developing ability to elaborate.

5. Unevaluated practice and experimentation.

6. Developing creative leaders.

7. Guided planned experiences.

8. Historiography and a search for truth.

9. Descriptive research and a search for truth.

10. Experimental research and a search for truth.

There are times when a teacher is able to involve an entire class in an atmosphere that is a creative one. Usually, however, the different levels of creative functioning can be observed among pupils in any particular classroom unless creative behavior is severely repressed. From a list of 230 different signs of creative classroom behavior compiled by 200 students. in E. Paul Torrance's classes in creative ways of teaching, he offers an abbreviated check list which you may find useful in assessing the creative involvement and perhaps to some extent the creative abilities of children.

- intense absorption in listening, observing and doing.

- intense animation.

- use of analogies in speech and writing.

- bodily involvement in writing, reading and drawing.

- tendencies to burst out to complete teacher's sentences.

- tendencies to challenge ideas of authorities.

- habit of checking many sources.

- tendency to take a closer look at things.

- eagerness to tell others about discoveries.

- continued creative work after time is up.

- tendency to show relationship among apparently unrelated ideas.

- follow-up at home or in community of ideas generated at school.

- manifestations of curiosity.

-spontaneous use of experimentation and discovery of purpose.

- imaginative play.

- excitement in voice about discoveries.

- habit of guessing outcomes and checking accuracy.

- honesty and intense search for truth.

- less distractibility.

- manipulation of objects and ideas to obtain new combinations.

- tendency to lose awareness of time.

- penetrating observations and questions.

- self-initiated learning projects.

- tendency to seek alternatives and exploring possibilities.

- willingness to consider or toy with novel ideas.

## Teacher's Role

Calvin W. Taylor, in an article, "Developing Creative Characteristics," has offered a number of illustrations on how teachers can create situations to identify creatively gifted individuals. The following are a few of them:

1. At times let students do most of the planning on their own and make most of their own decisions and observe which ones are most dependent and which ones have the least need for training and experience in self-guidance.

2. Develop exercises to which children report their feelings and impulses and then have them see how well they can intuitively anticipate the correct course of the action.

3. Pose complex issues and see which children take a hopeful attitude rather than a position that things are in an impossible state of affairs and nothing can be done about them.

4. Have idea generating sessions to he who comes up with the most ideas. Whose ideas bring out the strongest negative reaction from the class and who tends to believe in expressing strong negative reactions. Observe who has the most courage to hold his ground or even move ahead instead of retreating or giving up in the face of negative reactions.

5. Ask students to do a task which they have
   done before but take away most of the facilities previously available to see who will be
   the most resourceful in improvising or accomplishing the task without the usual facilities.
   Structure some classroom task with those who
   tolerate uncertainty and ambiguity and see if
   they do better than those who are unable to
   do so. In other words, a situation in which
   the rewards go to those who keep the problem
   open and keep working on it with their own
   resources until they eventually obtain a solution.[21]

## Principal's Role

In schools, change is often facilitated best by
encouragement from personnel in higher ranking positions. Although some teachers may wish to try out
new ideas, they may hesitate or may do so secretly
unless supervisory, consultants, principals or other
supervisory personnel openly approve of change.
Therefore, in order to encourage more creativity in
teachers and children, supervisory personnel need to
make teachers feel their creative endeavor is valued
and wanted. Schools must be a life experience, human
and honest. Part of the creative process is the
willingness to learn from each other. Teachers and
administrators should not be so sophisticated that
they cannot learn from each other. The administrator does not have to be creative but must be
accepting of the creative process, condone it and
allow it to happen. The administrator must present
things so that people can come up with the affordable
solutions and allow them to buy into these solutions.

The administrator who recognizes creativity in
the classroom should make a consistent and conscientious effort to comment to the teacher about the

---

[21]Taylor, Calvin W., "Developing Creative Characteristics." The Instructor, 1964: p. 99-100.

creativity. An administrator might help the creative
process by allowing the faculty to brainstorm. When
focusing on a problem they should not be allowed to
use any solutions that have been used before. Looking at the old problem in a different setting is a
good administrative technique for developing creativity. THis would suggest that retreat type situations
are effective in helping the process. In brainstorming
it is helpful to solve the problem with no constraints and then once solutions are generated, plug
in the constraints.

Finally, we provide for the creative by supplying
highly motivated, well trained teachers and administrators. Generally, successful educators are found to be
interested in scholarly and artistic pursuits, have
wide interests, possess a sense of humor, are student-
centered, are enthusiastic about teaching and recognize the need for advanced study for themselves.
These same traits are highly essential for success
in challenging the creative.

Inservice programs to help all teachers understand the creative does much to assure better opportunities for them and reduce tensions regarding the
program. Administrators who understand and identify
with the creative generally assure success of creative
programs while those who don't usually spell failure
for such programs.

Among ways for supervisory personnel to encourage
changes towards more creative teaching practices are
as follows:

1. Projecting of attitudes which reassure the
   teacher that creative teaching is important
   and desired.

2. Helping teachers to identify creative behaviors.

3. Providing emotional support during the process
   of change.

4. Establish an atmosphere in which children and teachers feel free to try creative processes.

5. Suggesting ways to approach creativity whenever these suggestions seem pertinent and appropriate.

Principals and supervisory personnel should examine their own beliefs, prejudices and inclinations as honestly as possible before attempting to help teachers teach more creatively. In the same way that perfection cannot be supplied on demand by others, neither can perfection be supplied on demand by self. Knowing about one's own approach to education can help one be more effective in the role of consultant to the teacher who may be attempting to break habits of long years (or short months for that matter, since patterns can be established) of practice of techniques or methods.

No one can say with assurance that certain environments stifle more creative teachers or children. Creative teachers have in the past worked well in the non-supportive atmosphere. Creative children have produced under non-sympathetic teachers. It seems certain, however, that both groups function more easily, happily and productively under conditions in which their unique contributions are valued, recognized and encouraged. Supervisory personnel have the obligation of helping provide such an atmosphere.

We must begin with the hypothesis that every individual is capable of divergent ideation. It is a bold hypothesis but an essential one for a school administrator if there is to be any teaching for creative endeavor on the part of teachers working in the school. It is essential for the administrator and all of those with whom he works to understand fully the precise meaning of creative endeavor and its implications for those who read it, say it or practice it. As expressed in this chapter, creative endeavor is that effort which enables an individual to bring into being something from his own thought or imagination

which is new, unique, original, non-existent before.
With this acceptance of this concept of creative endeavor, one may readily distinguish between the
process of discovery which involves learning something
already in existence and creativity which encourages
the mind to manipulate and experiment with knowledge
that will serve as a springboard for new ideas.
Creation is a completely personal matter. Teaching
for creative endeavor is an attitude, a basic set of
values, a way of life. Some teachers find it easier
than others to accept these values. If teachers can
accept the premise that all individuals are creative,
then administrators can assist teachers to accept
those principles which lead to the cultivation of
creativity and creative teaching. Great benefits
accrue within a school when the administrator genuinely has the creative spirit or is in the creative
spirit.

Provision for the use of imaginative facilities
converts the conforming complaint team into effer-
vescent spontaneous individuals seeking originality
inventiveness and creative expression wherever possible. This in no way is to say that there is no place
for conformity, but rather a need for an atmosphere
that will provide the freedom to think, to do, to
discipline and to direct one's self toward evermore
creative individuals using their human potentials to
the greatest extent. Environment and orientation to
life conducive to creative endeavor may be thought of
as an attitude toward self and towards the world in
general that is willing to accept the unique, the new,
the different and the sometimes bizarre as unexplored
experiences as a challenge rather than a threat.
Erich Fromm describes the conditions essential for the
creative attitude as a capacity to be puzzled, the
ability to concentrate, the sense of "I" as the true
center of my world - the originator of my acts - and
the ability to accept conflict.[22]

---

[22]Fromm, Erich, "The Creative Attitude," pp.
44-54, Creativity and Its Cultivation, edited by Harold
H. Anderson, New York: Harper and Bros., 1959.

The educational implications of this conceptualization of creativity are significant for everyone concerned. It negates the idea of either/or, the haves or have nots, for it recognizes creative ability in all individuals. It challenges leadership to release what may be suppressed potential and develops creative personality. The administrator needs to ask, "How much is left, how much can be recovered, how can I insist in the development of this potential?"[23]

Administrators and supervisors can do much to facilitate the creative process. Although timing is very important, much of the success can be encouraged if:

1. The administrator allows for an easier access to materials and budgets for special purposes.

2. The administrator gives the teacher an amount of money without any stipulations.

3. The administrator is willing to allow teachers to reproduce teacher and aid material.

4. The administrator encourages out-of-school activities.

5. The administrator encourages human activities.

6. The administrator allows release time for conferences and professional activities which allow the teacher to gain new ideas and insights.

7. The administrator encourages and promotes research by individual teachers.

---

[23]Woodfin, Mary Jo, "Supervisory Personnel," pp. 266-281, Teaching For Creative Behavior, edited by William B. Michael, Bloomington: Indiana University Press, 1968.

8. The administrator encourages creativity by establishing a "Share an idea" board in the staff lounge.

9. The administrator encourages creative teachers to post ideas on creativity.

10. The administrator promotes a degree of equality between administration and staff.

### Suggestions for Creativity in The Classroom
### Helpful Hints from Happy Teachers

Teachers are concerned with creativity both as a product and as a process. To be aware of creative expression, there is a need to watch for drawings, paintings, handicrafts, poems, stories, dramatizations, or ideas that have the stamp of originality. Teachers are also concerned with creativity as a process and welcome any idea that is new to the child and represents, for him, a creative experience. There must be an availability of materials and tools that invite exploration. These may include the following items:

1. Paper of all sizes and texture

2. Cardboard

3. Crayons

4. Arithmetic measures and devices

5. Dictionaries

6. Story books

7. Pictures

8. Museum items

9. Microscopes

10. Flasks

11. Mounted specimens

12. Collections

13. Hobbies

Learning is a creative process. The creative process can be supplied to all areas of learning and function. Performing in a highly creative way within an area of human activity necessitates the use of certain skills and knowledge. There is hardly an area of skills development neglected when the daily program includes a variety of independent activities focused on creative power. A core study involving science, social studies, literature, and other subject areas holds great promise for expanding children's ability to think creatively.

We should not try to reduce creative teaching to patterns of forumulas, or to specific "know hows" or set methods. The following references are suggested merely as catalysts to trigger your creative power and are only a small sampling of the limitless possibilities in every classroom. They are divided into four broad areas for convenience only and are not meant to imply that one area can be divorced from another.

## Language Arts

It is essential that the classroom be one in which children are encouraged to express their unique, individual reactions without undue restrictions. The teacher plays a significant and vital role in fostering creativity. Creative work flourishes under teachers who strive to develop a classroom in which security, understanding, mutual respect and opportunity to express ideas are all-prevailing.

The rewards of creative writing are rich and varied. Children learn to share experiences and gain in their ability to communicate clearly.

1. Discuss magazine pictures which have been mounted on construction paper. Pass them around and when anyone finds one which interests him, let him keep it for a nucleus for his story.

2. Place several objects on the desk in front of the class. Suggest that the class might like to invent a chain story--one person telling a little, and then letting someone else go on weaving the objects into the plot.

3. The "open-end" story - A type of story teachers may compose from incidents reported in newspapers or magazines. Children are invited to write an ending to the story or are requested to write letters telling what they thought should be done about the situation.

4. Collect cartoon pictures and cut off the captions. Let the children write their own captions. Variation: Block out the conversation and let the children write their own version.

5. Put on the chalkboard descriptive phrases such as the following:

    a. Fat as a pig
    b. Blue as the sky
    c. Sweet as candy
    d. Busy as a bee
    e. Strong as an ox

Children write a story using as many of the phrases as possible.

6. Post an advertisement. Have your class write a critical opinion of it (pro and con)

7. Read and discuss riddles. Children are then asked to write one of their own.

8. Take the letters that spell the name of a holiday. Write about something that each letter might stand for.

9. Occasionally have your class write what they like or dislike about school.

10. For the child who is yet to feel, we must provide experiences before we can hope for much expression. A delicious smell is coming from the cafeteria. How can we tell someone else what it is like? How do we describe smoke coming from a high stack? The design of a row of roofs? For these children let's have more saying time.

11. In spelling, prepare a booklet of word origins, hunting for strange and interesting words, and determining their significance to people.

12. Rewrite a story into play form.

13. Write character sketches.

14. A single word can give a child an idea for a story. Write a number of words, each on an individual slip of paper. Sample words are:

   a. Tiger
   b. Blizzard
   c. Peace

   Drop the words into a bowl. The children draw from the container at random, and each child writes a story or a poem about the word he draws.

15. Most record shops have sound-effect records that provide marvelous stimuli for creative writing.

16. "The Box of Feels." Things in the box change ever so frequently. No one is allowed to re- move the lid unless he has first put on a blind- fold. (It might be an old Halloween mask.) In- teresting stories can be written about the feel of things.

17. Prepare story sheets with titles and lots of space for illustrations. Here are some starters for stories.

> a. If I could invent
> b. If I hibernated
> c. If I followed an ant

18. Divide the room with a visual barrier. On one side of the barrier place an art object. Since different people have different ways of viewing an object, all are encouraged to view the object, everyone's perspective and perception is enjoyed and considered by the class.

19. Create a sound for each of the four basic punc- tuation marks - the period, comma, colon and semicolon. Divide your class into groups and have the groups learn the rules for each punc- tuation mark. Have them write a script and appoint people to make the noise sounds through the various punctuation marks. This can then be presented to the remainder of the class and the remainder in order to understand the script, will have to understand the rules.

20. Have students write an essay on such topics as: Why is a Sunkist orange best, or have them compare two different forms of newspaper adver- tisements.

21. Have the students write a poem in the shape of an art object, such as an apple. They can write the lines of the poem as they form the outside of an apple. Possible one line could be a worm going into the apple or coming out

of the apple; the next might be a bite out of
the apple; then have them write the lines of
their poem about the apple in the shape they
they already created.

22. Have students listen to a pre-recorded sound
or groups of sounds and ask them to create
their ideas, either written or orally, where
they might have heard that sound.

23. Have students pair off. One of them should
be blindfolded. From a pre-prepared sack
students will be allowed to taste a food
item and then they will be asked to guess
what the item is and verbally describe when
or where they last tasted the food.

24. Students often see themselves as an object.
List several distinctive cars and ask the
students to describe why they are like
one of the cars. (Make up categories.)

25. Establish a joint effort book club where
students and parents are both reading and
sharing the same book. Plan follow-up
activities that allow the parent and student to discuss their ideas together.

26. Have the students write a letter to an object,
such as a coat hanger.

27. In cooperation with nearby elementary school,
have the middle school student interview
1st and 2nd graders about things they like.
Have the students write a story and create
a book based upon the interview. Plan a day
when the books can be read to and given to
the student.

28. Ask students to write their philosophy and
then have an exchange with students from
another school who have also written their
philosophy. THis not only gives the students
a purpose to write, but will allow them to

share with people who have like interests.

29. After visiting a city museum or returning
    from a field trip, allow students time to do
    creative writing about their experiences or
    ideas.

30. Plan a scavenger hunt to take place in your
    classroom or other places in the building,
    or outside. Have pre-planted items, stories,
    etc. and ask the students to do an academic
    task, such as find the various parts of
    speech.

31. Ask students to secretly bring a favorite
    thing or object and put it up in the class-
    room. Then have students write or tell to
    whom an object belongs and why they feel it
    belongs to that person.

32. Take a topical paragraph, cut up each of the
    sentences, give each of the sentences to a
    different person and then have the students
    as a group create the paragraph by finding
    other students who have the sentences that
    will go to their paragraph.

33. When students are asked to do research or a
    research paper, have them do it in the form
    of a research board that can be displayed,
    both in writing and with pictures and illus-
    trations. Various pieces of the picture
    board can then be taped together to provide
    an illustrated research report. Students
    might also be expected to give talks to
    other classes in elementary schools by using
    this display board.

## Science and Mathematics

The area of a direct contact around us can be so
surprising and exciting that its possibilities for
creativity go beyond all other experiences for a

child.  At the very lowest level of inventiveness,
three things can happen:

1. Awareness
2. Identification
3. Association

An awareness of the many unfoldments and developments
that quietly, but constantly occur.  An identification that lays the base for comfortable expectations.
An association that helps the child know why.

1. Provide a science table (change regularly)
   which is more than a display table.  Leading
   questions, direction cards and demonstrations
   provided by the teacher lead children to seek
   answers.  Prepare and leave on the table a
   booklet that has space for individuals to write
   their discoveries and sign their names.  Name
   it a "Science Discoveries" book.  Let children
   examine items on the science table and voice
   their hunches about properties, functions,
   structure or origin before reading for veri-
   fication.

2. Encourage children to discover answers to
   problems and extend their concepts as they
   set up experiments for research.  They may
   record their discoveries in picture or chart
   form.

3. Have the children draw a picture of a machine
   that will do a job they don't like to do, and
   write a story about the machine.

4. Read Zim's What's Inside of Me.  After you have
   concluded reading the book, have your class
   draw a picture of a skeleton.  Under the picture have them write as much as they can recall
   about the story.

5. Let a group dismantle a clock or a mechanical
   toy.  After a thorough examination period, ask
   the group to write what they have observed and

noticed.

6. Present a science experiment and discuss the principles involved. A few days later present a different experiment demonstrating the same principles. This time ask the children to write an explanation of the experiment. Do not discuss the experiment prior to writing.

7. Rub balloons with different materials to learn about electricity.

8. Make a calendar of the months with a design or original drawing for each month.

9. Create a new number system using conventional symbols or make up original symbols.

10. Answer questions in a "What Does It Really Mean To You" booklet.

   a. A million
   b. A mile
   c. A dollar
   d. Freedom
   e. Family

11. Make up time zone problems.

12. Do research in the history of arithmetic.

13. How to make a gallon:

   a. Illustrate ways to get a gallon of liquid, using small measures and large measures.

   b. Draw something which people purchase by the gallon.

14. Develop an individual book of original problems.

15. Write and illustrate a page of arithmetic problems for a class book.

16. Prepare and make reports on money of other countries.

17. Analyze the school building in terms of dimensions.

18. Compare land, water, and air speeds in transportation.

19. Make calculations relative to beginning astronomy and space studies.

20. Construct and play number puzzles and games.

21. Provide all the necessary data in a paragraph or two and have the children make up problems using this data.

22. On a rainy day, ask children what "wetness" is. Ask them, "Can you touch it? Feel it? What are the scientific facts we know about wetness? Could you paint wetness? (Art)

23. Try to find out various ways that men communicate with one another. Instigate this research by determining a social need for communication. The following topics are suggested:

    a. Braille
    b. The musical notation system
    c. The Morse code
    d. The symbols used by pilots on planes
    e. Indian smoke signals
    f. Manual alphabets of deaf mutes.

24. Provide a box of simple toys that will illustrate some scientific principle. Instruct the student to think of as many things as he can that these toys can do and explain them. Do not give up when you have discovered one use; there are several possible uses for each toy. The toys can be combined, if needed.

25. Ask questions such as these:  "Is air real?" and "How do you know?" Have students prove their hypothesis  or write why they do or don't think so.  Allow experiments to find out.

26. Allow each child to select a special phase of interest to him and work out a project on it.

27. Have the children prepare experiments to prove a scientific principle and demonstrate them.

28. Create a "how do you measure up" chart where students are allowed to find the height of the world's shortest and tallest people and height of other famous people.  Using a graduated rule, allow the students to place the names on a chart and ask them to see how they measure up in height to these people.

29. Enlarge  a photo, cut out a small section of it and have students respond to what the entire photograph might be.

30. Allow students to create materials to teach other students in their class, different classes or possible even between different schools.

31. Place the direction to an activity or experiment in unusual places around the room, such as on the ceiling, under a chair, the edge of the chair, edge of the table, etc. This will not only stimulate activity, but also creativity.

32. Create a physical barrier and have students create ways of getting an object over the physical barrier.

33. A simple but fun experimental activity is to have students study with something distinctive, such as a lollipop, while eating foods,

while watching TV, reading music, etc. and
then during testing time have them replicate
that distinctive sound, taste or idea while
testing.

## Social Studies

In an ever-expanding world, we cannot hope to
"cover the ground" but can familiarize learners
with self-directed ways of getting at resources and
using them creatively.  In a creative approach to
the social studies, children can find meaning in many
types of social experiences, and clarify meaning by
giving it some form of expression.

1. Divide your class into groups or teams.  Each
   group pantomimes some situation, pertaining
   to the country which the class is studying,
   for another group to write about.  No discussions or spoken clues are given.

2. Use an opaque projector to present pictures
   such as children from other countries, objects of art from other countries or economic
   conditions.  Ask your class to compare and
   describe the items you have presented.

3. Prepare research papers on county, state
   and country.

4. Compile statistics to use in making graphs
   or charts.

5. Create skits on the history, culture, ways of
   life, etc. of people in other areas of the
   world.

6. Creative drama concerning areas being studied.

7. Think of ten man-made features on land.

8. Pretend you are a business man opening a
   business in a country you are studying.
   How would you develop it?

9. Present a radio or T.V. newscast of any important events that are in the recent news.

10. Write a letter to someone telling them about your visit to a country which you are studying. (Imaginary)

11. Pretend to have a T.V. program interviewing some important person in the history of a country.

12. Have a panel discussion on some phase of economy or problems encountered in regions studied.

13. Use the tape recorder for recording imaginary interviews with natives of countries studied.

14. Present important events in a "You Were There" manner.

15. Keep an itinerary for countries studied as though you took the trip.

16. Write a few paragraphs on whether the student would like to visit the country under study and why.

17. The requiring of collateral for an object borrowed, such as a pencil, lunch money, etc. is a creative activity in the area of economics.

18. When assigning your students to watch a historical or adventure show, add a little twist to it by having the students figure out logistically how they can do that film or show.

19. Allow students to get some sayings from a tombstone epitaph and write about the lives of people or the times of people.

20. To encourage cooperation, give students each a puzzle piece as they complete their assign-

ment. The puzzle can be made from a chart or
map, or other materials that you are currently
studying.

21. Take a picture of a super-hero, blow it up
    larger than life size, cut it into a puzzle
    and give people different pieces of the puzzle.
    Ask them to color their piece. Those students
    who combine the puzzle with others before they
    begin to color will have learned the skills of
    cooperation necessary to create a coordinated
    picture. Those who did not will understand the
    necessity of cooperation when the puzzle is
    put together.

22. Have the students create a society by identify-
    ing artifacts of that society. Then have that
    group bury the artifacts; another group can
    then have an archaeological experience by
    digging up the artifacts and reconstructing
    the meaning of the society.

23. Have a costume day when faculty members or
    guests are dressed up in costumes of famous
    people of history and have these teachers and
    guests go around and tell students about this
    person.

24. When students have an understanding of the
    cause and effects of the Civil War, let them
    generate the solutions during the reconstruc-
    tion period, then go back and compare them
    with the actual solutions that are recorded in
    history.

25. When planning a field trip or overnight exper-
    ience, allow students to be responsible for
    studying the government and the rules to
    govern them on these activities.

26. Allow students to plan a small business that
    can be operated at school, seek a loan to
    start the business, mark it a product, show
    a profit and then be allowed to spend the
    profits on a worthy project.

27. Display a historical picture with several people in the scene. Allow students to choose to identify with the person in the scene and then have them write about that person.

## Music and Art

In music, as in all art, there is need for expressive feelings, experiences, or skills.

1. Listening initiates intellectual or physical response. Even the shyest child in the room will want to try the Russian kicks in the "Nutcracker Suite."

2. Making musical instruments is one creative project that is particularly interesting to elementary school children. Each child presents his instrument and tells how it was made and why certain features were employed.

3. Composing original songs is another activity with strong appeal. In preparing for the composition of a song, much initial poem construction is needed.

4. Illustrating a recording through the uses of various art media.

5. Have your class draw and exchange pictures about trips, hobbies or other subjects that interest them. Each writes a story to go with the picture he gets. Interesting discussions can also be based on this activity.

6. Children draw a rainbow at the top of their writing paper. The rainbow should include all of the primary colors plus some of the other popular hues. You then ask the children each to write a short paragraph telling how they feel about each color, and why a certain color is their favorite.

7. After your class has experienced a successful art project or craft lesson, ask them to write directions telling another class how to make it.

8. Pass out or exhibit examples of modern abstract art. Let your children write what ideas and thoughts one of the pictures gave them.

9. Display inanimate objects such as a doughnut, a flag, an apple, a leaf. Let children pretend to be one of these and write how they might feel if they were that object.

10. Make ink-blot designs on paper (about 6" x 4"). Staple each ink-blot to a sheet of lined paper. Work with the class on interpreting some of the blots, then let each child about what he visualized as he examines one.

11. Have a child see and mimic a variety of dances on T.V., after which the child is asked to dance freely to a variety of recorded music.

12. Allow the students to create a large mural to be displayed in the school. Several dried food items such as rice, beans, various forms of spaghetti and others will allow them to do the mural in a large format.

13. Start a permanent art collection for the school by purchasing students' works of art.

14. Set up contests for students to write songs, do a work of art, construct a project from the shops, or other activities. The important thing in any contest would be that students be allowed to do their own thing and receive an incentive for participating or an award for the best in each category.

## INDEPENDENT STUDY

Is independent study a myth or a reality in our
middle schools? A more basic question might be, is
independent study something that should be included
in the educational environment of the emerging adolescent learner?

The concept of independent study has been a part
of the educational scene for many years. It has been
instituted in a great number of secondary as well as
elementary schools in one form or another. In fact
in recent years more and more schools have implemented some type of independent study program. Overly,
Kinghorn, and Preston refer to independent study in
the following manner:

"It has become professionally fashionable to
institute some form of independent study.
Who can be against either independence or study?
Combined, independence and study makes an
appealing label. However, independent study
means different things to different people."[1]

By breaking the concept of independent study into
its two separate parts, it becomes evident how
value laden this concept has really become. A look
at how teachers and students might view independent
study would most likely support the statement that
"...independent study means different things to
different people."[2] For example, most middle school
teachers would agree that their students are
struggling with a new found desire for independence.

---

[1]Donald E. Overly, Jon Rye Kinghorn, and Richard
L. Preston, The Middle School: Humanizing Education
for Youth. (Belmont, California: Wadsworth Publishing Company, Inc., 1972), p. 105.

[2]Ibid.

Likewise, middle school teachers would substantiate
that studying does not have a high priority with
these youngsters. When putting the two terms
together, independent and study, middle school teachers probably would recognize a need but would question
the degree and method of implementation.

Then there is the attitude of the middle school
student toward independent study. For the most part
these students see a much greater need for independence than their teachers and usually have much more
confidence in their ability to handle such independence. However, when their feelings about studying
are revealed, the table suddenly turns; and whereas,
the teachers see a great need, the middle school student sees studying as a lesser priority. When the
total concept of independent study is presented to
the middle school youngster, the reaction is mixed,
as it is with the teachers. Independence, which
has a high priority, and studying, which has a
somewhat lower priority, are two terms which are
often hard to synthesize in the mind of the
emerging adolescents.

If these hypothetical reactions are accurate it
would appear that the teacher and student each has
his own feelings about independence and studying as
separate concepts. However,when the two are combined
into one concept there are not only differences of
opinions but also confusion as to the meaning and
relevance to the learning process of the emerging
adolescent. Thus, before talking about how independent study can be implemented in middle schools, the
question of why independent study should be implemented in middle schools must be resolved.


Relationship of Independent Study
to the Middle School

Probably the prime reason the middle school movement has been successful is due to the fact that the
middle school concept has been based on instituting
a unique educational environment which meets the

unique needs of the emerging adolescent learner.
If the needs of the emerging adolescent are at the
core of the middle school philosophy, then middle
school educators can not afford to fall into the
age old trap of accepting an educational innovation
such as "independent study" without first considering the reason for its inclusion into the curriculum.
It becomes extremely important that middle school
educators keep in mind the prime reason for the
existence of the middle school.  The decision to
include an independent study program can be no
exception to this cardinal rule which insists that a
program be developed to meet the unique needs of the
emerging adolescent.

The critical question then this:  is independent
study a viable means of meeting the needs of the
emerging adolescent and what needs will it meet?
The answer to this question will help establish the
philosophical foundation necessary for consideration
of its inclusion into a middle school curriculum.
In answering this question, it is assumed that one
accepts the fact that the middle schooler is unique
with unique needs and characteristics.  Volumes of
books, articles, and research could be cited substan-
tiating this assumption.  However, rather than elabor-
ating on what the literature has said regarding this
subject, let us focus our attention for a moment on
the implication of such an assumption for building
a case for independent study in the middle schools.

Diversity in Growth, Development, and Interest

Many things make the emerging adolescent different.  However, all these differences can be summarized
in one word, change.  At no other time in their
lives will these youngsters have to contend with so
many personal changes at one time.  They are making
significant changes in their physical, emotional,
and intellectual make-up.  To complicate matters
even further, these changes do not occur at the
same time or at the same rate.  At no other time in
schools are the differences in maturation levels as

evident even though the chronological ages may be the same.

Thus, differences in levels of maturation might be justification enough to warrant an individual approach to instruction such as through independent study. It stands to reason that the diversity found in a certain age level would demand diverse methods of instruction. The old adage that no two people learn in the same way would certainly apply to emerging adolescents. For example, a child who is at a concrete stage of thinking might respond much differently than a child who has attained formal operation level according to Piaget's theory of cognitive development.

Not only do emerging adolescents find themselves in the midst of physical, social, emotional, and intellectual transition; but, they are also in the midst of developing new and diverse interests. These are often short in duration but never-the-less may be one of the biggest assets a middle school teacher can have as a means of accomplishing an educational goal with a student.

On the surface it would then appear that independent study would have significant implications as a means of meeting the needs of groups of youngsters with such diverse interests. However, to justify independent study for this reason alone would not be altogether accurate. It would be more accurate to justify individualized instruction for the middle school, but not necessarily independent study. Alexander and Hine point out that these two concepts are definitely not synonymous. They further explain that individualizing instruction can be extremely teacher centered, i.e., tutoring. Independent study, on the other hand, although it may be used as a means of accomplishing individualized instruction connotes more than a one to one mode of instruction. Preferably independent study should nurture some type of self-directed or independent learning on the part of the student.[3]

This by no means diminishes the role of independent study in providing for the individual needs of students. In a survey of 300 schools done by Alexander and Hines, teachers and administrators indicated that the most beneficial aspect of independent study was that it provided for the needs and interests of the individual student.[4]

## Meeting the Need for Independence

Although justification of independent study as a means of meeting the diverse needs and interests of the emerging adolescent certainly is an important reason for implementing such a program, one must be careful that the essence of the concept is fully realized. One of the most important needs of the emerging adolescent is that of independence. By merely focusing on an individual student's interest and/or abilities does not necessarily mean that his/her needs for independence will be met. The need for independence might even be stifled.

Even though a teacher recognizes that a student has discernible interests or a particular learning ability (exceptional or remedial), unless the teacher provides that student with a certain amount of autonomy for making decisions and accepting the responsibility of his/her learning, this need will not have been met. Completing questions in a workbook independently of the teacher's directions does not necessarily foster independent learning on the part of the student. Working with a student on a one to one basis, where the teacher is the primary source of direction and information, also fails to foster

---

[3] William M. Alexander and Vynce A. Hine, Independent Study in Secondary Schools. (New York: Holt, Rinehart, and Winston, Inc., 1967), pp. 9-11.

[4] Ibid., pp. 92-93.

independent learning.

Independent study begins to make even more sense
as a part of a middle school program when it is
viewed in terms of how it can benefit the emerging
adolescent in his/her struggle to make the needed
transition from the dependency of childhood to the
relative independence expected of a mature adult in
our society. Margaret Mead points out that this
transition is extremely important and in a technological society, such as ours, it tends to be prolonged.
Thus, it becomes a period when the rights and
privileges of adulthood are gradually and sometimes
reluctantly given to our youth as opposed to other
less advanced cultures which bestow all rights and
privileges at the onset of puberty.[5]

A survey of a typical group of middle school
youngsters revealed some interesting insights about
their feelings of independence. The following questions were asked of 150 middle school youngsters
in a sixth through eighth grade middle school in a
suburban community of 50,000 people.

1.  I see myself as being: (a) dependent on others,
    (b) more dependent on others than independent,
    (c) more independent of others than dependent,
    (d) independent of others.

2.  I feel my teachers:  (a) are too restrictive,
    (b) allow me the right amount of independence,
    (c) are not restrictive enough.

3.  I feel my parents:  (a) are too restrictive,
    (b) allow me the right amount of independence,
    (c) are not restrictive enough.

4.  I would like to be more independent to make
    my own decisions.  (a) agree  (b) disagree

---

[5] Margaret Mead, "Early Adolescence in the United
States," NASSP Bulletin, (April, 1965), pp. 5-10.

TABLE I:  How the Emerging Adolescents View Themselves in Relationship to Independence.

|  | 6th grade | 7th grade | 8th grade | Total |
|---|---|---|---|---|
| Dependent | 5.0% | 0% | 4.2% | 3.1% |
| More Dependent than Independent | 13.0% | 4.5% | 24.9% | 13.9% |
| More Independent than Dependent | 46.1% | 67.6% | 57.1% | 58.0% |
| Independent | 35.9% | 27.9% | 13.8% | 25.0% |

This survey tends to affirm the idea that the
emerging adolescents see themselves as being more
independent than dependent.  As can be seen, approximately 83% of the students who responded saw themselves as being either independent or at least more
independent than dependent.  On the other end of the
scale a very small percentage (3.1%) of the students
saw themselves as being dependent.

TABLE II:  How Emerging Adolescents View Independence
With Respect to Their Relationship to
Teachers

|  | 6th grade | 7th grade | 8th grade | Total |
|---|---|---|---|---|
| Teachers Are Too Restrictive | 13.0% | 25.5% | 21.2% | 20.1% |
| Teachers Allow About the Right Amount of Independence | 84.5% | 72.0% | 72.3% | 75.9% |
| Teachers Are Not Restrictive Enough | 2.5% | 2.5% | 6.5% | 4.0% |

TABLE III:   How Emerging Adolescents View Indepen-
             dence with Respect to Their Relation-
             ship with Parents

|  | 6th grade | 7th grade | 8th grade | Total |
|---|---|---|---|---|
| Parents Are Too Restrictive | 10.0% | 27.9% | 14.9% | 17.7% |
| Parents Allow About the Right Amount of Independence | 85.0% | 67.6% | 85.1% | 79.1% |
| Parents Are Not Restrictive Enough | 5.0% | 4.5% | 0% | 3.2% |

The figures in Tables II and III would seem to
indicate that there is a basic satisfaction with the
amount of independence allowed by teachers and
parents.  However, when comparing the two extremes it
is evident that the emerging adolescents involved in
this survey felt that teachers and parents where much
more restrictive than non-restrictive.

TABLE IV:   The Emerging  Adolescents' Perceptions of
            Need for More Independence

|  | 6th grade | 7th grade | 8th grade | Total |
|---|---|---|---|---|
| Need for More Independence | 97.5% | 93.0% | 83.0% | 90.7% |
| No Need for More Independence | 2.5% | 7.0% | 17.0% | 9.3% |

The final question of the survey substantiates
the notion that independence is an important need of
the emerging adolescent.  As can be seen in Table IV,
there was only a small percentage who did not perceive a need for more independence (9.3%).  Even

though Tables II and III did not indicate that there was a great deal of conflict in what the students saw as a need for independence and what teachers and parents permitted, Tables I and IV indicate that emerging adolescents see a need for more independence. It would seem logical that if independence is a perceived need of the emerging adolescent, then middle school educators should develop strategies to help them cope with this need.

In this era of the knowledge explosion, it is impossible to know all there is to know about anything. In fact, what knowledge we have at our disposal now might not be applicable or even true a few years hence. Thus, to base education entirely around the idea of disseminating knowledge would be an extremely futile, if not impossible, task for an educator to effectively accomplish. Might not a more realistic goal be one of helping a child learn how to learn and thus equip him with learning tools to which he can readily adapt the ever changing and expanding knowledge base. However, in order to do this the learner must gain some sense of ownership for his/her learning. It would be presumptuous to think that youngsters could assume any type of responsibility for their own learning if they are not given the opportunity to do so.

Middle school students are typically under constant direction of a teacher who not only determines what they learn but when and how they learn it. This type of educational environment tends to breed dependent learning rather than independent learning. Dependent learning in turn tends to restrict the learner rather than move him toward a more adaptive self-directed learning process.

Independent study thus has an important function in providing a meaningful learning environment for the emerging adolescent. Not only does it provide a flexible method of meeting the diverse needs, interests, and abilities of emerging adolescents but it also provides a method by which teachers can facilitate the transition of their students from the

dependency of childhood to the independency expected
of adulthood.

## Implementation of an Independent Study
## Program in a Middle School

Now that a basic rationale has been established
for the inclusion of an independent study program in
the middle school curriculum, let us turn our attention to ways in which such a program can be effectively implemented. It should be stressed that independent study activities and experiences are not
reserved for only the exceptional and gifted students.
Unfortunately some schools have viewed independent
study programs as a means of expanding the educational horizons of accelerated students. This
approach implies that the students with average or
below average abilities need more direction and
guidance and would not benefit from such a learning
situation. In Beggs and Buffie's book, Bold New
Venture, William Rogge writes:

> "The real problem is not to decide who shall
> be included or excluded in the program but
> to determine what kinds of adjustments must
> be made for individual students so that all
> can be reached and properly challenged."[6]

This statement would have to be particularly applicable to the pre and early adolescent. The diversity
of maturation and interests plus the need for independence are characteristics found in all emerging
adolescents. Thus, independent study should be
looked at as it meets the needs of each individual
student in terms of each one's personal abilities,
interests, maturation level, and cognitive level of
thinking.

---

[6]David W. Beggs and Edward G. Buffie, ed.,
Independent Study, Bold New Venture. (Bloomington,
Indiana: Unversity Press, 1965), p. 23.

Teachers have had students they felt could not be
trusted or could not assume responsibility even when
the learning activity was teacher directed. How then
can students be expected to assume responsibilities
to learn independently of the teacher? The familiar
saying that "practice makes perfect" may have some
relevance in this case. If students are never given
the opportunity to assume some degree of responsibility for their learning, how will they develop into
independent learners? Certainly teachers have to
expect that some students will not readily respond
or will even take advantage of such freedom. However, a teacher must also recognize that a majority
of the middle school students' reactions are caused
by peer influence. Therefore some students may seem
irresponsible in class but might respond quite
differently given the opportunity to work on their
own with minimum peer influence.

The success of an independent study program is
determined by a variety of factors. Two of the most
important, however, would be the ability of the
teacher to recognize the needs and interests of
each student and the willingness of the teacher to
give a commitment of class time to independent study
activities. Independent study activities and
learning situations will not happen by accident in
the classroom. The teacher must be prepared with
ideas, equipment, materials, and class time to aid
each student in developing his/her independence
in learning to the fullest.

## Three Types of Independent Study
## Programs for the Classroom

Three alternative for implementing an independent study program in a classroom will be discussed
in this section. Perhaps you will find one of these
or a combination of these suggestions applicable to
your own classroom situation.

Independent Project Day. One approach to independent study in a classroom might be through the

development of project days for the entire class
on a regular basis.  On these days the teacher must
be prepared to step aside from the role of an
instructor of students and assume the role of a
facilitator of student activities.  This is not meant
to imply that the student is not at the center of
the class learning situation everyday.  It is meant
to point out that on project days the students'
interests and concerns become the focal point of
that day's learning activities instead of the teacher
pre-determining what will be covered in class.  The
regularity of these project days will vary from program but for the moment give consideration to the
possible inclusion of a project day once a week.
Weekly project time will satisfy several basic needs
of a successful independent study program.  First of
all, a weekly commitment of time in the classroom
emphasizes the importance placed upon the opportunity
to develop personal interests and experiences of the
student by the teacher.  Students are quick to
respond to the apparent enthusiasm toward a progrsm
shown by their teacher and react accordingly to the
value and importance placed upon these activities.
Weekly independent study time also allows the
student to become more deeply involved in appropriate projects with each unit of study since a
project may be developed over several weeks of work
and thus encourages more in depth research.

At the beginning of the project day, the teacher
should spend a limited amount of time setting the mood
and importance of independent study time.  This is
when the teachers' own enthusiasm for the upcoming
activities and commitment to the importance of each
student's independence can make or break the program.
This is a time also when some students will put to
the test the sincerity of the teacher in accepting
the right of each student to pursue an independent
acitivity or project, for the activities suggested
by the teacher should be just that—a suggestion or
starting point.  If a student has independently come
up with a research problem or activity of his own,
this should be readily accepted by the teacher and
encouraged to the fullest for this is the blossoming

of independent study and learning.

Once the independent study time has begun, the teacher should assume the role of the resource person for those students who are in need of such help. Perhaps a student has decided to research a related topic of personal interest but has difficulty in using the card catalog in the library. The teacher then needs to help the student develop these skills and locate the needed information. This should be done in a teaming situation with the student and teacher as partners only until the student has located the needed information and is clearly capable of pursuing the remaining research independently. At this point the teacher should move away from the partnership giving the student encouragement to continue the project as he/she sees fit.

Another opportunity which may be developed through project days is peer interest groups. Several students may discover they have interests in the same area and may wish to develop a project as a team. There is no reason why this should be discouraged as long as the students sincerely work on the project and do not get distracted along the way. Peer enthusiasm and peer teaching can be valuable additions to any classroom and many times are not utilized to the fullest.

Daily Independent Project Time. Another way of approaching the implementation of an independent study time in the classroom might be to devote a certain portion of the class period each day to independent study. This would work extremely well where the teacher has an extended class period in which more time is available. The type of independent work a student did during this time might vary. However, the majority of the time would be devoted to each student working on his/her own project with limited teacher direction. This time would also enable the student to work on an independent project on a continuous daily basis as opposed to the weekly or periodic project day. However, unless students are given sufficient time to work on their projects,

this time will result in them just getting started
and then having to stop and go onto another class
activity. Where daily time is too limited for the
task on which the students are working, it might be
better to designate an entire day for independent
study such as a project day.

In scheduling independent study time into the
classroom on a daily basis the teacher must not only
consider the amount of time bu the logistics of
providing the proper environment conducive to
independent learning. In other words, it would be
very difficult for a student to study independently
in the back of the room while other students are
engaged in a classroom activity in the front. If
a teacher is going to attempt to have some students
doing independent study while there is another class
activity going on, it is best to have the independent study students in a separate area where they
won't be disturbed. If this is not possible, the
teacher might consider having independent study for
all students at the same time or at least backing
the independent study time with a non-distracting
activity.

The one drawback with having some students
on independent study while the teacher is working
with the rest of the class is the obvious elimination of the teacher as a resource person for the
students. This problem is not easily resolved when
there is only one teacher in the class. However,
in a team teaching situation, multiple classroom
activities work very effectively. One teacher can
devote his/her time to working with the students
on independent study while the other(s) engage in
other classroom activities. This type of cooperative teaming lends a dimension of flexibility to the
class that allows the students to have the opportunity to engage in independent learning activities
as well as other more teacher directed activities.

Independent Project Units. Yet another way of
implementing independent study into the classroom
is through an independent project unit approach.

In such an approach the teacher makes a commitment
that the material covered on a certain topic will
be studied by the students on an independent basis.
The role of the teacher thus becomes one of a
resource person who helps the student design the
manner in which they wish to investigate the topic
under study.

A teacher needs to be cautious not to over-use
this type of approach. Although some students would
react very well to this type of independent instruction, most students at this age need to be involved
with their peers in class. This need for interaction is not only common among emerging adolescents,
but also essential to their growth and development.
Thus, to use the independent project unit exclusively
might provide the youngster with the opportunity to
develop independent learning skills, but at the same
time it might not provide the needed opportunity to
interact with peers. The unit approach could be
used as a method to study a subject once or twice a
year with an entire class. If there was a student
who did well with such an approach, he/she could be
given the opportunity to pursue other units independently of the rest of the class.

### Independent Study Activities That Can Be
### Included in a Middle School Classroom

Now that some of the alternatives for implementing independent study into the classroom have been
presented, let us turn our attention to the types of
activities that can be incorporated into these time
blocks. This section will describe four types of
activities that would lend themselves to independent
study periods in a classroom.

Independent Study Projects. Not all material
needs to be presented to all students in the same
way. In fact if one accepts the premise that the
emerging adolescent is at a stage of development
marked by diversity in ability, interest, and maturation, then to present the same materials the same

way to all students is obviously not the most
effective way of teaching or learning. To let
the student have some degree of determination in the
design and implementation of his/her learning
environment is an essential component in helping
the student become an independent learner.

Independent study projects can be used in two
different ways. First, the project can be designed
as the principle means by which the individual student learns about the topic under investigation.
Secondly, the student with the help of the teacher
can design a project which would supplement what is
being covered in class. No matter how it is used,
there are certain steps which should be followed
before a student embarks on such an independent
educational adventure.

Prior to the beginning of each unit of study
the teacher should determine possibilities of high
interest projects which could be pursued by the
students in the class. In deciding project possibilities, thought must be given to the various modes
of learning used by the emerging adolescents and the
variety of levels of cognitive thinking present in
a class. Suggested activities must cover a wide
spectrum so that each student has the opportunity
to become involved in a learning situation which is
geared to his/her individual needs.

One method which works effectively with the
emerging adolescent is brainstorming. This is a
process of getting students to generate as many
ideas as possible in a short amount of time on a
particular topic. For example, if a teacher were
about to embark on a current events unit on "Great
Persons in the World Today," he/she might divide the
class into small groups and have each group come up
with a list of as many noted people they could think
of in four or five minutes. After each group reports
the names on their list, they would be assigned the
task of dividing these names into categories. The

the students could be regrouped and put into a
second brainstorming activity to determine possible independent projects based on these personalities.
One of the rules of brainstorming is to accept all
ideas without making value judgements as to its
acceptability or usefulness; thus, the teacher should
be receptive to all ideas.  From this list of names
and activities the students could select who they
would like to investigate and what form their
projects would take.  Once these topics and activities have been determined the teacher must assemble
the materials and equipment needed to complete the
projects so that the class time may be spent with the
students involved in the learning process and
research rather than in their search for needed
materials.

The teacher becomes a resource person for each
student in the development of his/her project.  The
teacher must also be able to recognize students who
are having difficulty in completing the tasks they
have chosen.  If for example, a project requires the
student to use the school library and he/she does not
have the basic library skills, then it is the job
of the teacher to help that student develop the
skills necessary to complete the project.

If the intent of the teacher is to use these
ideas generated by the students as a jumping off
point for an independent study unit, then the teacher
should allow the students the majority of class
time for completion of their projects.  However,
if the teacher's purpose is to use these ideas to
develop independent study projects that would
supplement a class unit, then a project day and/or
a daily independent study time would be adequate to
complete the projects.  This would allow the teacher
to carry on with the classroom activities planned
for this unit.

Independent Study Resources. Besides having
different needs, abilities and interests emerging
adolescents also have different modalities of learning.  Some youngsters may learn more readily

visually than auditorily. If a teacher recognizes this, he/she may want to establish different ways in which a student may obtain needed information and thus facilitate these different styles of learning. A good example of allowing the student to independently gather information may be shown in the following summary of a unit in American history on the "Causes of the Civil War."

The students were given the task of studying the causes of the Civil War. The class was first given some of the major differences between the North and South, such as, slavery, tariffs, states rights vs. central government, etc. They were then divided into two smaller groups, one representing the southern point of view and the other the northern. The task was to research this topic from a northern or southern point of view and be prepared to debate that particular topic.

The teacher then set up several different ways in which the students could obtain the material they needed to support their case. The students could select one or a combination of the following to gain the needed information.

1) View filmstrips on causes of the Civil War
2) Read suggested books
3) Participate in small group discussion focusing on one point of view (North or South) of the Civil War. The discussions would be directed by the teacher.
4) Listen to tapes and records on the Civil War

Several days were devoted to the task of collecting data. Some students drifted from one station to the next while others stayed with one method of information gathering. This information was then organized and put to immediate use in their debates.

Allowing the students to select the way in which they felt most comfortable in gathering information is a form of independent study. Although the teacher organized and set up all the needed resources the

student was still given the option to select the
type of information gathering mode which fit him/her
best. The student most likely did not work strictly
on his/her own. However, with the exception of the
small discussion groups, the student did work independently of the teacher. This type of independent
study, although it does not nurture true independent
learning as an independent project might, does
provide the student with some independence in how
he/she learns.

   Independent Learning Labs. A similar approach
to independent learning, but on a more permanent
basis, is the independent learning lab. Too often
teachers expect their students to become independent
learners without giving them either the time, place,
or materials to fulfill this expectation. Learning
labs, if established permanently in a classroom and
equipped with the proper resources, can provide the
place and materials to facilitate independent learning. It is still the teacher's responsibility to
give the time. Learning labs may be set up in any
classroom no matter what the content area. These
labs should have a designated purpose, should provide
the materials needed to accomplish that purpose, and
they should also be readily available to all students.
When the students are given the opportunity to use
labs, the exact purpose of each lab should be presented in a manner which the student can easily understand. Complete directions for the use of the lab
and available materials must always be present.

   Some examples of independent learning labs
which might be offered in various academic areas
follow.

| Social Studies | Math | Language Arts |
|---|---|---|
| reading | reading | reading |
| use of maps | math games | writing |
| writing | basic functions | word games |
| simulations | geometric design | poetry |
| social studies | geo-boards | spelling |
| games | | challenges |
| listening tapes | calulators | listening tapes |

There are a variety of activities which could be
put in each one of these labs enabling students to
work independently or in small groups. These could
be commercially made or teacher made materials such
as in the area of creative story starters in language
arts.

Independent learning labs are usually designed to
enhance or at least give the students the opportunity
to work on basic learning skills or skills related
to that discipline. In some areas automated equipment might be used such as a listening lab or computer
terminal.

Independent Reading. One of the areas mentioned
as a possible learning lab was reading. This seems
obvious because reading is an important skill which
is essential to all content areas. This approach
to providing an independent study time for reading
can certainly have an impact on building reading
skills if the lab is equipped with high interest
material.

However, in addition to skill development, just
as important at this age is the development of a
positive attitude toward reading. In order to do this
students must first have the opportunity to read and
secondly, be given an opportunity to read materials
geared to their abilities and interests. There have
been various attempts to do this on both a school
wide basis and a classroom basis.

One approach is to set aside a certain time
during the day when everyone in school (students,
teachers, administration, custodians, etc.) stop and
read silently for a certain number of minutes.
Another such approach is to take a few minutes,
preferably at the beginning of each class period,
for students to selently read self-selected materials.
Once the students get into the habit of bringing
their reading materials each day, they tend to come
in, sit down, and begin reading. This enables the
class to begin with a common activity and also
provides a transiton period from one class to another.

Using an independent reading time in class in these ways could certainly be classified as a type of independent study. The students are not only working independently of each other and the teacher but they are also pursuing materials which are of interest and relevant to them.

One of the aforementioned approaches to independent study could be incorporated into the middle school classroom through any of the three methods of implementation described in the previous section. The following chart illustrates some of the possible combinations.

IMPLEMENTATION INTO CLASSROOM

|  | Project Days | Daily Independent Study Time | Independent Project Units |
|---|---|---|---|
| Independent Study Projects | Devote entire class period to work on project at least once a week.<br><br>Supplement with teacher directed class activities between project days.<br><br>Number of project days determined by project. | Devote part of each class period to working on independent project.<br><br>Sufficient time should be allowed to accomplish certain tasks required to complete project.<br><br>Class may be divided so that some are working on independent projects while others are involved in teacher directed activities. | Devote each class period during an extended unit to working on an independent project<br><br>Brainstorming may be used to determine possible projects.<br><br>Options should be available to students both in the process and materials used. |

|  | Project Days | Daily Independent Study Time | Independent Project Units |
|---|---|---|---|
| Independent Study Resources | Devote one class period per week to allowing students to use a variety of resources to gain information.<br><br>Students would have time to use resources outside the classroom, i.e., library. | Devote part of each class period to allowing students to use a variety of resources to gain needed information.<br><br>Resources would probably need to be available in the class room because of time limitations. | Devote each class period during an extended unit to providing different independent resource options for collecting needed information on a unit. |
| Independent Learning Labs | Devote one class period a week to working in independent labs.<br><br>Each lab should have a specific learning purpose. | Devote part of each class period to having students work on independent labs set up in class. | Independent study labs may be set up to assist students in their projects. |
| Independent Reading | Devote entire day to letting the students read independently. | Devote part of each period to letting students read independently. First 10 minutes usually works best. Paperback books should be available in classroom. | Students may choose to read and report on certain materials as a project. |

## Independent Study on a School Wide Basis

Up to this point we have investigated the possibilities of implementing independent study in the individual classroom. We have seen that implementation of such a program takes a commitment from the individual teacher. Let us now turn our attention to the implementation of independent study on a school wide basis, which demands a much broader commitment from the total teaching staff of the middle school.

If a middle school is to offer the emerging adolescent learner an opportunity for independent learning during the school day, several key factors must be considered, most important of which is the role of the teacher. No longer is the teacher the disseminator of knowledge but rather he/she is a resource person who must be able to diagnose individual learning problems and motivate students to become independent learners. Other major factors to consider are scheduling facilities and materials. Various middle schools may choose to institute a school wide independent learning program in various ways and to various degrees. Some may decide to design their entire school curriculum around the independent learning philosophy, while others may decide to commit only a portion of the school day to such an endeavor. To whatever degree schools devote themselves to the idea of independent learning, the staff must be committed to making it work.

The teacher's role as a resource person during this time would alter the traditional type of student/teacher contact. While working with students on an independent study basis, the teachers might find themselves more in a helping capacity than in a traditional instructional capacity. The teacher must help each student identify his/her own unique interest and abilities and then work with each on developing appropriate activities which will enhance each individual's style of learning.

To put the teacher in such a position seems to have some benefit for both the student and the teacher. However, to implement such a program on a school wide basis might seem to be more idealistic than realistic. In order for the teacher to be effective in this role the schedule would have to be flexible. Time would have to be available for the teacher to meet with students on a one to one basis while at the same time the students must be given time to work independently on projects.

Places within the school must be designated where students have the opportunity to study independently. This does not necessarily imply that all students would work completely independent of other students or even other teachers. It does suggest that a variety of places be designated throughout the school where the students have the opportunity to work on a variety of independent activities. For example, students might be given the opportunity to go to one of the following areas:

Learning Labs (writing, reading, listening, etc.)
Learning Centers (math, social studies, science, etc.)
Small Group Discussion Areas
Study Centers
Library
A.V. Center
Interest Centers
Computer or Math Room

They might also wish to meet with an individual teacher or a resource person within or outside the school.

There is no one plan for implementing an independent study program in a middle school. This would depend on the particular school and its needs. As a rule most middle schools have chosen not to design their entire curriculum around the philosophy of independent study. Rather, they have chosen to emphasize the idea of independent learning through various classes and/or by committing a portion of the

school day to a general independent study program.
This gives the students some time during the day to
engage in some form of independent activity.  THis
is not considered a free period for the teachers or
the students but a period where teachers and students
have the opportunity to work together in a more independent learning environment as opposed to a teacher
directed classroom situation.

Independent study may be scheduled in many
different ways.  A school may have the entire population on independent study at one time or they may
spread the independent study periods throughout the
day.  Spreading it throughout the day usually has a
significant drawback in that not all teachers are
available.  However, if the independent study time
was divided so that each grade level had independent
study at the same time, it would minimize this
problem due to the fact that the teachers for that
grade level would be available at that time.  On the
other hand, freeing up all students at one time or
at least by grade level also frees up the facility.
Thus, a student may wish to work on an independent
project in science so he/she would report to the
science area where both the material and resources
are available.  The classrooms then become independent learning labs where students can take advantage
of the resources available in that area.  The classroom then serves a dual purpose as an instructional
area and also as an independent learning center
where students can go during their independent study
time.

Overly, Kinghorn, and Preston present an
interesting plan to convert a traditional school
facility into a facility designed specifically for
learning laboratories.  Most classrooms serve only
as a space where traditional instruction takes place.
Their proposal still suggests a single function.
However, they see the primary function of the classrooms as open laboratories.  Their plan first presents a diagram of a section of a traditional school
composed of two social studies rooms, two science
rooms, two math rooms, and two language arts rooms.

They take each of these rooms and reassign the
purpose of the room to fit a certain learning activity rather than a subject area.  The signs on each
classroom door might read audio-visual lab, small
group learning lab, science lab, large group presentation lab, individual study lab, etc.  Each area
would be equipped with study tables, round tables,
lounge furniture, stage, A.V. equipment, etc. which
would be appropriate for that area.[7]

    This type of unique learning environment although
it is an extreme departure from a traditional school
arrangement would provide an optimum physical
arrangement to enhance independent learning.  Using
such an arrangement to its fullest potential would
depend on many factors (number of students, number
of teachers, length of day, etc.)  The logistics
of developing a schedule is a large task but not an
impossible one.

    This type of arrangement would definitely be
the exception and not the case for most middle
schools.  If a middle school were to make a school
wide commitment to an independent study program it
would most likely be on a more limited scale.  In
many cases, it might be only for a limited number
of students for a limited time during the day.  This
type of program probably benefits those students
involved and helps them become independent learners.
However, as presented in the first part of this
chapter, all emerging adolescents have a need for
independence and thus a much broader approach might
be warranted which would include all students.

    How can this be done?  First, a time block
during the day must be set aside when all students,
or at least all students having the same teachers,
can meet on an independent basis.  This is probably

---

    [7]Donald E. Overly, Jan Rye Kinghorn, and
Richard L. Preston, The Middle School:  Humanizing
Education for Youth.  (Belmont, California:
Wadsworth Publishing Company, Inc., 1972), pp.105-119.

easier said than done because for most middle
schools this would mean that something would be
deleted from the curriculum. How and where such a
program would fit into a particular middle school
would have to be determined by that school.
Assuming that at least one period could be found,
let us investigate the possibility for implementing
learning periods in a typical middle school.

### Independent Acitivity Period, A School Wide Approach to Independent Study

This might best be done by citing an example of
an existing program. This program is rather
unique because it has been integrated into an
Independent Activity Period. This program was
instituted at the middle school level of the
University of Northern Colorado Laboratory School
by the middle school staff. Since then it has
undergone many changes and is still being altered to
better meet the needs of the emerging adolescent
learner.

The Independent Activity Period was first
designed for many of the same reasons which have
been mentioned before as being vital to a successful
independent study program. However, the focus was
much broader and incorporated more than just an
emphasis on independent study. This program not
only gives a student an opportunity to work independently but also allows students to pursue high
interest activities.

One of the most important prerequisites for a
good independent study program is that it allows
students time to pursue areas which they find
interesting and stimulating. The activities
which have been developed for the students during
the Independent Activity Period are for the most
part student generated. These are coupled with a
particular teacher's talents. Each year before the
schedule for the Independent Activity Period is
developed, the students are asked to submit

suggestions of activities in which they would like
to participate or learn more about. This list is
then screened carefully and resource people are
sought to sponsor a workshop on each activity. For
the most part teachers are the primary source of
sponsors. However, parents, teacher aides,
school secretaries, the principal, and other resource
persons from the community have also been used. Not
all the ideas generated by the students can be
offered in a workshop format. If it is determined
that there is a significant number of students to
warrant a workshop in a particular area then every
attempt is made to offer that workshop. This by no
means eliminates that student who marked on his/her
survey an unusual or uncommon interest. Even though
this student might be the only one who chooses that
particular area, he/she will be encouraged to pursue
a project on that topic using independent study. As
with any independent study project there would be
unlimited activities from which the student might
choose to complete his/her project.

In addition to participating in various workshops on an independent project, the students are
given a third option which is participating in intramurals. This means that intramurals become part of
the school day rather than an after-school activity.
Too often middle schools find themselves in a position of having to offer intramurals after school or
if they do offer a program during the school day,
they have no options for students who do not wish to
participate. By making the intramurals a part of the
Independent Activity Period the risk was taken that
it would drain off most of the students and thus
leave few students to participate in other workshops
or work on independent projects. This was not
necessarily so. Although on an average about 50%
of the students chose to participate in intramurals,
there was a significantly smaller percentage which
chose to participate in intramurals every session.
Generally it was found that the students participated
in intramurals one session, interest workshops
another, and independent study during another session.

Before examing the logistics involved with the
Independent Activity Period, let us first look at
each of these three options offered to the students.
These must be examined with respect to how they contribute to helping the student pursue independent
interests and also become independent learners.

Workshops.  Although workshops offer the students the opportunity to pursue high interest
activities, they do not necessarily allow them to
pursue these activities on an independent basis.
Many of the workshops are planned and directed by
the person responsible for them.  Thus, the student
is an active participant in a workshop designed and
implemented by another person.  However, some workshops have been designed by the students and
teacher.

These workshops have many distinct advantages
which help foster independent learning on the part
of the student.  Probably the most significant
advantage is the opportunity it gives the student to
work with a teacher or another resource person on a
more informal basis and on a common area of interest.
This is a particularly good situation in which
preservice teachers can gain valuable knowledge about
teaching.  These experiences are usually very positive because the teacher aids are not only teaching
something about which they have interest but the
students  in each workshop, by their own selection,
have indicated their interest in the area also.
This usually makes an unbeatable combination.  Other
school personnel such as the principal, school
secretaries, school nurse, custodians, could each
offer workshops relative to their interests.  This
gives them an opportunity to work with students in
a different capacity and at the same time gives
the students the chance to get a different perspective of them.

There are a variety of resource people within
the community from which to draw.  Two that deserve
special mention are senior citizens and the boy
scout and girl scout troops.  The elderly people of

the community have both a rich background from
which to draw and also some unique interests and
hobbies.  Likewise, the scout organization of
which many middle school students are members are
very willing to have the opportunity to offer
workshops on various merit badges.  The biggest
drawback of using these groups of people is the time
commitment required on their part.

Some of the workshops which have been offered
during the Independent Activity Period are listed
below.

| | |
|---|---|
| Model Rocket Building | Creative Drama |
| Backpacking | Golf |
| Macrame | Leather Work |
| Holiday Cooking | Fossils |
| Needle Point | Chess |
| String Art | Weight Lifting |
| Creative Writing | Judo |
| Model Making | Tall Tales |
| Fly Tieing | Plant and Animal Caring |

Some of these workshops culminated with an
extended field trip.  The backpacking workshop, for
instance, went on an overnight backpack trip, the
golf workshop went to the public golf courses one
afternoon to play a round of golf, and the weight
lifting workshop group toured a local health spa.

Intramurals.  Intramurals have become a vital
part of the Independent Activity Period.  All intramural activities are designed so both boys and
girls have an equal opportunity to participate.  An
effort has also been made to coordinate intramurals
with the physical education program.  If a unit on
basketball is being taught in physical education
class, time can be devoted to working on the
basic skills of the game whereas the intramural
period provides an outlet for playing the game.

Although a variety of sports are offered, the
most popular sports are those which require participation by a large number of students.  The

following is a list of games which seem to be the
most popular with this age level of students: flag
football, soccer, basketball, softball, floor
hockey, volleyball.  Other games which are also
part of the intramural program but do not have as
high a level of participation are:  gymnastics,
swimming, table tennis, wrestling, and track.

After the students have signed up for a particular intramural activity, they are bracketed in a
round robin tournament.  Each tournament is culminated with a championship game in which the winning
team or individuals are awarded a traveling trophy
or certificates.

Independent Study.  A student may also choose
to use the independent activity time to work on an
independent project.  If this option is chosen, the
student will be assigned to work with a teacher.
The project may relate to a particular class and
thus the teacher of that subject may also decide
to do a project which is related to an interest of
his/her own rather than something directly related
to a class.  This is definitely a viable alternative and a teacher or some type of resource person
would be assigned to work with this student.

A student may want to work on an independent
project with a fellow student(s).  These students
should be encouraged to pursue such a project as
long as the group size is kept workable.  This
again would depend on the type of project.

It is essential that each student or group of
students be assigned to work with a resource person.
These will usually be a teacher but could be an
outside resource person.  The teacher's role must be
clearly defined as an advisor to the project.  The
teacher should help the student(s) clarify the
following questions.

1.  What type of project do I want to do?
2.  What form will the project take?

3.  What resources will I need?
4.  How much time will it take?

To help the students answer these questions and
establish some guidelines for their project the
following form might be used.

## Independent Study Project

Name of  student(s)  working on project:_____

Statement of type of project you intend to complete:
_____

_____

What form will your project take?

| | | |
|---|---|---|
| ____written report | ____drawings | ____notebook |
| ____oral report | ____maps | ____diary |
| ____audio report | ____timeline | ____diarama |
| ____video tape | ____collage | ____experiment |
| ____play or skit | ____poster | ____film |
| ____other (explain)_____ | | |

What resources will you need to complete your project?

____art supplies (list)_____
____A.V. equipment (list)_____
____records or tapes (list)_____
____books (list)_____
____magazines (list)_____
____others (explain)_____

Develop a timeline for the completion of your project.

Date                         Activity

_____          _____
_____          _____
_____          _____


_____
Signature, Supervising Teacher

Once the project has been defined and a procedure
for completing it has been identified, the teacher
then becomes merely a resource person on whom the
student can rely for assistance.  It is important tha
the teacher give the students a degree of autonomy
to develop their own projects.  However, it is also
important that the teacher be available to support,
encourage, and lend assistance when it is needed.
Students may need help in getting materials or they
may just need someone on which to try out their
ideas.

Logistics.  Now that the three components of this
program have been briefly presented, let us turn our
attention to the logistics of setting up such a
program.  One of the most important aspects of this
program is the commitment of a certain segment of
the day for this purpose.  A commitment such as this
on the part of the staff assures the availability of
the facilities.  The various classrooms thus become
resource centers where workshops or independent
study activities take place.  For example, if students wish to work on a science project they would
report to the science room and work with the science
teacher.  Another science room might become an area
where a workshop takes place.  Once a period of the
day has been identified for the implementation of
such a program, it then becomes a matter of scheduling teachers and students in a manner that will
meet students' needs and utilize the teacher's
talents.

The students are allowed to sign up for either
an independent activity, a workshop, or intramurals
every six weeks.  The sign up sheets are then compiled into attendance lists for each teacher for
that six weeks.  Mr. A, for example, may have fifteen students signed up for his model making workshop while Ms. B may have four students signed up to
work on an independent project.  Mr. C and Mr. D
may have forty students signed up with them for
intramural basketball.  If a teacher does not have
any students signed up for his/her workshop then
he/she would be reassigned to help with another

workshop or intramurals, or assigned to work with
students on an independent project.

   This sign up is done the week before the beginning of each six week session. On the sign up sheet
each workshop is listed, plus the intramural activity
for that session. In addition the maximum number of
students for each activity, the sponsor, the room,
and a short description are also listed. The students are asked to indicate a first and second
choice, in case their first choice is full. A
typical sign up sheet might resemble the following.


   Independent Activity Sign Up Sheet

Student's Name_____

Workshops
1.____Leather Work (12 students) Mr. Smith, Shop
        Students will be given the opportunity to work
        with various leather processing tools to make
        belts, coin purses, key cases, etc. Students
        must provide their own leather.
2.____Backpacking (20 students) Mr. Black, Room 204
        Students will learn to prepare a pack, tech-
        niques of outdoor cookery, first aid, and how
        to pitch a tent. The workshop will culminate
        with an overnight backpack trip.
3.____Macrame (15 students) Mrs. Jones, Room 202
        Students will work on various macrame knots
        and make flower pot holders.
        String will be provided. The final product
        will be used to decorate the various class-
        rooms.
4.____Rocket Building (20 students) Mrs. White, Room
        104
        Students will build their own model rockets.
        The students will need to provide their own
        model rocket. The rockets will be fired on
        the last day of the workshop.

## Intramurals

_____ Basketball (48 students) Mr. Blue and Mr. Green
There will be eight teams of six players each.
A tournament will be established in which each
team will play several games.  A traveling trophy
will be awarded the winning team.  Teams will be
co-educational.

## Independent Study

Teachers available to supervise an independent
study are:

_____ Mrs. Taylor
_____ Mrs. O'Brien
_____ Mr. Nash
_____ Mrs. Williams

Name of Project: _____

## Study Area (upon request) Mr. Lewis, Room 200

_____ Students may sign out for this area for the
entire sessions or on a one or two day basis if
they have work to make-up.

One of the problems that arise in trying to
establish any independent study program is the problem of keeping the student/teacher ratio low for those
students on independent study.  By offering other
options, such as intramurals and workshops, the number of students working on independent study projects
are kept to a more workable number.

The Independent Activity Period presented here
is only one way in which a school wide system was
established to provide the emerging adolescent an
opportunity to pursue learning on an independent
basis.  It not only gives the students an opportunity
to engage in independent study but also allows them
to pursue high interest activities.  It is hoped that
citing such an example might generate ideas by the
reader as to how independent study periods may be
implemented in his/her particular school.

## Summary

In this chapter a rationale for independent study in a middle school was first established. Built on the premise that middle schools are designed to meet the unique needs and character- istics of the emerging adolescent, the following were recognized as important needs which might be met by an effective independent study program.

1. Meeting the diversity in growth and develop- ment of the emerging adolescent.

2. Helping the emerging adolescent pursue high interest activities

3. Providing an opportunity to move from depen- dency of childhood to the independency of adulthood

Assuming that independent study was a viable means of meeting these important needs felt by the emerging adolescent, attention was then turned to possible means of implementing such a program into a middle school curriculum. First, different ways and means for including independent study in an individ- ual middle school classroom were mentioned. Secondly, the institution of a school wide indepen- dent study program was investigated.

The ideas presented in this chapter are not to be viewed as a panacea for independent study in the middle school. They are rather presented as points of departure to help stimulate other ideas of how independent study can best be incorporated into your particular middle school in such a way as to aid each student in the process of becoming an independent learner.

## Other Sources

Thomas E. Curtis and Wilma W. Bidwell, Curriculum and
    Instruction for Emerging Adolescents, (Reading,
    Mass:  Addison-Wesley Publishing Co., 1977.)

Adam M. Drayer, Problems in Middle and High School
    Teaching, (Allyn and Bacon Co., 1979.)

Paul George and Gordon Lawrence, Handbook for Middle
    School Teaching, (Chicago:  Scott Foresman and
    Co., 1982.)

## Bibliography

Alexander, William M. and Paul S. George,  The
    Exemplary Middle School; New York:  Holt,
    Rinehart and Winston Co., 1981.

Alexander, William M. and Hines, Vynce A.  Indepen-
    dent Study in Secondary Schools.  New York:
    Holt, Rinehart, and Winston, Inc., 1967.

Beggs, Donald W. and Buffie, Edward G., ed.  Indepen-
    dent Study, Bold New Venture.  Bloomington,
    Indiana:  University Press, 1965.

Eichhorn, Donald H.  The Middle School.  New York:
    The Center for Applied Research in Education,
    Inc., 1966.

Lounsbury, John H. and Vars, Gordon E.  A Curriculum
    for Middle School Years.  New York:  Harper and
    Row, Publishers, 1978.

Noar, Gertrude.  Individualized Instruction:  Every
    Child a Winner.  New York:  John Wiley and
    Sons, Inc., 1972.

Romano, Louis G.; Georgiady, Nicholas P.; and Heald,
    James E., ed. The Middle School. Chicago:
    Nelson-Hall, Company, 1973.

Thornberg, Hershel D., ed. Preadolescent Development. The University of Arizona Press, 1974.

EVALUATING PROGRESS IN THE
MIDDLE OR JUNIOR HIGH SCHOOL


A topic frequently appearing in the media is that
of accountability in education. Examination of
reports in newspapers and on television provides
ample evidence of public concern for more assurance
that educational programs are producing desirable
results in terms of learning and growth on the part
of students. Concern on the part of the public is
prompted by constantly rising costs of operating our
schools and by painfully visible evidence of students
leaving our schools lacking necessary skills of functional literacy needed for employment in the world of
work. Others are students so discouraged by what, to
them, appear to be irrelevant programs that they drop
out of school prior to high school graduation.

Underlying these conditions is the failure of
many schools to provide evidence of the success of
their efforts to educate youth. Indeed, in far too
many instances, there is a lack of evidence of any
kind concerning program effectiveness. For too long,
schools have operated, largely on the basis of
inertia of previous practices without analyzing their
effectiveness or of justifying it! Study, discussion
and debate regarding the most appropriate role and
nature of effective educational evaluation continue
into the present.

In education, evaluation is the process of
collecting and studying data and other information
which will indicate growth and other changes in
pupils. Consciously or unconsciously, schools and
teachers carry on evaluation. Sometimes it is
referred to as "feedback." It may be carried on as
a combination of testing, examining, assessing and
is often expressed in the form of grades or comments
as well as other statements. Some of it is formal
and at other times it is informal. Whatever form it
takes, it is necessary to provide the basis for
determining the next steps to be taken in the educational program. Without evaluation, any planning

becomes questionable in terms of its appropriateness.
It is an indispensable activity in any educational
endeavor. Evaluation is also an indication of how
well the goals and objectives of education are being
attained. It is an essential part of the educational
process and an important activity in the middle and
junior high school. Evaluation in any educational
program, and certainly no less in the middle school
levels, is carried on for several important purposes.

1. Evaluation is conducted for purposes of
   determining the appropriateness of the
   curriculum or education plan for the goals
   which are sought. It should provide information which makes it possible for pupils
   and teachers to more clearly see their objectives and to relate their learning activities
   more clearly to these. If the goals are not
   being met, then part of the problem may very
   well lie in the curriculum which has been
   developed and if this is the case, revision
   of the curriculum becomes necessary to
   assure better attainment of the goals
   sought.

2. Evaluation is also conducted as a means of
   determining the effectiveness of the teaching
   which is going on, whether this is by an
   individual teahcer or by a team of teachers.
   Certainly, the failure to attain goals may
   very well be due to the inappropriateness
   and hence ineffectiveness of the teaching
   process being carried on. This is not a very
   flattering prospect for esteemed members of a
   valued profession, but it is a reality which
   middle school educators must courageously
   face.

3. Evaluation is also conducted for purposes of
   determining the progress shown by students
   in their growth and development. This information is essential for the guidance of
   students. Again, this growth is measured in
   terms of goals sought by the school program
   but at the same time, it must take into

account the particular and unique capabilities of each individual student. To
disregard this essential human characteristic of individuality is to doom any evaluation for its failure to provide for the
personal and human qualities so essential to
effective education in the middle school.

4. Evaluation should give assurance to teachers,
pupils and parents by providing continuous
evidence of growth shown by pupils in school
activities. It should also serve to enhance
relations between schools and the public by
providing desired information to interested
and concerned parents and other citizens.

One of the major problems in evaluation in any
school program is that there are two major sets of
criteria to be considered. One has to do with the
relative performance of the student with respect to
the rest of his group or class. The second has to do
with the student's performance with respect to his
own capabilities and individual goals. Frequently,
the means used to evaluate and report pupil progress
are confined to the first point. The result, inevitably, is that the less able student suffers since he
is inappropriately and unfairly compared to more
capable students. The self-image of the individual
suffers under the constant pressure of expectations
which are inconsistent with his capabilities. In
time, this takes its toll and the struggling student
becomes discouraged, disillusioned and disinterested.
Failure and retention in the same grade is a frequent
outcome.

The crux of the problem may be illustrated with
the following exercise. This can be used by a middle
·school or junior high school staff as a way of
launching the study of evaluating and reporting
student progress. Using the traditional A-B-C-D-F
grading system familiar to most persons, ask staff
members to give each of the three students below a
grade based on the data and other information
provided.

Invariably, a range of grades will be given to each student. Some teachers even add a plus or minus as a further indicator. The problem of grading students on this basis is further confounded by the student effort as perceived by each teacher. Obviously evaluation is a complex matter and deserves careful attention to all of its aspects. On-going discussion about what criteria to use in evaluation, how much weight to give various factors, how to best use evaluative findings for improving student growth are among important topics for staff members to think and talk about as a continuing concern and activity.

Hypothetical Cases --
8th Grade Social Studies

1. John W. -- Age - 13 yrs. 10 mos.
    IQ - 108
    Scored 88 out of 100 on a true-
        false test.
    Scored 79 out of 100 on a comple-
        tion test.
    Scored 8 out of 10 on 1st pop quiz.
    Scored 9 out of 12 on 2nd pop quiz.
    Participated actively in class
        discussions.
    Turned in an 8 page paper on apar-
        theid policy of South Africa.
        Paper was satisfactory.
    Attendance good.
    Course grade for 1st term____.

2. Mary D. -- Age - 14 yrs. 2 mos.
    IQ - 126
    Scored 92 out of 100 on a true-
        false test.
    Scored 87 out of 100 on a comple-
        tion test.
    Scored 9 out of 10 on 1st pop quiz.
    Scored 11 out of 12 on 2nd pop
        quiz.
    Participated actively in class
        discussions.

Turned in a 12 page paper on apartheid policy of South Africa.
Paper was outstanding, but parts may have been copied as they were far superior to her general work and written at a near university level.
Attendance good.
Course grade for 1st term_____.

3.  Bill J. — Age - 15 yrs. 9 mos. (retained once)
    IQ - 91
    Scored 72 out of 100 on a true-false test.
    Scored 63 out of 100 on a completion test.
    Scored 5 out of 10 on 1st pop quiz.
    Scored 6 out of 12 on 2nd pop quiz.
    Participated in few class discussions.
    Turned in a paper with numerous errors and misspelled words.
    Absent (sometimes truant) about 25% of the time.
    Course grade for 1st term_____.

## Some Points for Discussion

1.  Were there differences of opinion on the letter grade for each student?  If so, how was each differenct grade justified?

2.  Was the IQ a factor in the grade?  Should it be a factor?  Why or why not?

3.  How much, if any, copying of library materials is permissible?  What if library research is strongly encouraged by the teacher?

4.  Should absence be a factor in the grade?  Why or why not?  How much absence (percentage) is permissible, if at all?

6. Should any thought be given to effort on part
   of student? What part of a course grade
   should be due to effort? How should this be
   shown so that it is clearly understood by all?

There are many other points for discussion. These
will undoubtedly be suggested by teachers, parents and
students. Discussion of these ideas can help to bring
all concerned to a better understanding of what kind
of a grading system is best for that school district.

It is interesting to note that while retention in
grade or "flunking" students is a common practice in
many schools where it is viewed as a solution to the
problem of lack of progress, the evidence forthcoming
from research in this area does not support this
practice. In their investigations, Cheyney and Boyer[1]
noted that students exhibiting a lack of readiness
for a given kind of school work were not helped to
overcome this weakness when they were retained and
had to repeat a grade. This is further supported by
the investigations of Saunders, who studied the
effects of non-promotion upon school achievement and
reported:

> "It may be concluded that non-promotion of
> pupils in elementary school in order to assure
> mastery of subject matter does not often accom-
> plish its objective. Children do not appear
> to learn more by repeating a grade but exper-
> ience less growth in subject-matter achieve-
> ment than they do when promoted. Therefore
> a practice of non-promotion because a pupil
> does not learn sufficient subject matter in
> the course of a school year, or for the pur-
> pose of learning subject-matter, is not

---

[1]W. Walker Cheyney and Philip A. Boyer. Division
of Educational Research Philadelphia. Extracts quoted
in Elementary School Journal, 33, May, 1973,
pp. 647-651.

justifiable."[2]

This does not mean that such evaluation is to be avoided. In fact, parents as well as teachers, if not the students themselves, want to know how well the student is performing with respect to others in his group. Therefore, it is necessary to determine this and to report it accordingly. One way of doing this is to make use of standardized tests which have been used with large numbers of students. The use of such tests of achievement will provide information as to the standing of each student in his class or with respect to a large population as in the case of nationally standardized achievement tests. It provides parents, teachers and students with an indication of where the student ranks in his age or grade group.

Another kind of information coming out of the use of standardized tests is the identification of areas of subject matter or skills where the student may show weakness. This information is very useful in making possible better planning of a program of work for that student.

One of the important characteristics of the true middle or junior high school described in this book is concerned with the individualization of instruction. There is ample evidence to support the notion that each student is a unique individual, equipped with or characterized by a set of interests, strengths, weaknesses, fears, creative talents and other traits which make him different from all other students. Recognizing this, an effective educational plan should take these into account and provision for his growth and development made accordingly. Similarly, expectations of learning outcomes are shaped by the nature of this unique individuality.

---

[2] Carleton M. Saunders, Promotion or Failure for the Elementary School Pupil? New York: Bureau of Publications, Teachers College, Columbia University, 1941

One of the earliest and most notable efforts to provide individualized instruction was developed by Burk and Washburn in the Winnetka[3] Plan. The program developed and carried on there for many years and the model for many similar, later programs in other communities involved a series of instructional objectives, tests to assess pupil mastery of these, instructional materials, individual lesson plans, and steps for checking pupil progress through the sequence. Progress was made by pupils on an individual basis and was checked by the pupil himself utilizing tests accompanying the work materials. Careful records were kept of each step covered by the pupil and his teacher in analyzing progress and in making further plans.

Similar programs of more recent date which also stress some of the same elements of the Winnetka Plan include IPI or Individually Prescribed Instruction and IGE or Individually Guided Education. In each of these, as in the Winnetka Plan, the evaluation like the instructional activities are carried on individually with a wide range of variations as to rate of progress on emphasis on specific learning activities as individually needed.

In any program of individualized instruction, the major function of evaluation is to provide an analysis of pupil performance so that this information can then be used to plan further activities for the individual.

One important aspect is the use of tests which recognize that each student is possessed of a unique set of capabilities and these became the basis for determining his progress. In other words, the student sets as his goals whatever he is capable of achieving and this is different for each individual. Progress

---

[3]Carleton W. Washburn, "A Program of Individualization," Adapting the Schools to Individual Differences, (Twenty-fourth Yearbook of the National Society for the Study of Education, Part II, Bloomington, Illinois, Public School Publishing, 1925), pp. 257-72.

is then determined on the basis of how well he is
progressing towards his own unique sets of goals
and objectives.  These tests must, of necessity, be
individually developed and while this is a demanding
task, there is no alternative if the spirit of the
middle or junior high school is not to be violated.

One effective way of undertaking this task is
through the use of behavioral objectives.  Educational
objectives should be stated in terms that are
measurable.  To be measurable, objectives should be
stated in terms of what the student will be doing when
he demonstrates the achievement of an objective.
This should be readily observable by the teacher and
by the student himself as well.  If he can do what
the objective calls for, he has demonstrated mastery
of that objective.  As an illustration, consider the
following objective-----a student will be able to write
and spell correctly a prescribed list of 20 words in
ten minutes with 80% accuracy.  There is not much
question about what is expected of the student and
his readily observed performance either meets or does
not meet the criteria stated.  The author as well as
others have written more extensively on the use of
behavioral objectives in evaluation[4] and this may be
referred to for a fuller explanation.

With all evaluation, there must be a beginning
point, a point from which progress is measured.  As
stated earlier, this varies with each individual.
One way of accomplishing this is the use of a pre-test.
This provides benchmark data, a starting point for
determining progress towards a goal or objective.
Following the planned activities which are concerned
with those skills and knowledge which he was not able
to demonstrate mastery of on the pre-test, he moves
on to the next unit of study in the sequence.
One way of illustrating this procedure is provided
by the following schematic or flow chart.

------------------

[4]Nicholas P. Georgiady, "Behavioral Objectives
As An Aid to Evaluation," The Review, Spring, 1972,
School of Education, Miami University, Oxford, Ohio.

Flow Chart for Evaluating the Progress of
Pupils In Middle and Junior High Schools

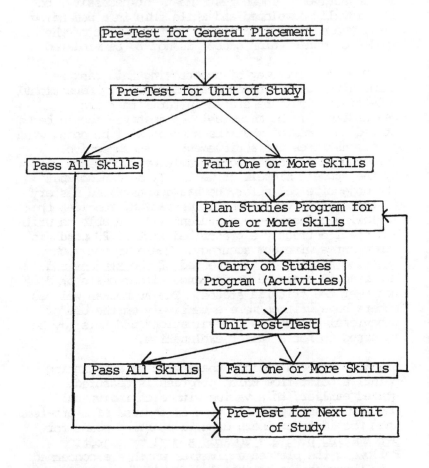

Examination of the flow chart leads to the inevit-
able conclusion that its adoption and implementation
will facilitate an individualized program of instruction and evaluation which is consistent with the
middle or junior high school concept. One excellent
technique along these lines is the use of the student
contract for planning the work of each student on an
individualized basis. Further, the flow chart fits
one of the important characteristics of a good middle
or junior high program, the principle of continuous

progress. If learning is accepted as being an
individual matter, differing with each person as to
rate and intensity, then by the same token, progress
is also an individual matter. The idea that all students at a given grade level are to be ready for
promotion at the end of the school year flies in the
face of what we know about human growth and development. In continuous progress, students are not
"flunked." Rather, each progresses as well and as
rapidly as he can and at the beginning of a new
school year in September, he resumes his progress at
the point at which he stopped in June or, rather,
at the point where he is ready to resume work. The
disastrous blow to the self-image of a student who
has not quite made the grade in his school work is
avoided and he is not forced to repeat the entire
year's work because he was retained in grade.

While only a few techniques for evaluation have
been discussed, there are many more worthy of our
attention. The team of teachers has the responsibility for meeting regularly not only to plan the
work of the team, but also for sharing in the evaluation of the students entrusted to their care.
Through the pooling of their respective assessments,
a composite picture of the strengths, weaknesses,
needs and accomplishments of each student will develop.
The data shared will be gained from a variety of
sources including the use of standardized tests,
teacher-made tests often utilizing behavioral objectives, and from continuous, subjective observation
of the students in a variety of situations. In
addition these data may be periodically augmented by
input from other staff members including the principal, guidance counselors, psychologist, remedial
teachers, school nurse, etc. The importance of
carefully kept records in the process cannot be
overstated. A longitudinal file on each student is
a necessity for evaluation and effective planning
for that student.

With the present public concern for accountability, the importance of effective evaluation is

immediately more evident to educators. Parents are
calling for evidence to assure them of the quality of
the programs in the schools their children attend.
The gathering of data from evaluation is of limited
value unless these data are communicated in meaningful, intelligible form to parents. To many parents,
this means they want to know how well their children
are doing with regard to class or group norms. To
educators, effective evaluation must be based on
individual differences. Both kinds of data cannot be
reported by a single set of grades. Therefore, any
reports to parents must recognize the inherent differences between these kinds of data. To facilitate in
dealing with the problem, written reports should
include how the student stands in his group and how
well he is doing with respect to his own capabilities.
In addition, since written reports suffer from inherent shortcomings due to language semantics and other
factors, conferences with parents and with students
should be held by teachers to facilitate communication. This personal contact not only aids in understanding of evaluation but serves as a powerful
public relations asset as well. It also gives added
emphasis to the important humanistic dimension of
the middle school.

Continuous examination by teachers of the means
for more effective evaluation of the middle school
student and his program provides for the exercise of
their professional expertise and can bring added
dividends in their growth professionally. The values
to students will certainly be a better understanding
of themselves as individuals and of their role in
society. Parents will be assured that their children are in good hands and that schools are indeed
responsive to their concerns and wishes. In all
respects, evaluation is an activity which holds great
promise for a better future if it is pursued on a
logical basis consistent with our knowledge of effective education.

Evaluation is concerned with the total development of the middle school student, with broad personality changes, with the attainment of major objectives

of the educational program of the middle school.
Included in evaluation are not only subject matter
achievement but also attitudes, ideals, interests,
ways of thinking and working, and personal and social
adaptability. Not only must the teacher in the middle
or junior high school evaluate how well the objectives
of the school are producing desired behavior on the
part of students, but she must also evaluate the
learning experiences that best promote and produce
these desired behaviors. Students, too, have an
important role to play in evaluation. They ought to
evaluate their own progress and growth towards goals
that they understand and accept.

The general procedure for pursuing a program of
evaluation includes several steps as indicated below.

1. The teacher needs to examine the objectives
   of a school program and with these in mind,
   to establish criteria. This can begin with
   a realistic knowledge of what each student
   needs and what behavior patterns are most
   logical for him in light of his make-up.
   This requires a thorough knowledge of the
   principles of human growth and development,
   of the psychology of learning and an accurate
   knowledge of community expectations of education. One way of preparing such criteria is
   to express these in terms of abilities expected at each age level, desirable habits that
   can be attained, and attitudes and under-
   standings that may be achieved. With this
   knowledge, a better selection of learning
   experiences can be made. Evaluation of progress becomes clearer as both teacher and student in the middle or junior high become
   more familiar with what the student actually
   does.

2. The teacher proceeds to collect data and
   information. The source of this can be from
   a testing program which supplies objective
   data on each student. It can also come from
   observing the behavior of the student in a

variety of situations, both formal and informal, providing valuable subjective information.

3.  The teacher studies and analyzes the data,
    making appropriate interpretations. How well
    is the student progressing towards desired
    objectives?  Is his behavior constructive and
    desirable?  Is the student's self-evaluation
    consistent with the teacher's evaluation?  In
    what areas is further progress desired?

4.  Using the information thus gained, the
    teacher plans a course of action.  Changes
    in learning activities and materials may be
    necessary.  The assistance of resource per-
    sons available to the middle school may be
    called for by the plan, including guidance
    counselors, school nurse, the principal,
    psychologist, or parents, as well as others
    including subject matter specialists.

The building of a body of data and other
information about each student can be aided by the use
of a variety of techniques for learning about the
student.  Again, some of these are subjective in
nature while others are more objective.

1.  An assessment of readiness for contemplated
    learning activities.  While a great deal
    has been written about the matter of readi-
    ness, there still remains a great deal more
    to be learned.  Nevertheless, it is regarded
    as essential to successful learning despite
    the fact that it is elusive and highly subjec-
    tive.  The training, experience and intuitive
    insights of the teacher into the nature of
    each individual are important to accomplishing
    this assessment.

2.  Using achievement tests, mental maturity tests
    and intelligence tests.  While there are
    dangers inherent in relying too heavily upon
    a single test score as an accurate indicator

of a quality, there is value in having such
test results to be considered <u>along with</u>
other information in better understanding the
individual student and his make-up.  This
diagnostic aspect, identifying areas of
strength and weakness can be useful in planning learning programs for the individual.

3.  Using the case study approach.  By keeping
notes on incidents concerning certain
observed behavior on the part of students, it
may be possible to identify clues which will
assist the teacher in arriving at conclusions
and plans for needed further activities.
This can be time-consuming but every teacher
makes these observations either formally or
informally, consciously or unconsciously.
The systematic recording of these behavior
incidents can provide much valuable information of great use to the teacher in understanding the uniqueness of every individual
student.

4.  Using sociometry.  Each individual exists
not only as an individual but also as a
member of his society.  Careful study and
analysis of how he functions in a group can
also provide valuable information about his
true nature.  Most teachers have an on-going
knowledge of the social make-up of a class.
This may or may not be accurate.  Along with
this informal approach of observing how the
individual functions in a group, added information can be gained from the use of widely
recognized sociometric instruments to objec-
tify such observations.

5.  Additional techniques may be used.  There are
a variety of other techniques for use in
evaluation.  One of these is the Parent-
Teacher Conference.  While this may be viewed
simply as a technique for verbally reporting
pupil progress to parents, it is also a
potential source of additional valuable

information about the student. In the conference, there ought to be ample opportunity for the parent to express an opinion on the progress of the student as observed in the home or neighborhood. Such information added to that already possessed by the teacher can round out the evaluation of the student and increase the effectiveness of plans made for further progress.

Parent interest in schools has never been greater than at present. Parents expect and are entitled to full information about school programs and particularly to information about the progress of their children. The use of the parent-teacher conference is an important vehicle for this kind of communication. It provides for a two-way exchange of information about the student. It may be used as a supplement to the report card but because it can do much more than a report card alone, it is becoming more increasingly used. However, to make the best use of this technique requires careful planning on the part of middle or junior high school staff. In some schools, the student also participates in the conference making it a three-way exchange of information.

## What Parents Want to Know

1. What subjects the students will study—the curriculum for the year.
2. An explanation of the grading system and how it works.
3. How much emphasis is placed on the basics and on other studies.
4. Pertinent school policies, school rules and procedures, including discipline.
5. How parents can help students learn.
6. Homework policies
7. What you, the teacher, expect of the student.
8. How well the student gets along with others, i.e., is he/she well-liked?

## What Teachers Can Learn From The Conference

1. Information about how the student is treated at home.
2. How the student feels about school, teacher and other students as reported by parent.
3. Strengths or interests the student has that may not have shown up in school.
4. Any problems regarding homework or study habits that show up at home.

## Tips For Better P-T Conferences

1. Prepare for the conference! Have an outline covering major points you want to discuss. You might want to send a copy of this brief outline of topics home to parents after they have confirmed the PT Conference date and time. Stick to the outline!
2. Be courteous and cheerful.
3. Give the parents a chance to talk <u>first,</u> to share <u>their</u> views and their problems.
4. Be a good listener.
5. Be truthful but tactful. Don't forget that a child is a <u>most</u> precious possession!
6. Try to avoid prescribing solutions. Offer suggestions and alternatives. Give parents a part in deciding any action to be taken.
7. Begin and end on a positive note.

The value of the PT Conference is quite apparent when one examines the lists of expectations held by parents and teachers. Both parents and teacher learn more about each student. Teachers learn how the child is treated at home and what, if any, bearing this may have on behavior in school. Parents can learn about the year's work for the student, what is expected of students, how the teacher and the school function and most importantly, that teacher and school are there to help in every way possible. Besides the direct benefits for learning by students, the PT Conference brings great public relation value that cannot be overlooked.

## Examples of Evaluation Forms

The preceding general discussion of evaluation and
its important role in a successful middle or junior
high school program provides a setting for the development of specific measures for accomplishing this
task.  Given the understanding of the nature of the
problems of effective evaluation, the task of the
middle or junior high school faculty is to adapt
these to their own school situation.  Needed are consideration for the teaching staff and their capabilities as professional educators, consideration of
the expectancies of the parents of the students as to
kinds of data and information they desire regarding
pupil progress and consideration for the information
which will be meaningful to students as they seek to
utilize their talents in understanding their goals
and working towards their attainment.

Examination of several middle schools and their
staff efforts to come to grips with their responsibility for effective evaluation can provide further
insight into the nature of the task and of the means
for dealing with it.  On the following pages are
contained the several evaluative forms developed by
middle schools seeking to do just that.  These forms
take the important aspects of evaluation and deal
with these in a way which is both understandable and
also consistent with the nature of human growth and
development.  Although they vary widely in the way in
which they perceive their evaluative functions, this
is not inconsistent with the principle of local
determination based on local  needs and other conditions.  Obviously, these samples are offered for
analysis and discussion rather than as models for
replication.

Explanation of East Lansing, Michigan,
Middle School Progress Report

The Middle School Progress Report is designed to
inform parents of their youngsters' progress, effort
and overall performance.

## Progress

In the upper right-hand box the teacher indicates a
student's progress in relation to the expectations
for the course. One of the three statements regarding
Progress will be checked for each reporting period:

exceeds expectations for the course
meets expectations for the course
is below expectations for the course

Whenever the teacher checks the statement "exceeds
expectations for the course" he is reporting that
the child's progress is greater than one would expect
from a typical student, of similar age, enrolled in
that course. If the teacher checks "meets expectations for the course" he is reporting that the
child's progress is at the pace one would expect of a
typical youngster of similar age. If the teacher
checks the statement "is below the expectations for
the course" he is reporting that the child's progress
is less than one might expect of a typical student of
similar age.

## Effort

In the upper left-hand box the teacher indicates the
effort a youngster puts forth in the particular
course. One of two statements regarding Effort will
be checked for each reporting period:

is satisfactory
is unsatisfactory

Whenever the teacher checks the statement "is
satisfactory" he is reporting that the student is
putting forth a reasonable effort in that course.

A student of high ability or aptitude may exceed the
expectations for the course without much effort.  If
the teacher believes that such a student's progress
would have been significantly greater with more effort
he will inform the parent that the child's effort
"is unsatisfactory" and indicate why in the Comments
sections.  Another student may be putting forth
sufficient effort but may be progressing below the
expectations for the course.  Again, the teacher will
so indicate by checking the appropriate statements and
also note why the youngster's progress is below the
expectations for the course.

## Comments

The Written Comments and Other Comments sections on
the Progress Report give the teacher an opportunity
to sum up a student's overall performance and to
indicate areas that may affect his progress.

Parents are encouraged to contact the teacher for
a conference whenever they have any questions
regarding their youngster's progress.

SVD:en
10-5-51

*1st 2nd 3rd 4th* — *Reporting Period* — *1989-90* — *TEAM*

## EAST LANSING MIDDLE SCHOOLS – PROGRESS REPORT 1972-1973

| STUDENT'S NAME | SUBJECT | INSTRUCTOR | HmRm | TEAM |
|---|---|---|---|---|
| | | | | |

### EFFORT

REPORTING PERIOD
1st  2nd  3rd  4th

☐ ☐ ☐ ☐  is satisfactory

☐ ☐ ☐ ☐  is unsatisfactory
(see comments below)

### PROGRESS

REPORTING PERIOD
1st  2nd  3rd  4th

☐ ☐ ☐ ☐  exceeds expectations for the course

☐ ☐ ☐ ☐  meets expectations for the course

☐ ☐ ☐ ☐  is below expectations for
the course (see comments below)

## WRITTEN COMMENTS

**1st REPORT**

**2nd REPORT**

**3rd REPORT**

**4th REPORT**

## OTHER COMMENTS

Items in the following general checklist may indicate areas affecting student performance and progress. A minus (−) indicates the student needs improvement whereas a plus (+) indicates especially positive behavior. If the box is not marked the student is performing satisfactorily.

REPORTING PERIOD
1st  2nd  3rd  4th

☐ ☐ ☐ ☐  1. Is attentive
☐ ☐ ☐ ☐  2. Follows directions
☐ ☐ ☐ ☐  3. Brings necessary materials to class
☐ ☐ ☐ ☐  4. Makes use of class time
☐ ☐ ☐ ☐  5. Completes assignments on time
☐ ☐ ☐ ☐  6. Cooperates in large and small groups
☐ ☐ ☐ ☐  7. Has a positive attitude
☐ ☐ ☐ ☐  8. Works independently
☐ ☐ ☐ ☐  9. Takes care of property, his own and others'

REPORTING PERIOD
1st  2nd  3rd  4th

☐ ☐ ☐ ☐  10. Contributes in class
☐ ☐ ☐ ☐  11. Demonstrates reasoning ability
☐ ☐ ☐ ☐  12. Consistent in quality of work
☐ ☐ ☐ ☐  13. Practices self-control
☐ ☐ ☐ ☐  14. Is courteous, respects rights of others
☐ ☐ ☐ ☐  15. Is punctual
☐ ☐ ☐ ☐  16. Relates with peers
☐ ☐ ☐ ☐  17. Displays decision-making ability

CLASS COLOR

HOMEROOM

TEAM

STUDENT NUMBER IN HOMEROOM

TEAM SUBJECT

SPECIAL AREAS TEACHER

John A. Hannah Middle School

S T U D E N T   P R O G R E S S   R E P O R T

Date_____

Dear_____,

We know that you are interested in the educational progress of your son/daughter at all times. We have indicated on this sheet some of the observations we see now and wish to inform you that
_____is:
(student's name)

| | |
|---|---|
| Doing very good work in | |
| Progressing satisfactorily in | |
| Doing unsatisfactory work in | |
| Related Comments | |
| Fails to make up work after absence | |
| Doing poorly on tests | |
| Lacks adequate daily preparation | |
| Having difficulty following directions | |
| Performing tasks carelessly and inaccurately | |
| Not seeking extra help | |
| Lacking participation in class activities | |
| Not using time constructively | |
| Lacking motivation | |
| Having reading difficulties | |
| Showing immature behavior | |
| Having difficulty in meeting deadlines | |
| Work hindered by unnecessary talking | |

If you wish to discuss this report, please contact us at 332-0848.

Sincerely yours,

The problem of proper evaluation is closely related to effective communication. Parents are frequently disturbed when they are informed students are not performing satisfactorily or are actually failing. They are most disturbed when this kind of news reaches them without prior warning. Therefore, <u>frequent</u> communication with parents is desirable, particularly when there are problems in performance. Here are some sample forms used in a school program, including a "sad" note and a "glad" note.

_____

Dear Mr. and Mrs. _____,

Because we know that you are concerned parents, we wish to inform you that _____

_____ Does not have necessary supplies.

_____ Is not using class time constructively

_____ Lacks adequate daily preparation.

_____ Is often tardy.

_____ Exhibits disruptive behavior

_____ Has difficulty in meeting deadlines.

_____ It is necessary that lost time be made up afterschool on _____ from _____ to _____.

_____    _____

Please sign and return this card so we know that you have received this communication.

_____

Date_____

Dear_____/

While_____ is performing

adequately in other areas, _____

deserves special commendation for:

_____ doing an outstanding job in_____
          class.

_____ demonstrating outstanding qualities of
          citizenship in class.

_____ performing important services for the class.

_____ demonstrating outstanding qualities of
          leadership in class.

_____ demonstrating outstanding qualities in
          athletics.

_____ dramatic improvement in_____.

_____ other:

Sincerely yours,


Another school in Reading, Ohio, has used skills check lists, one list for each academic area for each quarter of the school year. Student evaluation is done with respect to individual ability, that is, indicating whether or not the student is exerting reasonable effort. In addition to the check list, teachers may also add comments regarding student progress or effort. The listing of skills has previously been worked out by a teacher assigned to each academic area and further defines the objectives sought for that grade level.

READING COMMUNITY MIDDLE SCHOOL
Reading, Ohio

NAME_____ LEVEL_____        ADVISOR_____

SCIENCE SKILLS CHECK LIST                          Second Quarter 1921-72 90-91

On the basis of his/her ability, he/she:

| | Outstanding | Acceptable | Not Acceptable |
|---|---|---|---|
| 1. Can observe and write reports about experiments. | | | |
| 2. Shows ability to gather needed background information from the Learning Center through written and/or oral reports. | | | |
| 3. Shows ability to use Science Vocabulary. | | | |
| 4. Can collect, classify, evaluate, and report information orally and in writing. | | | |
| 5. Can write an explanation of magnetism. | | | |
| 6. Can write or illustrate the law of magnets. | | | |
| 7. Can list the different kinds of magnets. | | | |
| 8. Can explain and/or demonstrate the use of a directional compass. | | | |
| 9. Can write & demonstrate electromagnetism. | | | |
| 10. Can write an explanation of static electricity. | | | |
| 11. Can write an explanation of electricity. | | | |
| 12. Can write an explanation of parallel and series circuits. | | | |
| 13. Can write an explanation of fuses. | | | |
| 14. Can write an explanation of insulators. | | | |
| 15. Can apply the safety rules of electricity. | | | |
| 16. Can solve problems of measurement in electricity. (ohms, amperes, volts, watts, and kilowatts) | | | |
| 17. Can label the parts of a dry cell. | | | |
| 18. Can explain the operation of a storage battery. | | | |
| 19. Can detect the harmful effects of electricity in and out of the home. (lightning) | | | |

READING COMMUNITY MIDDLE SCHOOL
Reading, Ohio

LANGUAGE ARTS SKILLS CHECK LIST                    First Quarter

On the basis of his/her ability, he/she:

| | Outstanding | Acceptable | Not Acceptable |
|---|---|---|---|
| 1. Recognizes a ballad by its basic characteristics. | | | |
| 2. Reads silently and then writes at least the main idea and the supporting ideas of the poem read. | | | |
| 3. Writes a newspaper story from the given facts, after reading a selection of poetry involving an historical event. | | | |
| 4. Describes orally the author's point of view on a poem with a specific topic. | | | |
| 5. Can identify the events in sequence after listening to a poem. | | | |
| 6. Relates the content of poems to major themes of life. | | | |
| 7. Can retell in written form a poem he has read or heard, changing the ending. | | | |
| 8. Writes a poem of at least one rhyming couplet. | | | |
| 9. Can rewrite the story of a poem in prose form in a modern setting. | | | |
| 10. Reads, uses, and spells words specified in the story of poetry. | | | |
| 11. Participates in oral discussions, using acceptable speech patterns. | | | |
| 12. Uses correct punctuation and capitalization in written communication. | | | |
| 13. Is able to use subject-verb agreement in writing sentences. | | | |

READING COMMUNITY MIDDLE SCHOOL
Reading, Ohio

NAME_____ LEVEL_____          ADVISOR_____
                                                       Second Quarter

SOCIAL SCIENCE SKILLS CHECK LIST

On the basis of his/her ability, he/she:

|  | Outstanding | Acceptable | Not Acceptable |
|---|---|---|---|
| 1. Can describe the destruction caused by the Civil War. | | | |
| 2. Can locate on a map where major battles took place, and other areas important to the Civil War. | | | |
| 3. Can describe the feelings or attitudes of soldiers involved in the actual fighting of the Civil War. | | | |
| 4. Can distinguish between the effect the Civil War had on the South from its effect on the North. | | | |
| 5. Can describe how the Civil War changed farming and the plantation system in the South. | | | |
| 6. Can describe how the transportation system of the South was affected by the Civil War. | | | |
| 7. Has demonstrated a responsible degree of effort on the packet series. | | | |

COMMENTS:

READING COMMUNITY MIDDLE SCHOOL
Reading, Ohio

MATHEMATICS SKILLS CHECK LIST                         First Quarter

On the basis of his/her ability, he/she:

| | Outstanding | Acceptable | Not Acceptable |
|---|---|---|---|
| 1. Has mastery of addition and subtraction of whole numbers vertically and horizontally. | | | |
| 2. Can solve multiplication problems with at least 2-digit multipliers. | | | |
| 3. Can solve division problems with at least 2-digit divisors. | | | |
| 4. Has a proficient knowledge for use of the least common multiple and greatest common factor of a number. | | | |
| 5. Can apply an understanding of equivalent of fractions. | | | |
| 6. Can add and subtract fractions. | | | |
| 7. Demonstrates the relationship of improper fractions to mixed numbers. | | | |
| 8. Demonstrates the relationship of mixed numbers to improper fractions. | | | |

READING COMMUNITY MIDDLE SCHOOL
Reading, Ohio

NAME_____ LEVEL_____        ADVISOR_____

PHYSICAL EDUCATION SKILLS CHECK LIST              Second Quarter

On the basis of his/her ability, he/she:

|  | Outstanding | Acceptable | Not Acceptable |
|---|---|---|---|
| 1. Dresses appropriately for Physical Education Activities. | | | |
| 2. Has coordination in body movements through running, jumping, walking and other basics. | | | |
| 3. Has a sense of rhythm in body movements. | | | |
| 4. Is a good sport and team player. | | | |
| 5. Has developed skills, habits, and attitudes that will help in their social and emotional growth. | | | |
| 6. Exercises caution in a safety - sense in all activities. | | | |
| 7. Accepts responsibility of leadership by acting as squad leaders, scorekeepers, and captains. | | | |
| 8. Accepts physical education as integral part of their school life. | | | |

In considering what is expected of an evaluation and reporting system, the following list of criteria may provide an indication of its potential scope and complexity.

Tentative Statement of Criteria
for Selecting an Evaluation System
for a Middle School

1. Does the system fit purpose (or purposes) of middle school/junior high school education?
2. Is the system explicit and clear in exactly what qualities are being evaluated?
3. Will the system communicate to the student what he wants or needs to know about himself?
4. Does the system recognize differences in individuals and provide for evaluating progress or growth in terms of each individual's capability?
5. Is the system sensitive to a wide variety of capabilities of students, i.e., creativity, diligence, intelligence, independence, interest, articulateness, human relations?
6. Would the system promote the kind of instruction desired?  i.e., close interaction between students and teachers?
7. Is the system adaptable to the special needs and requirements of different segments of the community?
   i.e., a) can it deal with the matter of student retention?
        b) can it deal with the needs of special curricula or courses?
8. Would the system provide maximum encouragement to students i.e., be stimulating to the non-motivated without stifling the independent or frightening the insecure?
9. Would the system provide useful information to high schools?  or to other schools for transfer students?
10. Would the system communicate to the parents (a) what they want to know and (b) what they need to know in order to assist the student?
11. Would the system operate at minimum cost in time and money to the school district?

Any system of evaluating and reporting student
progress requires careful thinking and planning by
school staff. There are many questions to be dealt
with if the system is to do all that is expected of
it. Planning an evaluation system requires that
planners need to be aware of all aspects and provide for each of these. To do this properly often
requires a variety of forms. There is no simple
system such as many schools now use that can do this.

## SOME USEFUL REFERENCES

1.  Baughman, M. Dale, editor, Pupil Evaluation in
    The Junior High School, Danville, Illinois,
    Interstate, 1963.

2.  Drayer, Adam M., Problems in Middle and High
    School Teaching, Allyn and Bacon Inc., Boston,
    1979.

3.  A Guide to Successful Parent-Teacher Conferences,
    Franklin Publishers, Inc., Milwaukee, Wisconsin,
    1964.

4.  Lewy, Arieh, Editor, Handbook of Curriculum
    Evaluation, UNESCO, Longman, Inc., New York,
    1977.

5.  Middle School/Junior High School Evaluation
    Criteria, Revised Edition. National Study of
    School Evaluation. Arlington, Va., 1978.

6.  Rothney, John W. M.; "Evaluating and Reporting
    Pupil Progress" What Research Says to The
    Teacher Series, no. 7 N. E. A., Washington, D.C.

PLANNED GRADUALISM

Let us begin this chapter on <u>planned gradualism</u>
by eavesdropping on a conversation involving an elementary teacher, a middle school teacher and a high
school teacher.  The elementary teacher and the
high school teacher are trying to come to grips with
"the middle school concept" and the middle school
teacher wants to assist.

| | |
|---|---|
| ELEMENTARY TEACHER | As a fifth grade teacher, I am often asked at parent-teacher conferences to explain what goes on at the middle school.  Those who have not had a youngster in the middle school before are sometimes rather anxious about it.  I have to admit that I am not very well informed about the middle school myself.  Do you have any questions? |
| MIDDLE SCHOOL TEACHER | One suggestion would be to come over and spend some time with us to see for yourself what our program is like.  Regarding parents who seem uneasy or who just want more information, you might see how they would feel about your passing their name along to us for follow-up.  I know we welcome questions and are happy to contact people directly if they are comfortable with that.  Is there anything that comes to mind now that you would like to know more about? |
| HIGH SCHOOL TEACHER | Junior high I understand.  Is middle school a new term for junior high? |

| | |
|---|---|
| MIDDLE SCHOOL TEACHER | The middle school is different from the traditional junior high. The middle school is neither secondary nor elementary even though it has characteristics of both. |
| HIGH SCHOOL TEACHER | Sounds good to me. Why not start at the elementary level? |
| ELEMENTARY TEACHER | OK. We are organized into self-contained units at each grade level. I teach all the subjects except for music, art and gym. We have specialists who take the responsibility for those areas so that each group of kids has a special class on a rotating basis. In a way I guess I do really teach music, art and gym because we have classroom activities related to each of the three areas regularly. |
| HIGH SCHOOL TEACHER | You and I are really in different teaching worlds. I teach science, period. I have five classes of twenty to thirty students while you have the same students all day. I wonder why elementary schools are usually self-contained like yours. Wouldn't your kids learn more by having a specialist in each subject? |
| ELEMENTARY TEACHER | I have learned of departmentalized elementary schools but I don't like the idea. I believe young children need the stability of relating with one teacher. There is so much I would miss if I taught a different group every hour instead of keeping the same ones. My students aren't ready to change classes every hour. Your high |

school students are pretty independent. Most can take care of
themselves. Elementary children
need more adult guidance.

MIDDLE
SCHOOL
TEACHER

I would like to pick up on the
comment about your being in different teaching worlds. Although
we might agree that each world is
appropriate for its learners, it
is unlikely that the elementary
environment would suit high school
students or that elementary students could prosper in a high
school setting. If we could take
this line of thinking a step further, we would be in a position
to see the basis of the middle
school concept.

Pre and early adolescent youngsters have needs and characteristics which set them apart from
young children and from adolescents. They need more independence in decision making than
their elementary counterparts
but not as much as high school
students. Subject choices should
have a wider range than in elem-
mentary school but not as wide
as high school. Too many
choices lead to confusion for
these young people. Equipped
with skills from the elementary
years and with increasing maturation, they are ready to dig deeper
in study but not so deep as in
high school.

ELEMENTARY
TEACHER

One reason that my fifth graders
look forward to going to the
middle school is because it seems
that their world is growing

|                              | beyond what we offer at our school. We teachers call it "fifth grade-itis." |
|------------------------------|------------------------------------------------------------------------------|
| MIDDLE SCHOOL TEACHER        | Our eighth graders get an older version of the same affliction. I believe that they are telling us they are ready for more options and more independence. |
| HIGH SCHOOL TEACHER          | We experience the same thing with seniors. I didn't realize you had this happening all the way down in fifth grade. |
| ELEMENTARY TEACHER           | We need to remember that our kids by the end of fifth grade have been in self-contained rooms for about six years counting kinder-garten. They seem ready for contacts with larger numbers of teachers and students. |
| MIDDLE SCHOOL TEACHER        | Exactly! That's why we put our students in teams of two to four teachers. It's a change from the elementary but it doesn't over-whelm them as a high school sched-ule might. We build in more contacts with teachers and students than they had before but we still maintain that home base security factor of the elementary school. |
| ELEMENTARY TEACHER           | I'm glad we got together. I feel better able to respond to the questions of my students and their parents. |
| HIGH SCHOOL TEACHER          | I would like to visit both your schools. Could we set something up for this marking period? |

MIDDLE        That's a good idea.  There would be
SCHOOL        no problem on my end.  Maybe we can
TEACHER       get back together soon.

It is hoped that this imaginary conversation high-
lighted some of the realities of "schools in the
middle."  Middle school students really do have
characteristics and needs that make them special.
Elementary and secondary programs do not address their
special needs and characteristics.  Good junior high
and middle schools can and should help students make
the transition between two different learning worlds.

Planned gradualism is a concept which suggests
a bridging function by the middle school.  Inciden-
tally, according to Kindred, Wolotkiewicz, Mickelson,
Coplein and Dyson (1981), the junior high school was
meant to play this role, too.

Brod (1966) made a comprehensive list of sixteen
advantages of the middle school.  One advantage was
that it provides an opportunity for the gradual change
from the self-contained classroom to complete
departmentalization.  Alexander, Williams, Compton,
Hines and Prescott (1968) cited three examples of
middle schools which accomplished planned gradualism
(movement from self-contained to departmentalized).
Each school had an organization which included a more
self-contained arrangement for entering students and
variations of departmentalization for older students
before they went to the high school.  They cautioned
that such organizational plans could lead to as many
articulation problems within the school as exist
between separate schools.

The planned gradualism theme is also touched
upon by Stradley (1971).

The middle school exists to provide students a
more gradual transition from the elementary
school to the senior high school.  The
middle school curriculum must be planned and
developed in such a way that it builds on
and smoothly continues the program of studies

existing in the elementary school. In the
same manner, this curriculum must dovetail with
the high school program so there is no interruption of the learning process (p. 41).

It was Riegle (1971) who formally defined planned
gradualism in his dissertation.

Planned gradualism: A series of planned curricular and organizational changes designed steadily and
systematically to convert a student's educational
program from the single classroom design to the
departmental design (p. 3).

In assessing some critical issues facing middle
schools Romano (1978) stressed that the middle schools
should be elementary-oriented rather than secondary-
oriented because the students in middle schools are
predominantly still children. The program should
help these children understand more about their world
and enjoy life instead of trying to produce miniature
experts in the academic disciplines.

It may be worthwhile to examine each word in the
term, planned gradualism. "Planned" suggests that
the educators would have gathered and studied pertinent information before making decisions. Learner
needs and characteristics, prior elementary school
experiences and the district's curriculum structure
would likely be of interest. "Gradualism" projects
an unhurried, patient image connected with some
change.

By putting these different ideas together, a
more comprehensive definition for planned gradualism
is derived. Planned gradualism is a framework for
curricular and organizational decision-making which
takes into account the learner's elementary experiences, the learner's developmental characteristics,
and the K-12 curriculum. This is done in order to
provide experiences which are natural extensions of
prior experiences and which are responsive to learner
needs.

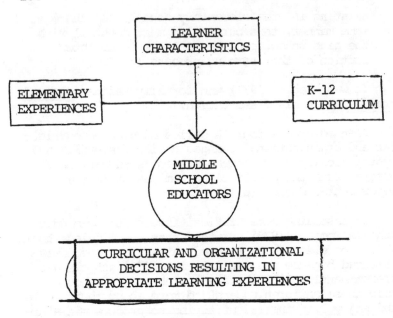

PLANNED GRADUALISM: A framework for curricular and
organizational decision-making.


The various components of the planned gradualism
decision-making system are variables. The learners
in different middle schools come with different
elementary backgrounds. K-12 curriculum structures
vary in different communities. The literature concerning the developmental characteristics of middle
school students points out the enormous spread
among students at any one time. Many claim that the
range is never greater than during the middle school
years. Finally, the educators making the decisions
are obviously different. The result of combining
these variables is that the decisions and the ensuing
learning experiences are also different. This is as
it should be.

Alexander (1977) warned against the danger
of copying features of "good middle schools" without
local experimentation and innovation.  He added that
basic guidelines should be used for regular planning
efforts but that diversity comes from "home-made"
programs.   "The diversity will exist because of the
unique nature of each school's population each year,
and the creative plans made by each middle school
faculty and community to serve its children well
(p. 39)."  Planned gradualism as an open-ended process
would appear to qualify as a basic planning guideline
mentioned by Alexander.

## Planned Gradualism--How To Do It

Since planned gradualism is a framework, its
purpose is to serve as a general guide for middle
school educators as they make decisions about curriculum and the organizational structure of the
building.  Let's return to the definition offered
earlier and examine each component more closely to
see how a middle school staff might become more able
to use the planned gradualism framework.  We will
consider the components in the following order:

1.  Middle school educators
2.  Elementary experiences
3.  K-12 curriculum
4.  Learner characteristics
5.  Curricular and organizational decisions
    leading to appropriate learning experiences.

## Middle School Educators

It is assumed that the professionals in a
building are involved in an ongoing process of program improvement.  It is clear that neither planned
gradualism nor any other concept in this book can be
implemented without professional working together.

## Elementary Experiences & K-12 Curriculum

These two sources of information are closely related. A middle school in a given community can begin to fulfill its mission only when it builds upon the program of the elementary school(s) and when there is curriculum articulation. We need to know our local setting thoroughly. We need to know what is happening in the other buildings which relate to ours. We need a feeling of trust and interdependence with colleagues in those related schools. We need to see our place in the overall scheme of things.

Although virtually every professional in a district should become involved in a communication network that connects the various levels, the responsibility for establishing the atmosphere and initiating and maintaining the process is administrative. Regardless of the size of the district, the building principals with the support of central administrators and with the participation of teachers would appear to be the people most able to keep cross-level communication active.

Listed below are eight suggested activities to open and maintain communication.

1. Establish exchange days for teachers, counselors, administrators, etc. between schools. This will help colleagues in different buildings see the bigger picture. Discussion is not enough. We need to experience what is happening throughout the district.

2. Send copies of building newsletters to related schools and invite each to do the same. This is one low cost way to help build bridges.

3. Have each school in a network establish a visitation group. Each group will make presentations at the other schools regarding philosophy, organization, plans, etc.

4.  Establish common in-service sessions with
    other schools.  It is healthy to recognize
    that selected issues touch all of us as
    educators regardless of our work setting.
    In-service activities can help remind us that
    we may have more in common than the increasing
    trend toward specialization might suggest.

5.  Invite representatives from related schools
    to your building curriculum meetings.  This
    is a good way to keep others informed and
    to keep us honest.

6.  Establish K-12 curriculum groups that are
    ongoing in the major areas.  This is a must!
    When each level does its own thing, fragmen-
    tation results with our kids being left to
    navigate a confusing K-12 set of expectations.

7.  Make the status reports from the curriculum
    groups a standard part of your school's
    communication.  Every educator should know
    what is happening in curriculum and it should
    not be left to chance.

8.  Invite representatives from related schools
    to your building's social functions.
    Having fun together is contagious.  Working
    and playing go hand in hand.

You will be able to think of others.  The important
idea is that we need a "feel" for the schools which
relate to ours, we need to know how those schools
are organized and we need a comprehensive knowledge
of the K-12 curriculum.

## Learner Characteristics

Most of us have had at least one course in
child development or adolescent psychology.  Unfortunately, many of the young people with whom we work
generally do not fall neatly into either category
(child or adolescent).  The result is that we really
lack important basic knowledge about our students.

McEwin (1977) stated the problem this way:

> Most teachers serving in middle schools have
> not undergone a program of preparation
> intended specifically for the teaching of
> transescents.  The overwhelming majority
> of those currently teaching at the middle
> school level have been prepared by depart-
> ments of secondary education . . . This
> lack of well-trained teachers prepared for
> and dedicated to teaching at the middle
> school level is in the opinion of this
> writer, the middle school movement's most
> crucial and long-standing problem, prevent-
> ing widespread acceptance and implementation
> of the middle school concept. (pp. 116-117).

There is a pressing need for those of us in
middle school education to buckle down in an
academic sense and take the responsibility to
become knowledgeable about the developmental characteristics of our students.  We continue to
operate without important information that is
readily available.

Three sources are suggested to help you grow in
this area.  The first is The  Middle School by
Donald H. Eichorn published by The Center for
Applied Research in Education, Inc., New York.

The second source is "Developmental Characteristics of Pre-Adolescents and Their Implications" by
Louis G. Romano, James D. Hedberg and Mark Lulich
(1973).  This readily usable work is essentially a
chart with three parts.  They are physical growth
characteristics, emotional and social characteristics
and mental growth characteristics.  Each set of
characteristics is accompanied by a discussion of
learner needs, curricular implications and guiding
questions.  Physical growth characteristics, one of
the main sections of the chart, will be included
to give you an overview of the organization of the
resource.

| Implications for the Pre-Adolescent (11-14 years) | Curriculum Implications for the School | Questions for the Teacher |
|---|---|---|
| I. PHYSICAL GROWTH CHARACTERISTICS | | |
| A. Body Growth The growth pattern is the same for all boys and girls but there are wide variations in the timing and degree of changes. The sequential order in which they occur is relatively consistent in both sexes. | Develop an awareness that individuals grow at varying rates of speed and begin this rapid growth at different ages. | Emphasize self-understanding throughout the curriculum. This can be done by: a. Providing health and science experiences that will develop an understanding of growth such as: (1) weighing and measuring at regular intervals and charting gains or losses; (2) observing growth of plants and animals; | Do I expect there will be a tremendous range of maturity levels in any one class, e.g. some 14 year old boys may be 19 years old biologically and physiologically? |

| Implications for the Pre-Adolescent (11-14 years) | Curriculum Implications for the School | Questions for the Teacher |
| --- | --- | --- |
| Each person rapidly accelerates before pubescence and decelerates after pubescence. | (3) learning about individual differences in growth. | |
| During the transition between childhood and adolescence, the greatest amount of physical (as well as psychological and social) change in an individual will occur. | | |
| Learn to accept one's own body; realize, too, that classmates may develop differently; each individual is unique. | b. Providing guidance at the classroom level and by utilizing school counselor(s) as a resource person. | Do I provide guidance within the classroom knowing that it's more important than help provided by the school counselor(s)? |

| Implications for the Pre-Adolescent (11-14 years) | Curriculum Implications for the School | Questions for the Teacher |
|---|---|---|
| a. growth hormone (anterior lobe of pituitary gland) stimulates overall growth of bones and tissue. This hormone is largely responsible for the growth rate. | c. During physical education classes providing for individual differences by having several groups of differing abilities. | Do I use pre-tests to group according to skills during team sports? Do I provide appropriate activities and objectives for each group? |
| b. gonad-stimulating hormone causes gonads (testes and ovaries) to grow, which | | |

| Implications for the Pre-Adolescent (11-14 years) | Curriculum Implications for the School | Questions for the Teacher |
|---|---|---|

produce hormones of their own. When gonads reach maturity they seem to dry up the growth hormone.

c. changes in thymus, thyroid, and possible adrenal glands result in changes in rate of energy production (metabolism), blood pressure, and pulse rate.

| Implications for the Pre-Adolescent (11-14 years) | Curriculum Implications for the School | Questions for the Teacher |
|---|---|---|
| d. bones grow fast, muscles slower; legs and arms grow proportionately faster than trunk. Hands and feet mature before arms and legs. This split growth is called asynchrony. | | |
| Understand that others will be changing as well as oneself and that all pre-adolescents have similar difficulties in coping with these changes. | Provide opportunities for interaction among students of multi-ages. | Do I provide activities which include the sixth, seventh and eighth graders? |
| Girls are usually taller and proportionately heavier than boys (ages 11-14. Some girls at this age are mature; menstruation begins | | |
| Understand that reproductive organs are developing. Girls should know that menstruation will soon occur and should know how to deal with it. | Provide instruction related to growth of the body so that one can better understand changes in himself and others and be prepared for future changes and problems. | Am I aware that the pre-adolescents may be extremely self-conscious during these physical changes, and minimize |

| | Implications for the Pre-Adolescent (11-14 years) | Curriculum Implications for the School | Questions for the Teacher |
|---|---|---|---|
| (12-13), and development of breasts and hips becomes noticeable | | | potentially embarrassing situations. |
| Boys are growing broad-shouldered, deep chested and heavier with a voice change being more noticeable than with girls. Most rapid growth has occurred by 13½-14 and most have experienced ejaculation. | Boys should know that they may have nocturnal emissions. | | Do I provide rules for entering or leaving the classroom that are flexible? |
| | Develop the habit of periodic visits to doctor and dentist. | Provide school examination of eyes, ears and teeth. Keep complete health records including height, weight, medications, and emotional problems. | Am I aware of special health problems in the classroom—diabetes, poor vision, students on medication, epileptics, etc? |

| Implications for the Pre-Adolescent (11-14 years) | Curriculum Implications for the School | Questions for the Teacher |
|---|---|---|
| Facial proportions change as the nose and chin become more prominent. | A nurse should be available on a full-time basis for first aid and as a resource for the teachers. | Do I know what to do in an emergency? |
| Secondary sex characteristics develop—hair appears on face and in genital area. | Health classes should especially emphasize exercises for good posture. | Do I encourage good posture habits and ignore awkwardness? |

B. Health
  Continues to enjoy comparative freedom from diseases; however, eyes, ears, and especially teeth may require medical attention. Minor illnesses of short duration are fairly

| Implications for the Pre-Adolescent (11-14 years) | Curriculum Implications for the School | Questions for the Teacher |
| --- | --- | --- |
| common during adolescence. | | |
| Poor posture and awkwardness become increasingly evident. | Learn to accept the fact that some awkwardness and accidents caused by it are likely to occur. Make an effort to improve posture. | Physical education classes should provide health instruction as well as exercise. Periods should be long enough to allow adequate time for showers—which should be required. | Do I require periodic rest especially during highly competitive sports? Do I provide adequate time for showers? |
| C. Body Management Endurance is usually not high, perhaps because of the rapid growth spurt. Pre-adolescents can overtire | Develop good habits for diet, exercise and rest. Nine hours of sleep is usually needed. | Formulate school policy regarding homework assignments to insure adequate play time. | In making homework assignments, do I consider the student's need for free play time? |

| Implications for the Pre-Adolescent (11-14 years) | Curriculum Implications for the School | Questions for the Teacher |
|---|---|---|
| themselves in exciting competition. | | |
| For many, this is a period of listlessness, possibly of an emotional or physical nature. | Develop a balance between mental and physical activities. | |
| Pimples and excessive perspiration become problems as glands produce oily secretion. | Learn good health habits such as to bathe regularly.<br><br>Be aware of sales propaganda for beauty aids which may be harmful. | |

The third source recommended for your consideration is from the work of Epstein (1977). He suggested that during the age span of twelve to fourteen years the brain stops or greatly slows its growth. The implications of these findings include the proposal that a moratorium be placed upon the introduction of cognitive skills in favor of refining and applying existing cognitive skills.

> Children should be given massive doses of interaction with nature, society, and people. I would, in essence, remove children from school most of the week and put them to work in public service projects, nature reclamation projects, helping with old age homes, day-care centers, etc. I would retain schooling for a couple days each week, but the emphasis would be on developing already initiated skills (pp. 10-11).

### Curricular and Organizational Decisions Leading to Appropriate Learning Experiences

The purpose of using planned gradualism as a framework is to translate what we know about our students and about our local curriculum into decisions which relate to how we organize the building and structure the curriculum. A thoughtful study of those characteristics leads to the discovery that planned gradualism is a unifying theme of the middle school concept. Analyzing these characteristics consistently yields the following:

1. Begin with learner needs.
2. Be flexible
3. Use imagination; be innovative.
4. The middle school concept is an ideal. It is an abstract target toward which the continuous process of goal setting, program development and evaluation is aimed.

By definition <u>planned gradualism</u> must happen at the individual building level. It is based upon professionals using their judgment to combine what they know about middle school youth with what they know about the unique local setting. The following questions and observations are not meant to offer ready-made answers to the question of how to implement <u>planned gradualism</u> in your school. Rather they are presented to help identify some issues that need to be faced as your middle school uses <u>planned gradualism</u> as a framework for making decisions.

1.  What is the role of the elementary school in shaping the middle school?
    It is considerable. The middle school should be a natural extension of the warm, caring elementary environment. The middle school provides a more diverse climate consistent with the needs of the changing young person.

2.  What is the role of the high school in shaping the middle school?
    A continuing trend has been to increasingly move components of the secondary curriculum into the intermediate and even into the elementary schools. Forces within our society seem to tell us that more and faster are better. We need to guard against this trend in our middle and junior high schools. The "gradualism" part of <u>planned gradualism</u> reminds us to respect the changes that our young people are having. They are not high school students and we should not emulate the high school.
    Romano (1978) has said it succinctly, "There is too much covering ground and not enough cultivating of the ground." He argues for more in-depth applying of skills such as drawing murals and writing plays instead of trying to get students into the high school curriculum. There is no need to hurry the change process. Constantly eyeing the high school curriculum makes hurrying a strong temptation.

3.  Should the student begin in a self-contained
    organization upon entering the middle school
    and finish in a departmental setting before
    moving to the high school?
    Although this has been one interpretation of
    planned gradualism, it is not the only alter-
    native. Many students enter the middle school
    expecting and needing something other than a
    self-contained environment. Having departmen-
    talization in the middle school may result in
    more disadvantages than advantages. It would
    give students a taste of the high school
    organization but perhaps at the expense of
    needed flexibility so essential to the middle
    school concept. Teaching teams in which
    teachers and learners share flexible blocks
    of time would appear to be an alternative
    worth trying. Team teaching is explored in
    detail in another chapter.

We will conclude with a look at how two school
districts have applied the planned gradualism framework. The first application comes from the West
Bloomfield Schools in Orchard Lake, Michigan. The
elementary and middle school physical education
curriculum will be the interest area. The second
application shows how a middle school's organizational
plan reflects planned gradualism. Northwest Middle
School in the Northwest Schools, Jackson County, Michigan, is the source for the organizational example.


Application #1 West Bloomfield Schools

The general scheme of the K-8 curriculum is that
the basic skills that are learned early are extended
and applied as the student grows. Each skill group
is introduced, developed and then reinforced at
pre-determined grade levels. Two examples, tumbling
and soccer, are illustrative.

Tumbling The elementary curriculum includes helping the student master skills such as the log roll,

side roll, forward roll, back roll, back and forward roll to different positions, cartwheel, and
roundoff. The sixth grader learns more skills and
then needs to choose three and combine them into a
sequence. The seventh grader adds more skills as
does the eighth grader who must combine any eight
skills into a routine. As you can see, there is a
logical progression with each subsequent level building upon the former.

Soccer  In the elementary program the emphasis
is on learning the component skills (passing, stopping
the ball, dribbling, kicking) and participating in
lead-up games. The middle school program (grades
6-8) reinforces the elementary skills and adds
specialized skills such as the volley kick, tackling,
heading and chesting. More stress is given to
strategy and the official rules of soccer. Not only
is there an orderly transition from the elementary
to the middle school soccer program, there is also
sequential development within the middle school soccer
curriculum itself. This culminates with eighth graders demonstrating their skill mastery and knowledge
of the rules in game play.


### Application #2 Northwest Middle School

Northwest Middle School serves approximately 575
sixth and seventh graders in an urban fringe district
with a K-12 student population of about 4,000. The
professional staff includes twenty-four classroom
teachers, six elective area teachers, a media center
director, an integrated classroom teacher (ICR), a
reading specialist, a counselor and two administrators.

The twenty-four classroom teachers are organized
into six planning teams with the auxiliary professionals as members of each planning team according to a
rotation which parallels marking period changes.
Each administrator works with three planning teams
while the counselor meets with all six planning
teams. A planning team is defined as a group of

teachers who serve a common group of students.
Each planning team meets weekly to deal with mutual
concerns through a problem solving process.

In addition, two thirds of the eligible staff
are engaged in team teaching. Team teaching means
that two or more teachers teach the same subjects to
the same students at the same time. All the team
teaching partnerships at Northwest Middle School
involve two teachers. All classroom teachers have
an assignment of at least three different subjects.
This non-departmentalized structure has eliminated
the concept of the subject matter specialist in
favor of the generalist.

The description which follows excludes elective
classes and teachers. One third of the teachers
are organized into self-contained teaming pairs.
The remaining teachers have students in two hour and
three hour blocks of time. Some of these teachers
are also teaming.

The students are dealing with more than one
teacher which makes it different from elementary
school, but they are not changing teachers every
period as they will in the secondary school which
follows. Half the students have two teachers per day
while another one third have three. The remaining
students have four teachers (two pairs of team
teaching partners).

This organizational plan has offered important
benefits. One is that the overall building climate
has calmed. Rather than having all students in the
halls at the end of each period, relatively few are
out of class at any time during the day. Some of the
common problems associated with large numbers of
middle school young people interacting during unstruc-
tured time are avoided. At the classroom level the
potential number could increase if educators would
dedicate themselves to providing learner centered
programs. The starting point must be the needs of
the learner. This is the essence of the middle
school concept and of planned gradualism, an essential component of any middle school.

BIBLIOGRAPHY

Alexander, W. M.  Alternative futures for the middle
    school.  In P. S. George (Ed.), The Middle
    School:  A Look Ahead.  National Middle School
    Association, 1977.

Alexander, W. M., Willimas, E. L., Compton, M., Hines,
    V. A., & Prescott, D.  The Emergent Middle
    School.  New York:  Holt, Rinehart and
    Winston, 1968.

Alexander, William M. and Paul George, The Exemplary
    Middle School, New York:  Holt, Rinehart and
    Winston, 1981.

Brod, P.  Middle school:  Trends toward Adoption.
    Clearing House, 1966, 40, 331-333.

Eichhorn, D. H.  The Middle School.  New York:  The
    Center for Applied Research in Education, 1966.

Elementary Physical Education Curriculum.  West
    Bloomfield Schools, Orchard Lake, Michigan.

Epstein, H. T.  A neuroscience framework for restruc-
    turing middle school curricula.  Transescence,
    The Journal on Emerging Adolescent Education, 1977,
    V, 6-11.

Kindred, L. W., Wolotkiewicz, R. J., Mickelson,
    J. M., Coplein, L. E., The Middle School Curricu-
    lum, Boston:  Allyn and Bacon, Inc., 1981.

McEwin, K. C.  The middle school:  an institution
    in search of teachers.  In P. S. George (Ed.),
    The Middle School:  A Look Ahead.  National
    Middle School Association, 1977.

Middle School Physical Education Curriculum.  West
    Bloomfield Schools, Orchard Lake, Michigan.

Riegle, J. D.  A study of middle school programs to determine the current level of implementation of eighteen basic middle school principles. Unpublished doctoral dissertation, Michigan State Unversity, 1971.

Romano, L. G.  Conversation of April 14, 1978.

Romano, L. G., Hedberg, J. D., & Lulich, M.  Developmental characteristics of pre-adolescents and their implications.  In L. G. Romano, N. P. Georgiady, & J. E. Heald (Eds.), The Middle School: Selected Readings on an Emerging School Program.  Chicago: Nelson-Hall Company, 1973.

Romano, L. G.  The middle school - An "emerging" cesspool?  Speech presented at the Michigan Association of Middle School Educators Convention, Lowell, Michigan, March 17, 1978.

Stradley, W. E.  A practical guide to the middle school.  New York: The Center for Applied Research in Education, 1971.

PHYSICAL ACTIVITIES AND INTRAMURALS

## Purpose

Middle school programs are developed to help
children meet their learning needs - physical, social,
emotional and mental.  Resources must be allocated
and staff efforts directed toward providing opportunities for those needs to be met.

The four areas of need are not isolated nor
mutually exclusive in nature.  They are highly
interrelated and interdependent.  However, for
purposes of study and analysis in this chapter
physical needs are separated for close attention.  In
that way, a clearer picture can be drawn regarding
the ways in which the physical needs of middle
school children might be dealt with effectively in
instructional programs.

Physical needs are frequently more important
than any others to middle school children.  The
reason is that in our society a high premium is
placed on physical ability, personal appearance,
size and good health.  Thus, what often happens to
children in terms of social acceptance, self-
concept and confidence for acquiring mental skills is
highly influenced by the degree to which physical
needs can be met.

A quick review of Abraham Maslow's hierarchy of
needs clearly indicates how important physical needs
are in the process of self-actualization.  Maslow's
hierarchy is noted below:

1.  The physical needs for food, sex, activity
    and the like.

2.  The need for safety, for a peaceful, orderly,
    predictable world.

3. The need for belonging and being loved, for close and affectionate relationships with others.

4. The esteem needs, for self-respect, as well as the respect and appreciation of others, based on one's own accomplishments.

5. The need for self-actualization, for the full realization of one's potential.

6. The need to know and understand the world.

7. The aesthetic needs for beauty and harmony.[1]

One can readily see how prominently in the hierarchy the physical needs are placed.

Frequently, physical needs are ignored in school programs and are, at best, generally assumed to be met. A partial physical education program, an interscholastic program and some minor intramural activities are the extent of any real attention to physical concerns. Often, even these programs are not clearly designed to provide equal opportunities for every child to meet existing physical needs.

There must be a clearly defined goal in middle school programming that has as its focus the physical concerns of transescent youngsters. The implementation of that goal must include as priorities: 1) a sound physical education program; 2) a thoroughly developed intramural program; and 3) directed attention to physical needs in every classroom, program and activity related to the middle school.

The Physical Needs of
Middle School Children

The needs of middle school children are not

---

[1] Maslow, A. H., Motivation and Personality, New York: Harper, 1954.

easily categorized or comparmentalized. The children vary in every conceivable fashion and so do their needs. The life of a middle school child is constant with change and of such intensity, that may recall the ages of ten to fourteen as the most difficult in their lives.

There are, however, some physical needs which can be identified and that seem to be common to middle school youngsters related to their development. Middle school aged students need:

1. A nutritional diet - this is extremely important due to the rapid growth taking place;

2. Regular physical activity - this is important due to the high energy level that exists between growth spurts, for fitness, for periodic stages of high restlessness, and for rapidly developing muscle groups;

3. Regular rest - During periods of rapid growth, both mentally and physically, body and mind need occasions for rest and relaxation. Often the individuals tire easily and may have a tendency to over-exert;

4. To be in physical proximity to peers - the approval of peers is critical and nearness is often a prelude to or a factor in gaining acceptance. Groupness is highly sought.

5. To have physical differences accepted - the middle school student needs to feel that differences in appearance and ability are okay and will not interfere with his/her acceptance level;

6. To have "time alone" - some time almost totally free from others, especially adults, is important;

7. To have relationships with the opposite sex - sex characteristics and needs are

developing. Interaction with the opposite
sex is important to test out new behaviors
and gain acceptance.

8.  To have a safe and secure environment - even
    though students are seeking independence,
    there is still a need to return to the phys-
    ical safety and security of the home and the
    adult world;

9.  To know, understand and manage feelings toward
    the rapid physical changes or lack thereof -
    perceptions and feelings are generally more
    important than the changes themselves;

10. To have skill activity at their level of
    development - the opportunity to succeed and
    to avoid frustration is maximized when stu-
    dents are able to work at their rate and
    readiness level.


### Growth and Development (Physical)

In addition to the characteristics noted in the
needs description above, there are some other observations which are important.

In middle school students, actual physical growth
tends to be well ahead of muscular strength. However,
rapid skeletal growth spurts begin during this period
and coordination may decrease for a time as muscle
growth catches up and bone growth continues.

Girls are often taller and more developed than
boys. Many girls begin to menstruate, although
irregularly, and this causes them some anxiety.
Secondary sexual characteristics are also developing
and personal appearance becomes a concern as rapid
growth may bring poor posture, acne and longer arms
and legs.

Competitiveness begins to increase with the
middle school years and worry about winning and

losing can be a critical factor in self-concept
development. Thus, it is very important to provide
an environment which supports success experiences in
competition.

## Some Reminders About Learning

Learning is essential in middle school students
and is the process by which change and renewal take
place. It occurs when experiences are need-ful-
filling relevant to values and analogous to past
experiences. As the individual interacts with his
environment, he learns. Although not always in a
positive direction, it takes place and does bring
about change.

Behaviors which are rewarded or reinforced are
those which are most likely to recur. The reinforcement must follow almost immediately after the desired
behavior if the learner is to make a connection
between reward and behavior. As a learning tool,
repetition is relatively ineffective unless the
learner can relate that repetition very directly to
his own experience. Threat and punishment have
varied and uncertain effects upon learning, and
generally accomplish very little; certainly less
than rewarding and reinforcing.

Students learn most effectively when they can
identify present and future use for the learning.
Learning also has a much greater chance of being
used in the future if it is utilized immediately
following the learning. Children, like adults,
also tend to remember information which confirms
previously held attitudes much better than information
which runs contrary to them.

There are variations among students regarding
1) readiness for any learning, and 2) how rapidly
an individual is able to learn a given skill or idea.
Readiness and speed of learning are a product of
many variables: physical maturation; prior learning
experiences; the student's value system; the student's

beliefs about the relevance of the learning and his
feelings about self, home, school and teachers.

Learning is more likely to be supported by the
learner if he or she feels a sense of choice or
participation in selecting the learning activity.
When a person is not involved in determining those
things which are to be learned, the commitment to
that learning is minimized. In addition, there
does not appear to be any subject in the school
which is superior to others in strengthening a person's learning skills. It depends on the individual.

## General Description of Behavior

The behaviors of middle school students are
clear evidence of the growing-up process. It is
important to recognize that one common element in
describing the behavior of middle school students is
diversity. The behavior of an individual is erratic
and often found at opposite extremes within a short
period of time. The behavior of a group of students
regularly shows that same diversity and extremes.
Behavior reflects the wide range in maturation
(developmental) levels found among middle school age
youngsters. The behavior which individuals exhibit
in the transescent years coincides with their needs.
More effort is expended to meet social, emotional
and physical needs prior to the meeting of mental
needs.

## Some Generalizations From the Literature

There are some generalizations which can be drawn
from the literature regarding physical activities
which are important in considering the development of
sound programs for middle school students.

Much of the psychological development and
socialization which occurs with the transescent is a
result of the entry he makes into the peer group
culture. Adult intervention in the arena of

children's games has questionable positive effect
on the growth of children. On the contrary, there is
a distinct possibility that adult interference (which
is frequently most intense in interscholastic
athletics) may cause damage to the natural process of
growing up.

Transescents are not physically mature adults.
Adult activities are frequently too strenuous for
the normal development of middle school age individuals. In addition, there are great differences in
physical development at this age. Chronological
age, certainly, is not an accurate indicator of
physiological age. Determining the level of
physical development is extremely difficult. Thus,
adults take great risks in providing highly competitive and strenuous physical activity for children
who may not be physically mature in bone development
and muscular strength.

Interscholastic athletics may, in fact, actually
reduce the opportunity for students to participate.
The exclusive nature of interscholastic activity is
one factor. The high degree of imposed structure
is another which reduces participation for the individual. The child's involvement is being directed
by others.

When the middle school age youngster is exposed
to experiences in which he cannot be successful
simply because of his physical or emotional maturity,
success is minimized and desire for further positive
physical activity often diminishes.

Intense competition for many students of middle
school age may cause severe emotional damage. Being
thrust into the competition of making the team or
being on the first team, when emotional readiness is
absent, will frequently end in a failure experience
and may cause permanent damage emotionally. The
same is true for physical readiness. Many individuals
are not ready emotionally and/or physically until
they are fifteen years or older in chronological age.

Late maturing individuals often have more
difficulty establishing positive self-concepts. Frequently, they feel more inadequate, rejected and
dependent on adults. Thus, increased adult sensitivity to the needs of both the late and early
maturer is critical.

## Opposition to Middle School
## Interscholastic Sports

Interscholastic athletics at the middle school
level are not appropriate. They are exclusive in
nature, incompatible with the developmental levels
of ten to fourteen year olds, consume an inordinate
amount of resources that could better be utilized
in programs for all students, and are mostly
adult oriented and directed activities.

## General School Environment
## Conducive to Meeting Physical Needs

The total school learning environment must be
developed in a manner which takes into consideration
the physical needs of middle school age students.
The school must provide an environment where they
can feel physically safe and secure so that other
needs can be addressed and met.

Every program and learning experience should be
constructed to include both active and sedentary
activities. It is important to provide adequate
and regular time for rest and relaxation. The physical activity which is planned should be frequent
and not based primarily on complex motor skills.

There are times when activities may need to be
varied for boys and girls, based on their developmental levels. Opportunity must be available for
individuals to choose those activities in which they
will participate. Therefore, there must be ample
and varied options from which they can choose.
Required activities for all students will be

effective only when they fit particular developmental
level and interest of the individual.

Time must be provided in many programs for students to study and discuss their personal growth and
development as well as their health and personal
care. Nutrition and healthy body care and an understanding of these are necessary areas of focus.

In addition to opportunities for rest and a break
in the day, there should be time to get a nutritional
snack during the school day other than during lunch.
High energy levels necessitate adequate diets and
nutritional fulfillment. A long school day usually
makes this a high priority.

A comprehensive guidance program should be
easily accessible to assist students in understanding
and coping with their intense and changing physical
needs and the problems which result. In addition,
guidance staff must make provision for all parents to
learn and understand about the physical needs of
their children. Often parents feel helpless and
frustrated regarding the rapid and drastic changes
taking place in their children. They usually welcome the chance to share and learn with teaching
staff and other parents.

All programs need to have readily available
materials which students can access to learn about
being a transescent. In particular, the media
center should be adequately supplied with appropriate growth and development related materials. It is
important that students have easy access to these
materials and not be placed in embarrassing situations in attempting to use them. Both fiction and
non-fiction materials are available and appropriate.

Sufficient opportunity must be provided for
middle school students to learn about posture and
grooming. In addition, every individual should
have the opportunity to learn and develop first aid
skills. Saving a life or a limb may be most
important.

The chance for middle school students to meet
physical needs is often greatest when activities
take place outside the walls of the school.  Outdoor
education, resident camping, survival activities and
community service often provide students new avenues
for successful physical endeavors.

School activities should stress the importance
of leisure time utilization and the role physical
activity can play.  All activities should stress
the Greek concept of "the ideal man being sound in
mind and in body."


### Physical Education Program Components

Physical education is a high priority for all
middle school students.  Thus, resources should be
allocated to insure that a quality program can be
provided.  Facility, equipment, materials, time and
staff must be available to provide for both individual and team activities.  Students should have
access to the activities and resources necessary
for developing the basic skills and positive attitudes necessary for effective use of leisure time,
life-long physical activity and sound physical health.

Facility for physical education instruction is
often more an idea than a place.  Physical education
activities can take place many places.  Gyms,
stages, cafeterias, play fields, classrooms, bowling
alleys, sidewalks, woods, fields, and swimming pools
are some places that creative physical education
staff utilize.  Facility for physical education
should certainly be the number one priority.
Intramural programs should have the highest priority
for facility use after regular school hours.  Other
school activities should generally be scheduled after
intramurals have been completed.

Equipment and materials must include much more
than balls and bats.  Racquets, bows and arrows,
gymnastic equipment, field hockey equipment, ping
pong tables are simply a few.  Video equipment is

also a valuable tool for helping students improve their skills. Physical education and intramural staff can cooperate in the use of materials and equipment for more efficient utilization.

Time may be the most important resource to develop. Middle school students should have physical education on a daily basis with time equal to any other required school program. The practice of using a nine week block for physical education alternative with a following block without physical education cannot be defended.

Staff members in physical education should be fully certified and qualified. The teacher must have the mastery of the specific competencies involved in teaching physical education along with the awareness of the physical, mental, emotional and social needs of the middle school student. The teacher has the responsibility to help the student develop the skills, master the knowledge and acquire the attitudes and social qualities that will help each student become all that he is capable of becoming. The teacher shares in the responsibility of program planning, evaluation, testing, counseling and caring for equipment and facilities.

In addition, the physical education teacher has the responsibility to provide inservice for the rest of the staff regarding the importance of physical education as an integral part of the student's life-long learning.

In order for full use of resources to occur, it is recommended the teachers team in planning and presenting the physical education program. In that manner, teacher strengths can be used effectively, flexible group sizes can be achieved and a diversity of offerings can be presented. Class sizes should be similar to those throughout the school. The proper pupil-teacher ratio allowing for individualizing instruction is as important in physical education as in any other program of the shcool. Overly large physical education classes are to be avoided.

Processes for student evaluation and measurement should be diagnostic in nature and designed to build upon the strengths of each individual. Individual goal setting and evaluation with guidance from staff is critical for the transescent. Letter grades are not necessary. However, progress reports on an individual basis and planned parent conferences are a key part of the program.

A written instructional program should exist for physical education. Included should be clearly defined goals, objectives, program descriptions and the plans for on-going program evaluation. The program should provide:

1. Opportunities to have success.
2. Opportunities for individuals to progress at their own rate and ability level.
3. Opportunities for students to direct some of their own activities and make choices regarding their program.
4. Opportunities for student interests to be pursued.
5. Opportunities for multi-aged and co-educational learning activity.
6. Opportunities for children to play.
7. Opportunities for participation without fear of put-down or reprisal due to developmental levels or ability.
8. Opportunities to develop physical fitness habits.
9. Opportunities for learning leisure-time skills.
10. Opportunities for team activity.
11. Opportunities for individual efforts.
12. Opportunities for competition which is primarily focused on one's self but also provides for team effort.
13. Opportunities to work with adults who model through activity and appearance sound concepts of physical fitness.
14. Opportunities to learn about one's bodily capabilities.

15.  Opportunities to experience some form of leadership.

The Southfield Public Schools[2] have developed a written plan for physical education at the middle school level. The staff outlined content and further expanded each activity in behavioral terms. They have further sub-divided the activities in team, individual and dual, and leisure-time sports. Listed below are the general objectives and content of their physical education program.

Southfield Public Schools

General Objectives

Team Sports
By the end of the eighth grade, the student will participate in three team sports with a degree of success.

Individual and Dual Sports
By the end of the eighth grade, the student will participate in six individual and dual sports with a degree of success.

Leisure Time Sports
By the end of the eighth grade, the student will participate in three leisure time sports with a degree of success.

---

[2]K-12 Physical Education Curriculum, Southfield Public Schools, Southfield, Michigan.

Southfield Public Schools

Content of Physical Education Curriculum

Team Sports
Basketball
Football (touch)
Soccer
Softball
Speedball
Volleyball

Individual and Dual Sports
Apparatus                    Physical Fitness (body
Archery                          conditioning)
Badminton                    Tennis
Bowling                      Track and Field
Dance                        Tumbling
Floor Exercise               Weight Training
Golf                         Wrestling

Recreational Sports
Chinese Soccer               Paddle Ball
Floor Hockey                 Shuffle Board
Four Square                  Table Tennis
Horseshoes                   Tetherball
Kickball                     Relays

The following three charts show more detail for three particular areas of the Southfield middle school physical education curriculum: 1) Apparatus, 2) Archery, and 3) Badminton.

Southfield Public Schools

Scope of Activities

Apparatus

| Activities | Apparatus (Co-ed) |
|---|---|
| GRADE<br><br>8 | **UNEVEN PARALLEL BARS**<br>Skills<br>1. Mounts<br>2. Supports<br>3. Swings<br>4. Dismounts<br>Knowledges<br>1. Create & perform a routine |
| GRADE<br><br>7 | **EVEN PARALLEL BARS**<br>Skills<br>1. Mounts<br>2. Supports<br>3. Swings<br>4. Dismounts<br>Knowledges<br>1. Create & perform an exercise routine.<br><br>**VAULTING**<br>Skills    Knowledges<br>1. Approach  1. Body control<br>2. Take-off<br>3. Clearance  2. Space awareness<br>4. Landing |

GRADE

6

BALANCE BEAM
Skills
1. Mounts        4. Running
2. Balances      5. Walking
3. Turns         6. Dismounts
Knowledges
1. Create & perform a routine

LONG HORSE
Skills
1. Mounts
2. Dismounts
Knowledges
1. Body control
2. Space awareness

Southfield Public Schools
Scope of Activities
<u>ARCHERY</u>

| Activities | Archery (Co-ed) |
|---|---|
| GRADE<br><br>8 | <u>Preparation</u><br>1. Selecting bow and arrow<br>   a. Proper bow length<br>   b. Proper arrow length<br>   c. Proper pull<br>2. Stringing a bow<br>   a. Stance<br>   b. String in nocks<br><br><u>Skills</u><br>1. Stance<br>2. Grip<br>3. Nocking<br>4. Drawing<br>5. Releasing |
| GRADE<br><br>7 | <u>Aiming</u><br>1. Horizontal<br>2. Vertical<br>3. Point of aim<br>4. Use of bow sight<br><br><u>Knowledges</u><br>1. History<br>2. Arrow retrieval<br>3. Scoring |

Southfield Public Schools
Scope of Activities
Badminton

| Activities | Badminton (Co-ed) |
|---|---|
| GRADE<br><br>8 | **Skills**<br>1. Forehand stroke<br>2. Backhand stroke<br>3. Serve<br><br>**Knowledges**<br>1. History |
| GRADE<br><br>7 | 2. Rules and scoring<br>3. Court markings<br>4. Singles game<br>5. Doubles game |

### Individual and Dual Sports

## Apparatus

A. Uneven parallel bars (girls)
   By the end of the eighth grade, the learner
   will demonstrate the ability to perform basic
   skills on the uneven parallel bars including
   mounts, supports, swings, and dismounts.

B. Vaulting
   By the end of the eighth grade, the learner
   will demonstrate the ability to perform
   basic vaults on a waist high side horse.

C. Long horse (boys)
   By the end of the eighth grade, the learner
   will demonstrate the ability to perform
   mounts and dismounts on the long horse.

D. Even parallel bars (boys)
   By the end of the eighth grade, the learner
   will demonstrate the ability to perform
   basic skills on the parallel bars including
   mounts, supports, swings, and dismounts.

   By the end of the eighth grade, the learner
   will demonstrate the ability to move the
   length of the parallel bars.

   By the end of the eighth grade, the learner
   will demonstrate the ability to plan and
   perform an exercise routine on the parallel
   bars.

E. Balance beam (girls)
   By the end of the eighth grade, the learner
   will demonstrate the ability to perform
   basic mounts, stunts, and dismounts on a
   regulation balance beam.

   By the end of the eighth grade, the learner
   will demonstrate the ability to perform a
   variety of stunts on the regulation balance

beam, using correct mounts and dismounts
in a continuous routine.


## Archery

A.  Preparatory task
    By the end of the eighth grade, the learner
    will demonstrate the ability to select
    appropriate archery equipment.

B.  Aiming
    By the end of the eighth grade, the learner
    will demonstrate the ability to explain an
    acceptable method of training.

C.  Scoring
    By the end of the eighth grade, the learner
    will demonstrate the ability to score
    target archery.

D.  Range Procedures
    By the end of the eighth grade, the learner
    will demonstrate the ability to follow
    correct range firing procedures.

E.  Skills
    By the end of the eighth grade, the learner
    will demonstrate the ability to fire arrows
    from a bow (stance, grip, nocking, drawing,
    aiming, anchor, and release).

F.  Participation
    By the end of the eighth grade, the learner
    will demonstrate the ability to participate
    in competitive target archery.


## Badminton

A.  Strokes
    By the end of the eighth grade, the learner
    will demonstrate the ability to execute a
    functional forehand stroke.

By the end of the eighth grade, the learner
will demonstrate the ability to execute a
functional backhand stroke.

By the end of the eighth grade, the learner
will demonstrate the ability to execute a
functional serve.

B.    Participation
By the end of the eighth grade, the learner
will demonstrate the ability to participate
in a singles and/or doubles game of
badminton.

The physical education program for middle school
students merits close study and evaluation by each
school district.  Carefully developed and thoroughly
written activities, goals, objectives are extremely
helpful in guiding staff in the implementation of
instruction.  In addition, a plan for annual evaluation provides a regular format for calling attention
to program strengths and weaknesses.

When physical education programs have the necessary resources for quality implementation, the
intramural program can be developed and implemented
to further enrich the learning experiences of
transescents.

When a high quality physical education program
is implemented and functioning effectively, a
school can study to determine those physical needs
which an intramural program might address.  In the
next few pages, intramural programs are examined
and ideas presented for implementing a quality
intramural program.


Intramural Program Components

An intramural program draws its strength from a
strong physical education program.  The materials
and resources used in developing physical education
programs naturally carry over to successful intramural programs.  But, as important as materials and

resources are, the real success of intramurals lies
in a school's philosophy, its desire to meet the
needs of the students, its understanding of student
behavior and the commitment of personnel involved
in the program.

Offerings should be geared to the interests of
the students and provide a variety of activities to
attract their interests. Frequently, these activities can take place away from the school. Canoeing,
fishing, bowling, horseback riding, cycling and
roller skating are some examples. In-school activities could include wide participation in leagues,
tournaments, ladder challenges, skateboard contests,
ping-pong, dance and the like.

Often intramural activities can be effectively
planned with other schools. If the activity is
low-key, informal and participation is not limited,
students can gain much from interaction with students from other schools.

As time affects participation, intramurals can
best be accomodated by prime time scheduling.
Students should be able to participate in one or
more activities each week and have an opportunity
to be exposed to individual and dual, as well as
team, activities.

An intramural program should have a designated
director as planning, scheduling and organization
are vital to its success. Those staff members
involved in intramural programs should be paid at
rates equivalent to those paid for other extra-
curricular activities. Many staff members can be
involved on a short-term basis to supervise those
specific activities in which they have an interest
and expertise. Frequently, persons from the community can become key members of an intramural program as well.

The Forest Hills Public Schools have written
and implemented an intramural program for their
two middle schools. That program is described here.

A calendar of activities for the fall quarter
is included.

Forest Hills Public Schools
Grand Rapids, Michigan

Middle School Intramural Program

BELIEF STATEMENT:

The purpose of the intramural program is to provide a positive recreational and athletic experience
for middle school students through a planned activity program which supplements and expands upon the
regular physical education program.

Emphasis in the intramural program will include:

1. Program planning which generates participation for the greatest number of students.

2. Equal opportunity for boys and girls to
   participate.

3. Development of interest and skills in
   athletic activities which carry over into
   high school athletics and/or leisure time
   activities.

4. Instruction and supervision by qualified
   personnel.

5. Providing individual, team and recreational
   sports.

6. Providing equal participation time for all
   players in a team situation as opposed to
   stressing a win-loss record.

Since the scope of the intramural program is
intended to be comprehensive, student and parent
input will be sought through a needs assessment
survey. An Intramural Advisory Board, made up of

students and parents, will also be developed at
Northern Hills Middle School and Central Middle
School.

OBJECTIVES:

1.  The intramural program will provide an opportu-
    nity for interested students to explore a
    variety of team, individual and recreational
    activities which extend beyond those offered
    through the physical education classes.

2.  Skills taught in the physical education program
    will be assessed and upgraded when necessary as
    a regular part of the intramural program.

3.  The intramural staff will try to provide an
    environment where students feel more secure in
    participating because no one can be cut or
    dropped.

4.  More students will be encouraged to participate
    because the emphasis of the intramural program
    will be on participation.  In some instances,
    students may even be referred to the physical
    education teacher or some other resource for
    specific skill instruction.

5.  Field Trips

    Groups of students may attend special athletic
    tournaments and exhibitions by amateur or pro-
    fessional athletes.


USE OF RESOURCES:

1.  Staff Organization

    Each middle school intramural director will be
    responsible for organizing and supervising the
    intramural program in his/her respective
    building.

Middle school staff members will be continuously encouraged to participate in the intramural program and to generage new ideas for intramural activities.

Intramural staff members will be paid on an hourly rate of $____ per hour. Allowances will be made for paid planning and organization time when necessary.

Staff will also have an opportunity for inservice activities and/or visitation to other intramural programs.

High school coaches or other qualified personnel will be invited to hold specialized clinics in their area of expertise as part of the skills portion of the intramural programs.

Parents and other community members will be involved on a volunteer basis, as specialty instructors, aides and assistants.

Ideas from the results of the needs assessment survey and input from the Intramural Advisory Board may warrant consideration for utilization of public or private (non-school) facilities and personnel for certain intramural programs. Additional costs for such ventures will be shared by the students involved and certain funds from the intramural program.

2. Facility Organization

Existing facilities, including the gymnasium, balcony and outdoor playing areas will be utilized as the primary source of space. Display cases and bulletin boards will also be used to promote student participation in the program.

3.  Student/Parent Advisory Board

    An Intramural Advisory Board will be developed
    at each middle school.  Initially, students will
    be chosen from a subcommittee of student council
    representatives.  Those positions will even-
    tually be elected positions.

    Parent members of the Intramural Advisory
    Board will be appointed by the middle school
    principal and the intramural director.

    The Intramural Advisory Board will assist the
    intramural director in designing and distribu-
    ting an intramural needs assessment survey.
    Results will be used by the intramural director
    in planning the activity program.  The Intra-
    mural Advisory Board will also be responsible
    for designing, distributing and analyzing an
    evaluation tool for use with students, parents
    and staff in the spring of 1980.  Results will
    be summarized and reported to the Board of
    Education.  The Intramural Advisory Board will
    also assist in communicating via the student
    newspaper, school newsletter and Focus.

4.  Equipment

    Attached are inventory lists of all school
    equipment presently available for intramural
    use.

5.  Participant Consent Form (Injury Waiver)

    In order to assure that all students participa-
    ting in intramurals are in good physical health,
    parents will be asked to submit a permission
    slip verifying that their child has no serious
    health problems.  The attached form is a sample
    of the type of consent form which will be
    developed.  Every student will be asked to
    complete a consent form before participating
    in each new activity area.

6. Activity Calendar

An activity calendar for the first nine weeks
of the 1979-80 school year, developed by each
intramural director is attached. The remaining
activities will be decided upon pending the
organization of the Intramural Advisory Board
and the results of the needs assessment survey.

7. Tentative Intramural Schedule - December - June

A tentative activity calendar for December,
1979 through June, 1980, is attached.


For purposes of protecting instructors and the
school as well as for purposes of clear communication with parents, a consent form may be advisable.
A sample form is indicated here.

Forest Hills Public Schools
Grand Rapids, Michigan

Middle School Intramural Program
Consent Form Example

NAME_____ PHONE_____ GRADE/
                                            HOMEROOM

DEADLINE: (Enter date)                      _____

For parents:

It is with our full knowledge and consent that our
son/daughter____(name)____ may take part in the
intramural ___(name sport)_ program. I further
state that he/she is in proper physical condition
to compete in this event, and we waive and release
all rights and claims for injury my child may sustain while participating in this intramural program.


_____    _____
Parent's signature           Date

Forest Hills Public Schools
Grand Rapids, Michigan

Intramural Activity Calendar
Fall

## CENTRAL MIDDLE SCHOOL

| | |
|---|---|
| October | Cross country Fun Run |
| | Cross country Poker Run |
| | Cross country True Grit Run |
| | Basketball clinics |
| | Racquetball clinic and play |
| | |
| November | Cheerleading clinic and Cheer Fest |
| | Pick-up basketball league play |
| | Co-ed flag football league and tournament play |
| | Punt-Pass-Kick contest |
| | Chess club clinics and tournament play |

## NORTHERN HILLS MIDDLE SCHOOL

| | |
|---|---|
| September | Punt-Pass-Kick contest |
| | Co-ed soccer (all grades) |
| | |
| October | Co-ed Husky Run (all grades) |
| | 7th and 8th grade girls basketball |
| | Boys pass ball and table tennis |
| | 6th grade co-ed passball and table tennis |
| | |
| November | 7th and 8th grade boys basketball |
| | Girls cheerleading and gymnastics |
| | 6th grade basketball |

Forest Hills Public Schools
Grand Rapids, Michigan

Tentative Intramural Activity Calendar
Winter-Spring

## CENTRAL MIDDLE SCHOOL

| | |
|---|---|
| December | Basketball |
| | Table tennis |
| | Cheerleading |
| January | Wrestling |
| | Volleyball |
| February | Gymnastics |
| | Bowling |
| April-May | Softball |
| | Track |
| | Golf |

## NORTHERN HILLS MIDDLE SCHOOL

| | |
|---|---|
| December/ | Boys basketball |
| January | Gymnastics |
| | Cheerleading |
| February | Boys Wrestling |
| | Girls table tennis |
| March | Co-ed volleyball |
| April | Special events |
| | Kickball |
| | Dodgeball |
| | Horseshoes |
| | Husky Run |
| | Golf |
| May/June | Softball |
| | Track and Field |

Well-run intramural programs generally have a
person designated as director. The effective implementation of an intramural program is not an easy
task.

One can readily see from the following Okemos
Public Schools intramural director job description
how much planning, implementing and evaluating effort
must be provided.

Extra Duty Position Description:
Middle School Intramural Director
Okemos Public Schools

I.  General Description
    A.  The director is responsible for the
        planning, implementation and evaluation of
        a comprehensive intramural program.

    B.  The director will actively promote and
        solicit participation of both boys and
        girls.

II. Specific Responsibilities
    A.  Whereas the intramural program will vary
        from year to year, the director will be
        responsible for programming the following:

        basketball              swimming
        gymnastics              floor hockey
        cheerleading            golf
        table tennis            volleyball
        tennis                  softball

    B.  In addition to the above, the director is
        encouraged to offer additional activities
        which supplement and enrich the total
        program. These may include archery,
        bowling, canoe races, chess, cycling,
        fishing, ice and roller skating, skate-
        boarding, fly tying, cross country skiing,
        soccer, racquetball and rocketry.

C.  The aforementioned activities shall be
    programmed into a yearly calendar, devel-
    oped by the director prior to the fourth
    week of the new school year.

D.  All activities which employ a specific
    skill should be consistent and coordinated
    with the regular classroom instructional
    program whenever possible.

E.  The director shall be responsible for the
    development of a preliminary intramural
    budget, to be submitted to the middle
    school principal and I.M. coordinator
    by March of each year, for the following
    school year.  This budget shall be revised
    as needed, and submitted with the yearly
    calendar.

F.  The director will be responsible for the
    scheduling of all facilities and be
    encouraged to coordinate said with the
    appropriate school system staff to eliminate
    facility conflicts.  Also included in such
    scheduling would be the arrangement for
    transportation to and from a particular
    activity whenever necessary.

G.  The director is responsible for the pur-
    chase, care and storage of all intramural
    equipment.  Similar responsibility exists
    for the use of all school district equip-
    ment.

H.  The director is responsible for the dissem-
    ination of all information publicizing the
    program, to both students and middle school
    staff.

I.  The director is responsible for the evalua-
    tion of the entire program.  This would
    include the evaluation of personnel
    assigned to special activities, a regular
    needs assessment administered to students

to ascertain interests and the recommendation for program revisions and/or
changes.

J.   The director is responsible for the hiring
of specific activity staff.

K.   The director is responsible for keeping
accurate records which would reflect
attendance, correspondence pertaining
to intramurals, budget, and personnel
hired to conduct specific activities.

L.   The director will supervise specific
activities only when other responsibili-
ites have been fulfilled.

M.   The director will work to coordinate the
middle school intramural program with
those being offered at the elementary
and high school levels.

III.  Working Conditions
A    The basic intramural program, although
varying by season and activity, should
consist of a minumum of one hour of program time per day, four days per week,
for a total of thirty-two weeks.

B.   Whereas the director is not directly
responsible for all day to day activity
supervision, he should work towards a
combination of administrative and specific
activity time to keep within the defined
one-hundred twenty-eight hours of contact
time.

IV.  Qualifications
A.   The director shall preferably have the
qualifications of a teacher for the State
of Michigan.

B.   The director shall preferably be a member
of the middle school teaching staff.

C. The director preferably should have intramural experience and shall have the ability to organize, communicate and implement an intramural program.

V. Appointment
   A. The director shall be appointed by the middle school principal, after consultation with the Director of Personnel and Communication Education Coordinator.

   B. The director shall be appointed yearly, subject to yearly review. This appointment shall be made prior to the last day of the school year so as to facilitate advance program planning.

VI. Supervision and Evaluation
   A. The director shall be jointly supervised and evaluated by the middle school principal and the Community Education Coordinator.

   B. This supervision shall take place periodically throughout the scheduled intramural program.

   C. The director shall be evaluated in writing prior to the end of the school year.

One important factor in developing a successful intramural program is to build on student interests. At Kinawa Middle School, Okemos, Michigan, a survey is administered on an annual basis to determine student interests and attitudes. The results of the survey provide staff with meaningful information upon which to build their programs.

Okemos Public Schools
Okemos, Michigan

Kinawa Middle School

DIRECTIONS:  Place an (x) in the blanks which tell
about your interest and your problems about stay-
ing for intramurals.

1.  Grade <u>243</u> 6th grade <u>237</u> 7th grade <u>218</u> 8th grade

2.  Sex    <u>341</u> Boy      <u>357</u> Girl      TOTAL = 698

3.  Kinawa Intramurals 1979-80...Place an (x) in
    front of one of the three choices below:

    <u>381</u> I would usually come to intramurals if I
        liked the activity.

    <u>259</u> I would come to intramurals if it didn't
        interfere with other activities.

    <u>54</u> I am not interested in intramurals at all.
        (List reasons below.)

4.  What do you usually do after school between
    3 p.m. and supper?  (Check as many as usually
    happen during a normal week.)

    <u>466</u> Go home on the bus

    <u>355</u> Go to my friend's house

    <u>248</u> Music lessons or practice

    <u>56</u> Other school activities

    <u>46</u> Scouts

    <u>576</u> Do homework

    <u>453</u> Watch TV

    <u>192</u> Baby sit

    <u>116</u> Work at home or neighbors

 159 Have hobby

  28 Dance lessons or practice

 252 Ride bike, mini-bike, etc.

  40 Ride horses

  42 Play practice

 246 Read books for fun

  47 Church activities

 132 Other activities

  29 OAKS football

  96 OAKS soccer (boys/girls)

  58 OAKS basketball (boys/girls)

  42 OAKS softball

  62 Chieftain football

   9 Interscholastic volleyball

  36 Interscholastic basketball (girls/boys)

   8 Interscholastic wrestling

5. The following is a list of activities we may offer this year. Your interest will help determine which events are planned or cancelled. Put an (x) in the blank if you would participate. Put an (o) if you may participate or are not sure. Leave blank if you would NOT participate.

| 230 Anything Goes | 177 Ice skating |
|---|---|
| 139 Archery | 153 Kickball |
| 56 Backgammon | 53 Kite flying contest |
| 79 Badminton | |
| 132 Basketball (boys) | 90 Mile run |
| 95 Basketball (girls) | 144 Obstacle course |
| 143 B.B. gun shoot | 166 Open gym |

230  Bowling (one time or league)

211  Canoe Race

45  Checkers

143  Cheerleading

81  Chess

234  Cross country ski

98  Cycle riding club

225  Dance (disco)

138  Dance (50's & 60's)

145  Diving

112  Fishing Derby

42  Fly tying

115  Floor hockey

111  Frisbee (tournament)

115  Golf

94  Group gym activities (parachute, cageball, etc.)

201  Gymnastics

399  Horseback riding

50  Horseshoe pitching

60  Horse show & competition

97  Ice fishing

102  Activities with other schools

105  Boat safety

96  Snowmobile safety

322  Open swim

218  Pinball bombardment

65  Physical fitness

88  President's physical fitness award

100  Punt, Pass & Kick

150  Racquetball

346  Roller skating

114  Skateboard derby

104  Skeet shooting

90  Self defense

154  Soccer

85  Snow shoeing

163  Softball

114  Swimming tournament

168  Table tennis

150  Tennis

225  Tobogganing (sledding & inner tubing)

122  Track meet

104  Water polo

50  Wiffleball

122  Water volleyball

117  Volleyball

91  Father/student night

123  Mother/student night

72  Hunter safety

## Summary

The physical needs of middle school children are intense. They must be provided for in the development of instructional programs. In order to provide effectively for physical needs, teachers, administrators and Board of Education members must understand basic, human needs and be knowledgeable about how children learn. It then becomes clear that physical needs can and must be addressed 1) in the total school including every classroom and school activity; 2) through activities in a well-planned physical education program; 3) in an intramural program for all children.

Planning instructional activities which provide opportunities for transescents to meet physical needs is an exciting challenge. It is a challenge that must be met if children are to have every opportunity to realize all of their human potential.

## References

Frank S. Blom, Addie Kinsinger, Glen K. Gerard,
    "A Middle School Belief System," MAMSE, 1974

Mary F. Compton, "After the Middle School...?",
    Michigan Journal of Secondary Education, Summer
    1971

Wayne E. Donnehl and Jack E. Razor, "The Values of
    Athletics-A Critical Inquiry," The Bulletin
    of the National Association of Secondary
    School Principals, September 1971, pp. 59-65

Leonard Ernst, "Revolution in Sports," The Education
    Digest, November 1973, p. 50.

Glen K. Gerard, Robert R. Schwenter, Fred Watters,
    "Focus on Physical Education, Intramurals and
    Interscholastics," MAMSE, 1978

Nicholas P. Georgiady, "The Emergence of the Middle
    School," Michigan Journal of Secondary Education,
    Summer 1971, p. 20

D.L. Martin, "Competitive Sports - Are They Wasting
    Dollars and Ruining Youngsters Too?", American
    School Board Journal, 159:16-20, August 1972

Michigan Department of Education, "Guidelines for
    Physical Education in Michigan Schools,"
    Lansing, MI, 1976

B.C. Ogilvie, "Personality Traits of Competitors and
    Coaches," Modern Medicine, Medical Aspects of
    the Olympic Games.  July 26, 1972, pp. 61-68

1952 Report of the Joint Committee of Representatives
    from the National Education Association, the
    National Council of State Consultants in Elemen-
    tary Education, the N.E.A. Department of Elemen-
    tary Principals, the Society of State Directors
    of Health, Physical Education and Recreation,

and the American Association of Health, Physical Education and Recreation

Louis G. Romano and Nicholas Timmer, "Middle School Athletics: Intramurals or Interscholastics?", Middle School Journal, May 1978.

Lauretta Woodson, "Student Activities Programs," chapter 14, The Intermediate Schools, Leslie Kindred, editor, Englewood Cliffs, NJ: Prentice-Hall, 1968, p. 321

## SOCIAL EXPERIENCES

Junior high and middle school students are perhaps the most interesting of all children to teach.
It is during these years that many dramatic and
exciting changes can be seen in these young people.
Physically they are about to enter puberty; their
bodies are changing reflecting the play activities
of childhood to the reproductive capabilities of
adulthood.  Psychologically they are changing as
they begin to deal with abstract concepts and apply
principles of inductive reasoning to complex problems.  Emotionally they are struggling with the
frustrations of escaping from adult domination and
experiencing the anxieties of accepting the responsibilities that go with independence.  The middle
school teacher has the opportunity to observe these
students as they make the transition from child to
adult.

The middle school child,  or transescent, is
caught between two worlds.  He is not a child,
he is not an adult.  He is somewhere in between,
and he fluctuates between the extremes.  At times
he is expected to behave in a grown-up manner making
responsible decisions, and at other times he is
expected to be submissive and willing to accept the
directions of his elders.  Confusion and frustration
can result when the transescent's perceptions of
appropriate responses conflict with the behavioral
expectations of his parents or teachers.  The
twelve year old who is expected to clean his room
without adult prodding, but yet, who is told he must
go to bed at 9:00 p.m. with no argument has
experienced this frustration.

As the physical, psychological, and emotional
needs of the transescent change, so do his social
relationships.  The social development of students
has long been recognized as an important aspect of
the school program.  Social development refers to
the ways an individual integrates himself into
society.  While this integration is a lifelong

process, certain crucial developments occur during
the transescent years which can influence how
successful social relationships will be in later
stages of development.  Some aspects of social
development include identification with appropriate
sex roles, clarification of values and attitudes,
initiation of responsible social behavior, the
attainment of social acceptance, and learning how
to achieve success in terms of one's desires and
goals.

## The Themes of Change

The program of social experiences which the
middle school provides must recognize the many
changes which are occurring within the transescent.  Four themes of change emerge as students
enter transescence.  Emerging from the problems
and stresses of transescence are (1) the theme of
self-acceptance, (2) the theme of sex role relationships, (3) the theme of independence, and
(4) the theme of broader horizons.  These themes
can be used to create a rationale for the development of social activities which are designed for
middle school children.  By providing activities
based on these four themes of change, the school
can help the transescent to engage in social
experiences which are appropriate for his unique
social needs and which will also lay the foundation
for successful social development in subsequent
stages of growth.

## The Theme of Self Acceptance

As students enter transescence, a number of
physiological changes begin to take place.  The
onset of puberty brings visual physical changes
which signal the end of childhood.  Bones and
muscles that used to work perfectly have begun to
grow, and the once coordinated child becomes a
clumsy, awkward transescent.  What was considered
to be a cute child turns into a creature who is half

child-half adult, subject to acne, baby fat in
the "wrong" places, and hormonal imbalances which
cause a rash of emotional outbursts. The menstrual
flow of girls and the appearance of facial and body
hair on boys are other signs that a new and different body is emerging.

These physical changes bring about a need within
the transescent to redefine his attitudes about himself. As the transescent struggles to gain mastery
of his changing body, he may begin to lose confidence in himself and his physical abilities. Unfortunately for him these changes occur with such
irregularity among his peers that comparisons give
him little concept of what is normal. In addition,
this lack of knowing what is considered to be normal
development can cause the transescent to experience a great deal of concern and anxiety in regard
to his own growth.

Physical growth changes do have an influence on
self-attitudes. For example, in his interviews
with transescent girls, Kagan found that the onset
of the menarche was regarded as a clear-cut line
that marked the end of childhood and the activities
associated with children.[1] Self-acceptance is at
the center of these changes in self-attitude. A
new and changing physical image, the regaining of
physical agility, and the recognition that adulthood with all of its responsibilities is impending
must be integrated and accepted by the transescent
as he perceives himself.

The theme of self-acceptance represents one of
the problem areas confronted by the transescent.
"Success" is the key word for social activities
that help the student to come to terms with his
changing body and which help him to accept a new

---

[1] Jerome Kagan, "A Conception of Early Adoles-
cence," in Twelve to Sixteen: Early Adolescence,
Jerome Kagan and Robert Coles (eds.), (New York:
W. W. Norton and Company, 1972).

concept of himself. Teachers must encourage social
experiences that provide opportunities for personal
success and promote self-confidence. For example,
if social recognition in school is based primarily
on athletic prowess, the slow developer who
already has questions of self-doubt and inadequacy
may never gain a feeling of confidence and self-
acceptance. But if teachers believe there should
be many ways to gain social recognition, they can
provide a variety of activities that call for
differing kinds of human strength.

## The Theme of Sex Role Relationships

The physical changes occurring within the
transescent's body have implications for changes
in his social relationships. The impending
capacities for reproduction call for certain
expected social behaviors. Society expects boys
to learn how to fulfill masculine roles and
girls to fulfill feminine roles. In addition,
there are expected courting behaviors that exist
between the sexes. During the transescent years,
boys and girls begin to learn the social behaviors
which are associated with each sex.

In order to learn these social behaviors, close
peer group relationships form. One of the functions
of the peer group is to help the transescent define
his appropriate sex role. Learning to conceptualize, react, and behave like a member of one's own
sex is very important to the development of the
individual's self-concept.[2] As the transescent
learns the appropriate behaviors for his own sex,
he also learns how to react and respond to the
opposite sex.

Two very important concerns need to be

---

[2] William M. Alexander and Paul S. George, The
Exemplary Middle School, (New York: Holt, Rinehart,
Winston, 1981).

considered as teachers develop social experiences which help the student define his sex role. The first of these concerns has been voiced by those who feel that many of the traditional behaviors society expects should not be in the exclusive domain of a particular sex group.[3] For example, there is increasing pressure for boys to learn to cook, to care for babies, and to assume other homemaking responsibilities. Girls are repairing automobiles, joining baseball teams, and learning how to participate more in the business world. The second concern deals with the tensions which are created when the middle school promotes social activities that encourage courting behaviors.

The school can provide a social context which allows boys and girls to understand that the concepts of masculinity and feminity refer more to biological rather than cultural differences. Certain cultural sex role distinctions between men and women change with time and circumstances. Thus women are driving trucks; men are doing the family shopping; and raising children is becoming more of a cooperative effort. Rather than teaching students to assume assigned sex roles, the school can help students study the nature of society today and the wide range of individual roles found in that society.

The transescent should be given opportunities to establish relationships with the opposite sex without the pressures of having to fulfill future sex roles. That is, at the age of eleven or twelve there should not be worries about dating, who is going

---

[3]Excellent discussions of the traditional sex role expectations held by society can be found in Michele Hoffnung Garskof (ed.), Roles Women Play: Readings Toward Women's Liberation (Belmont, California: Brooks/Cole Publishing Company, 1971); and in Cynthia Fuchs Epstein and William J. Goode (eds.), The Other Half: Roads to Women's Equality (Englewood Cliffs, New Jersey: Prentice-Hall, Inc., 1971).

steady with whom, or how to display sexual prowess.  Transescence is a good time for boys and
girls to learn to regard one another as persons
rather than as sexual stereotypes.  In the middle
school there needs to be an emphasis on social
activities that orient the goals of boys and girls
toward the accomplishment of common purposes.  Activities that call for students to participate in
the so-called "battle-of-the-sexes" should be
discouraged.

The theme of sex role relationships presents
several implications for the development of social
experiences in the school.  Projects and activities
that allow for the cooperative contributions of all
students can illustrate that both boys and girls
have much to offer.  Or, competitive events can be
very healthy so long as the competitors are evenly
matched.  Body size and physical development should
be given more consideration than age and sex when
matching competitors.  "Mixer" type activities can
introduce boys and girls to more adultlike social
roles without the pressures of one-to-one relationships.  A social program that provides cooperative
type activities, competitive events based on fair
contestant matching, and social events that promote
informal pairings can help students develop positive
sex role relationships.

## The Theme of Independence

The transescent's need for independence should
be considered in planning the social activities
of the middle school.  Many parents and teachers
have had anxious firsthand experience with the
transescent's often truculent demands for more freedom.  He wants to stay out later at night, he wants
greater financial resources, and he wants to make
more decisions regarding the development of his
own life style.  A challenge to any of these demands
brings that well known refrain, "But everyone does
it."

The transescent's striving for independence is a
source of frustration for both youngsters and adults.
In one sense the transescent wants to be dependent,
and in another he needs independence. Emotionally
he wants to be loved, he wants to be accepted, and
he wants to feel that he belongs. But he also wants
the adults who fulfill these emotional needs to
grant him social independence. Conflicting signals
occur when adults expect responsible social behavior
from the maturing transescent but treat him as a
child in other respects. In school, these conflicting signals are seen when teachers expect students
to work at their studies independently and with
inner direction, but yet demand that students ask
for permission to use the restrooms.

In addition to the dependence-independence
dilemma is the problem of helping the transescent
to understand that as he gains social independence
he must assume responsibility for his own behavior.
No longer can he claim the immaturity of childhood
as the reason for irresponsible acts. The transescent needs to be given opportunities to make decisions concerning what is regarded as acceptable and
unacceptable social behavior. The manner in which
he fulfills his desires and achieves his goals
must be in accordance with society's expectations
for responsible behavior.

A planned program of social experiences can help
students overcome many of the problems associated
with independence. As the transescent gains independence, he must make more choices regarding his
own behavior. Given opportunities to select from
among alternatives and to realize the consequences
of his choices, the transescent can begin to achieve
independence. Some of the ways to help students
with the problems of independence are to involve
students in the planning of activities, provide a
wide range of activities from which students can
choose, have students collect and manage money
related to their clubs or projects, and allow students to accept the responsibility for the success
of failure of their projects.

## The Theme of Broader Horizons

In addition to the physical and emotional changes occurring in middle school students, the school's program of social activities must also acknowledge some very important intellectual developments among transescents. For example, the transescent is capable of understanding more abstract concepts--abstract concepts which enable him to make generalizations concerning his place in the universe. Middle school students exhibit an interest in the problems of ecology, they question the workings of government, and they begin to show a consciousness of world problems. The transescent begins to understand that the world is larger than his immediate surroundings.

As the transescent's intellectual curiosity broadens, so do his social relationships. In his expanding explorations of the world, the transescent seeks out others with interests similar to his own. He will join groups that reflect his intellectual interests. Involvement in community service projects, student government, and clubs that promote specialized skills such as writing or photography play an important role in the student's social activities.

The transescent's widening intellectual interests present two suggestions for the social experiences offered by the school. First, the activities must have gradated structures which allow the student to explore specific areas of interest with a sense of direction. With a gradational structure to follow, the student can progress from simple to complex concepts. Second, the program of social experiences must be broad and it must offer much variety. To nurture his growing interest in the world, the transescent must be given opportunities to sample from many areas which will help to stimulate his intellectual curiosities.

Characteristics of The Social Experiences
for Middle School Students

The themes of change emerge from the unique
growth patterns of transescents. The characteristics
of the social activities appropriate for transescents are an outgrowth of the themes of change. By
providing social experiences with the following
characteristics, the school can develop a social
program which is unique for middle school students
rather than adopting modified versions of activities
that are appropriate for students in other developmental stages of growth.

1. Success oriented: With the pressures of
adjusting to physical changes, transescents do not
need a social system based solely upon athletic
prowess. They should be given opportunities to
receive social recognition for skill development
in many areas. Activities which allow the student
to gain social status and which help to enhance his
self-concept are very necessary. Recognition and
success can be achieved when students can exhibit
collections or show expertise in a particular hobby
area, contribute to the school newspapte, have art
work displayed in prominent places in the school,
participate in dramatic presentations, organize a
musical group, or join the debate society.

2. Group structured: Activities in which students can socialize without the pressures of pairing can help students achieve some social poise
with the opposite sex. Mixer activities where students participate together can help them to establish many types of relationships. A gradual introduction to dating can be achieved by providing
opportunities for boys and girls to socialize
together in group activities. Group activities
sucy as bowling, ice or roller skating, hiking,
gymnastics, folk dancing, chorus, and band can provide a wholesome social context for students.

3. Fair competition: Competitive events among
middle school students can sharpen skills, build

self-confidence, develop school morale, and provide
entertainment for spectators. However, care must
be taken to insure that contestants are evenly
matched. Pitting strong against weak, skilled
against clumsy, or intellectual against ignorant
for the sake of "separating the sheep from the
goats"is detrimental to developing youngsters.
Intramural sports, homeroom against homeroom service
projects, talent shows, arts and crafts fairs, and
noncontact sports can provide healthy and positive
competitive activities where boys and girls can
socialize.

   4. Goal directed: Social activities which are
directed toward the accomplishment of a goal will
help boys and girls learn how to work together to
achieve a common purpose. Students should be
given the opportunity to work at a common purpose
Students should be given the opportunity to work at
a common interest without pressures of developing
boy-girl relationships. Students who are socially
ready to begin predating activities may do so. However, the primary emphasis is placed on the achievement of the common goal. Sexual pairings should
be incidental to the attainment of the goal. Goal
directed social activities would include developing
ecology projects; preparing testimonial programs;
tutoring; presenting a consumer, job, clothing,
arts and crafts, or science fair; working with
school beautification projects; participating in
fund-raising projects; preparing for an inter-school
band, dramatic, or art contest; and organizing a
talent show.

   5. Provides for decision making and responsibility: Transescents need to learn how to make sound
decisions and assume the responsibility for their
behavior if they are to achieve independence.
Social responsibility comes when students establish
relationships with others based on fairness and with
a lack of prejudice. Examples of activities which
help students make decisions and assume responsibility are student council; fund raising projects that
hold students responsible for handling money; junior

achievement; the business aspects of clubs and
organizations; library, office, and audio-visual
helpers; associations for future teachers, farmers,
and homemakers; and career exploration clubs.

6. Organized structure: The transescent's
social activities should have an organized structure
to accommodate his developing intellectual abilities.
Structure provides a variety of entry points for students at different levels of intellectual development. Opportunities to experiment, develop problem
solving skills, and to learn new things in interest
areas can be accomplished by joining specialized
clubs and organizations. The transescent can progress from simple to complex or from beginner to
expert with others who have common interests and
who also have similar levels of understanding.
Social activities in the school which provide
structured intellectual experiences are clubs for
woodworking, debate, photography, creative writing,
science, ham radio, journalism, electronics,
geology, automotives, and art and music appreciation.

7. Wide variety: Social experiences ought to
reflect the transescent's growing intellectual
curiosities. By providing a wide variety of activities, the transescent can explore and enlarge his
horizons. As he turns his attention outward, the
transescent develops an interest in the world at
large. Social activities which can capitalize on
this intellectual curiosity would include clubs for
pen pals, service, school newspaper, stamp and coin
collecting, environmental conservation, debate,
travel, current events, world affairs, and scouts.

### Two Illustrative Programs

To illustrate how these concepts can be incorporated into a school's social offerings, two actual
school programs are briefly described below. The
faculties of these two schools worked many months to
present activities which would help their students
establish strong and healthy social relationships.

The most important part about these descriptions
lies in the fact that both of these faculties made
a concerted effort to develop unique social experiences for their students rather than to simpy
accept the traditional approach of imitating the
high school program.

The Andrew Jackson Junior High School in
Charleston, West Virginia is not a middle school
in the strictest sense, however, Andrew Jackson
does embrace the middle school concept. Much of the
school program is designed to provide a context for
the social development of its students. In a series
of planned intervals, students are given "free"
time to study, work on projects, tutor one another,
or to socialize. During these free periods small
groups of boys and girls work together at school
related tasks, discuss class assignments, and read
without peer group pressures to establish sexual
relationships. Associations and friendships form
because of common interests and goals rather than
the need to establish traditional masculine or feminine roles.

A commons area which doubles as a cafeteria,
provides a place for students to socialize, play
games, watch television, and just "horse around."
Since the commons is geographically removed from the
classroom area, the noise students make does not
disturb the rest of the school. Again, because only
small groups are free at the same time and because
of the flexibility of the area large segregated
groups of boys and girls are not given much of a
chance to form. The commons area with its television, juke box, games, and movable furniture provides a place for students to sharpen their social
skills.

Physical education classes at Jackson are
coeducational. Students are divided into various
groups by size, physical agility, and skill in
particular physical tasks. Students, regardless of
age or sex, learn to perform handstands, tumbling
moves, trampoline exercises, calisthenics, or play

team sports with others who are at a comparable
stage of development. Instructors, with the help
of student teachers, are able to provide a number
of physical activities at beginner, intermediate,
and advanced levels. Once the instructors show the
students in each group how to perform a particular
skill, the group goes to another area in the gymnasium to practice sessions without any apparent need
for boys to prove they are stronger than girls, or
for girls to allow the boys to out perform them.

Andrew Jackson actively uses the school curriculum to create a social context for students. With
flexible student schedules, the provision of a
social environment, and an emphasis on cooperative
goal achievement the faculty provides students with
many opportunities to work and play together.

Enslow Junior High School in Huntington, West
Virginia has been working toward a gradual adoption
of the middle school concept. Included in the first
phase of Enslow's conversion was the development of
a program of social experiences appropriate for
middle school students. After two years of inservice work, the Enslow faculty decided to provide
social activities in three ways.

The first way was to build an activity period
into the school schedule. Using a mini-course format, students are given the opportunity to pursue
new areas of interest every six weeks. A second
program of social experiences has been interwoven
into the school curriculum. This program presents
students with problem solving activities covering
such areas as decision making, career education,
self-awareness, and responsible social behavior.
The third set of activities follows the more
traditional cocurricular program of school dances
and athletic events.

The activity period, called the "Enslow House
Plan," has been included in the school schedule to
insure that all students have the opportunity to
participate. The emphasis of this program is to

provide interesting activities designed for middle
school students.  Every six weeks the faculty gives
students a list of fifty mini-course topics and the
students vote for the courses which interest them
most.  A total of fifteen different courses are
offered each six week period.  The list at the end
of this chapter includes most of the course offerings for a typical six week period.

The second group of social activities at Enslow
is a most imaginative program.  Commercially
prepared and entitled Bread and Butterflies, it has
been integrated into the school curriculum.  Intended as an approach to the teaching of career education to nine to twelve year olds, the program provides a number of activities which are used to
develop a wide range of social skills.

Activities for the following fifteen topics are
presented to students on both beginning and advanced
levels.[4]

1. Self Independence and    9. Life Styles
   the Economic System      10. Shaping One's
2. Why People Work              Destiny
3. Self-Clarification       11. People at Work
4. Decision-Making          12. Independency of
5. Relationship—School,         Workers
   Work, and Society        13. Human Dignity
6. The Responsible Self     14. Power and
7. Interpersonal Skills         Influence
8. What is Success?         15. Freedom to Hope,
                                to Choose, and to
                                Change.

Each topic is presented by educational television.  Before each program is aired, teachers are
·given ideas for readiness activities to prepare
students for the television lesson.  In addition,

---

[4]Debra Sharpe (ed.), Bread and Butterflies:  A
Curriculum Guide in Career Education (Bloomington,
Indiana:  Agency for Instructional Television, 1974),
p. 5.

there are long and short term activities which are
used to follow-up the main presentation.

The section on "Interpersonal Skills"[5] can
be used to illustrate how the program works. The
lesson has as its goal, "To help students identify
and begin to develop the social skills that form
the basis for present and future social interaction,
work satisfaction, self-respect, and achievement."
The readiness program has students clarify how they
feel when their friends treat them in different
ways. Afterward, by television, students are shown
a program in which two friends have a disagreement
and then reestablish their friendship. Students are
then given a series of questions which help them to
analyze the problem situation they have just seen on
television. Short term activities include a class
discussion of some case studies and a resource person who is professionally involved with helping
people who have problems with interpersonal relationships. A suggestion for how to develop a class
project and role playing situations is offered for
long term activities. Teachers are given further
aids for how to incorporate activities for the
development of interpersonal skills in mathematics
and science, language arts, music, social studies,
and physical education.

The Enslow program presents a more directive
approach to social development than does Andrew
Jackson. However, the descriptions offered here
are extrapolated from more complex total programs
at both schools. The common element between both
these programs is a belief that the youngsters for
whom these activities have been designated are
unique and that they deserve to have experiences
tailored to their particular needs.

---

[5]Ibid., pp. 58-64.

## Social Activities For The Middle School

The list of suggested activities at the end of this section can be used to develop social experiences for middle school students.[6] However, care must be taken to insure that the activities of the school are appropriate for transescents. The four themes of change discussed earlier in this chapter reflect the special problems of children between the ages of eleven and fifteen. Therefore, the characteristics of the social experiences for middle school children are different from those of other developmental groups.

All too often the unique needs of transescents are ignored in the rush to accelerate developmental growth.[7] There is more than a tendency to value social precociousness as a sign of advanced human development. Unfortunately, transescence is often regarded simply as an early stage of adolescence and not as an important and meaningful time in itself. Thus, the social program of the middle school often consists of watered-down versions of high school activities. The middle school student deserves to

---

[6] The author is indebted to the Robert Frost Middle School, Oak Park, Michigan, Andrew Jackson Junior High School, Charleston, West Virginia, and to Enslow Junior High School, Huntington, West Virginia for many of the suggested activities listed in this chapter.

[7] The dangers of accelerating developmental growth when students are not ready have been discussed by Ira Gordon, Human Development: From Birth Through Adolescence (New York: Harper and Row, Publishers, 1962), pp. 297-301; and Margaret Mead "Are We Squeezing Out Adolescence?" in The Middle School: Selected Readings on an Emerging School Program, Louis Romano et al., (eds.), (Chicago: Nelson-Hall Company, 1973), pp. 162-166.

have social experiences which have been designated
to accommodate his own needs and not those of other
age groups.

What is perhaps most frustrating in the construction of a social program for middle school students
is how to provide for the wide variations in
transescent interests, capabilities, and development.
In the middle school there will be boys with child-
like features, body and voice, and other boys, not
so much older, who are tall, well developed, and
ready to shave. Among the girls there will be just
as wide variances. Even wider variations can be
found when transescent boys are compared with girls.
Girls will tend to be more advanced than boys, particularly in terms of social development.

The social activities of the school must recognize the many differences in the developmental rates
of transescents. For example, some girls may be
ready to date when they are in middle school while
other girls are still playing with dolls. There
will always be boys playing cowboys and indians and
other boys who would rather organize an electronics
club. The school needs to have a broad program of
social experiences with many levels to accommodate
the many developmental differences among transescents.

Therefore, while the following list gives many
examples of appropriate middle school activities,
it is still necessary for the faculty to mold them
into experiences for middle school students. Understanding the themes of transescent changes, building
in the seven characteristics derived from them the
themes of change, and allowing for variations in
developmental growth are all a part of adjusting
these activities to transescent needs. Also, these
activities are for all students. There is no
need to restrict boys or girls from any of these
activities.

In many cases it is arbitrary to categorize
these activities as curricular or cocurricular. It

is hoped that the activities themselves will suggest
many wayt the school faculty can develop social
experiences regardless of how they are classified.


## Curricular Activities

| | |
|---|---|
| Career planning | Math puzzles |
| Consumer education | Mechanics |
| Contemporary problems | Modern music lyrics |
| Cooking | Money management |
| Creative writing | Nutrition |
| Current events | Panel discussion |
| Debate | Personal grooming |
| Electronics | Physical conditioning |
| Environmental problems | Public speaking |
| Gymnastics | Remedial or speed reading |
| Home management | Weight watching |
| Home repair | Woodworking |
| Interior decoration | World affairs |
| Journalism | |

Group and individual research or exhibition
projects in:

| | |
|---|---|
| Art | Science |
| English | Social Studies |


## Cocurricular Activities and
## Mini-Course Topics

| | |
|---|---|
| Art appreciation | Carving (wood, soap, corn |
| Arts and crafts | husks, apples) |
| Astronomy club | Ceramics |
| Automobiles | Chess club |
| Balsa Model | Chorus |
| Band | Cinema |
| Bible club | Coin and stamp collecting |
| Bicycle repair | Conditioning |
| Biology club | Conservation club |
| Book club | Copper enameling |
| Camping | Creative writing |
| Candle making | Crewel design |

Carving (wood, soap,
  corn husks, apples)
Ceramics
Chess club
Chorus
Cinema
Coin and stamp
  collecting
Conditioning
Conservation club
Copper enameling
Creative writing
Crewel design
Crocheting
Dancing, folk, modern
Decoupage
Dramatics club
Drawing
  Cartoon
  Commercial
  Graphic arts
  Mechanical
  Poster
Ecology
Electricity
Embroidery
Family history
Fashion design
Flying
Foreign language clubs
  French
  German
  Latin
  Spanish
  Russian
Games
Gardening
Geology
Guitar
Handicrafts
Hiking
Indian lore and arrow-
  heads
Jewelry making

Junior achievement
Knitting
Literary magazine
Macrame
Magic club
Math club
Model building
Motors
Music appreciation
Musical groups
Mystery club
Newspaper
Officiating sports events
Outdoor education
Pen pal club
Pet care
Photography club
Poetry club
Pottery making
Predicting weather
Puppet theatre
Puzzles
Radio club (ham)
Radio broadcasting
Reading club
Rocketry club
Rock collecting
Rock polishing
Rug hooking
Science club
Science fiction
Scouts
Sculpturing
Service clubs
  Audio-visual
  Library
  Messengers
  Office
  Ushers
Shop
Soap box derby
Spectator sports
Sports
  Archery

Baseball
Basketball
Bowling
Fishing (fly casting)
Golf
Gymnastics
Ice skating
Kickball
Roller skating
Self-defense
Skiing
Table tennis
Tennis
Touch football
Track

Tumbling
Volleyball
String art
Student council
Study habits
Talent show
Terrariums
Travel club
Tropical fish
Tutoring
Weight watching
Winter camping
Woodcrafts
Woodworking

Guidance Services and the Security Factor

To view guidance in today's middle school is to look at the middle school children. What are their unique characteristics? What are their needs? What kinds of programs should be planned to satisfy their developmental learning tasks? How should educational experiences be implemented to maximize cognitive, affective, and psychomotor skills growth? Finally, from what vantage point can accomplishment be best determined? Many of these concerns for the success of middle school youngsters can be effectively dealt with by those who are most responsible for the youngsters' guidance.

As it is applied to middle school aged children, it should be pointed out that guidance is not synonymous with counseling. Counseling is a component of guidance in much the same way that teaching is related to instruction. As with instruction, guidance should be viewed as an integral part of the middle school youngsters' total learning experiences. Thus, guidance becomes significant as it exists for the middle school student, not that the middle school exists for the sake of a guidance program.

In the middle school, the child is the central focus, with educational components such as guidance being brought to bear as needed upon the youngsters' development. This also serves to broaden the experiential environment of the youngster. In the case of "guidance," these resources are as many and varied as the encompassing life-space of the individual child. Therefore, it becomes a goal of the middle school to help the child through the use of all of the components of guidance.

KEY COMPONENTS

The key guidance components for the middle school youngster are the parents, the school administrator, the teachers, and the school counselor. While it would be expected that any one of these could exert greater influence than another, it is nonetheless important to recognize that in varying degrees each

makes a valuable contribution to guidance. For most
children, the parents provide nearly all of the assimilated guidance; yet, for some youngsters the parents
may actually be contributing very little in this
regard, leaving the school counselor, or other school
personnel, to become the "significant other" in
formulating guidance. Likely, however, the typical
middle school child receives guidance from all four
listed above, usually in proportion to the amount of
interaction the child has with each.

## Parents

Generally, those adults who have the greatest
impact upon the development of children are their
parents. Parents provide a home environment that in
many ways precludes all other efforts to influence
the youngster through non-parental guidance measures.
From the very beginning, parents are the child's
"first teachers," with this tremendous impact continuing throughout the youngster's lifetime. Their
guidance actions, deliberate or unintentional, vastly
shape the direction of attitude and self-concept.

To insure that parents are making effective
contributions to guidance for the middle school
children, these factors need to be examined:

1.  Are the parents providing a home environment
    that will enable the child to fit into
    society? It is most imperative that parents
    understand the extent of their influence upon
    their children. When children perceive
    divisiveness in the home, this may cause con-
    flict in their understanding of the world
    surrounding them. It remains for the middle
    school to encourage parents to use care when
    discussing issues wherein they disagree,
    particularly on matters such as the school.
    All children desperately need consistency,
    particularly in establishing a positive value
    system. If a child arrives at school with a
    confused or negative self-concept, it behooves
    the middle school to work with both the young-
    ster as well as his parents to develop more
    appropriate modes of coping.

2. As guidance facilitators, many parents need to receive specific training at parenting. Consequently, the middle school should establish a program for parent education. Here, parents can be given a better understanding of their important roles such as establishing a home environment conducive to study, along with help in dealing with the difficulties of raising children. Parents should not be asked to meet their responsibilities alone; the middle school should actively seek a partner relationship with parents through the availability of guidance services.

3. Every middle school should make its guidance services and expertise known to the home. Whereas there may be an excellent program in the school, its usefulness is restricted when the parents are unaware of its existence. Parents need to be informed about their roles in guidance so that an effective school-home relationship can be formed. When the school and the home work together, the child will be the beneficiary.

4. All members of the middle school staff should make a very deliberate effort to work with parents. Not only is this a prerequisite in keeping the home informed, it is also most necessary in maintaining a dialog between these two guidance entities. Here, communication will help dispel any criticisms between parents and school personnel as perceived or misperceived by the adolescent, along with building or reinforcing a bond of harmony. The emerging adolescent needs to feel that both the parents and the school are working together to provide constructive assistance.

5. Parents should feel favorably inclined toward their youngsters' utilization of the guidance services within the middle school. All too frequently parents arbitrarily view with sus-

picion any guidance programs available to
serve students, especially their own.  To
insure parents' support for the schools'
guidance efforts, they should be encouraged
to visit the school to openly discuss any
fears or concerns they may have about the
guidance process. Parental emotional irration-
ality is no excuse for child    underdevelop-
ment.

6.  In addition to allaying parents' real or
    imagined fears about the school's guidance
    program, visitations to the school by
    parents can also make a positive contribution
    to the overall progress of their children in
    school.  Professional staff can vastly in-
    crease their effectiveness in providing
    education to children when parents are
    encouraged to share valuable information with
    them about their children.  Even though school
    personnel generally have a good understanding
    of the children, parental input greatly aug-
    ments this knowledge for the benefit of the
    youngsters.

7.  Finally, parents need to be strongly aware
    that they can provide invaluable guidance for
    their children by setting appropriate stan-
    dards of expectation.  Unlike "making demands,"
    setting appropriate standards offers worth-
    while motivational targets that are achievable.
    Indeed, most children want to please their
    parents whether it be in academic accomplish-
    ment, discipline, or in becoming    integral
    members of society.

## School Administrator

In today's educational structure, the responsibilities of the school administrator extend far beyond their
previous stereotyped roles as school managers.  Current
administrative job descriptions and public expectations,
both written and unwritten, call for school administra-

tors to serve primarily as educational leaders.  In
this sense, leadership clearly includes accountability
for the entire educational operation of the school,
and as in the case of guidance, establishing the best
possible middle school program.  Moreover, as the
school would expand its guidance operation, administrative leadership should be at the forefront in the
role of change agent.  In today's middle school it is
not sufficient for the administrator to merely provide
information regarding the availability of services--
the current thrust of this leadership position becomes
one of inspiring and insuring the planning, implementing, coordinating, evaluating, and revising for
utilizing   the various guidance components:  parents,
school administrator, teachers, and counselors.

To a large extent, then, the middle school guidance
program will succeed or fail on the actions or inac-
tions of the school administrator.  The achievement of
those administrative tasks that are most essential for
success are included in the following:

1.  It is vital for the school administrator to be
    knowledgeable in the field of guidance.  In
    addition, this knowledge must be transformable
    to the promotion of a comprehensive middle
    school guidance program.  The administrator's
    applied knowledge of guidance, then, becomes
    one of the pivots upon which this whole effort
    hinges.  His knowledge of guidance and utili-
    zation to support such a program will most
    certainly insure its success, whereas a lack
    thereof will likely cause its ultimate doom.

2.  While others look to the administrator for
    support and direction in the development of a
    quality guidance program for the middle school,
    so, too, must the administrator look to those
    outside of his office for meaningful contribu-
    tions toward this effort.  The most effective
    educational programs--including middle school
    guidance programs--are those with input by all

those who have a stake in its outcome.  Even
the administrator who is quite knowledgeable
in the field of guidance would be wise to seek
the active involvement of parents, teachers,
students, and outside experts in developing
guidance for the middle school.  Such a flow
of information and exchange of ideas can only
serve to enhance the guidance program's
chances of success.

3.  In seeking to include others in developing an
exemplary guidance program, the school administrator must make it clear that this process
will be on a democratic, interactive basis.
Participants must be made to feel that their
contributions will be seriously considered in
building a representative-based guidance program, not just to make insignificant revisions
in the "administrator's brain child."  Since
the eventual guidance program will be a "tool"
for everyone affiliated with the school, it is
important that these individuals have an
opportunity to make meaningful contributions
to the program consistent with their collective
knowledge, beliefs, and attitudes.

4.  In any organization, some professional cohe-
siveness is necessary if constructive compromise and agreement are to be effectual in
leading to progress.  In the case of the
middle school, it would certainly be important
that the school administrator advocate a
penchant toward the "middle school concept" as
a commonality in recruiting all staff.  In its
later application to the development of a
middle school guidance program, professional
discussions would not have to deal with "if"
or "why" a program should exist; rather, "how"
or "what" should be its prevailing distin-
guishers for excellence.

5. Even a staff that is most congenial in its professional stance toward guidance may be uninformed or misinformed regarding its application. Once the guidance program's direction and focus have been determined, the school administrator should immediately take steps to establish a training function to enable staff to fully utilize this valuable educational component. Such inservice would certainly vary with the needs and personalities of the staff; however, it is suggested that sequentially phased in-service be provided to permit greater or lesser training for staff, depending upon their existing knowledge of middle school guidance and/or anticipated needs in this area.

6. Once staff training has been completed, the school administrator should encourage the full utilization of the guidance program: student schedules should provide maximum accessibility to guidance services; counselor loads should be reasonable and balanced; curricular and extra-curricular student activities need to provide for guidance opportunities; individual and group developmental counseling practices should be promoted; study skills and courses of study information—particularly as they affect life and career education—need to be provided; and suggestions toward improving the overall middle school guidance program should be encouraged. Above all, the administrator must set the tone toward maintaining growth in sound guidance efforts.

7. Finally, the school administrator should seek to broaden internal and external acceptance of the middle school's guidance program. One highly favorable avenue toward gaining support is through continuous, positive publicity. Here, the leadership role of the administrator can be used to overcome any "pockets of

resistance" to the school's guidance program,
as well as to maintain or increase support for
its continued development.  Such communication
may take many forms:  local radio, television,
and newspapers may be very willing to provide
"school news" to the citizenry.  Other proven
means for "spreading the word" are newsletters,
forums, conferences, coffees, and interviews
with influential persons.  Equally as important as the communication media, is the consistency and continuity of this "public
relations" effort.  Like all matters of
interest to the school, the guidance program
must be constantly promoted as a viable part
of the process of education if public support
is to remain in force.

## Teachers

In the case of the development of a middle school
guidance program, when the administrator and teachers
view their respective roles as conjunctive, a professional working partnership is more likely to be
formed.  Such a joining together enables both components (administrator and teachers) to bring their own
particular strengths to the guidance program.  When
working in tandem as described earlier, one of the
administrators' prime contributions would include
their responsibilities of support and leadership for
middle school guidance development; for teachers
working "on the line," they fulfill their duties as
they work directly on behalf of student guidance.
From both an organizational and applicational construct, it is the teachers who form the first level
of guidance for the middle schoolers.  As these
trained personnel interact with their students, they
assist these young people with personal and social
growth along with the day-to-day academics.  This
interaction of the affective domain with the cognitive and psychomotor is of crucial importance since
many potential "school" problems can be alleviated
through the teacher's efforts.  In particular, the

following teacher contributions are most important
in the development of middle school guidance:

1.  To be well prepared, the middle school teachers
    must be aware of the nature and needs of the
    adolescent.  Ideally, they see as "typical"
    the middle school youngster who possesses a
    unique complexity of social-emotional-
    intellectuality.  The classroom professional
    understands that the middle school's un-
    predictability is itself predictable.

2.  The middle school teacher must have a strong
    willingness to actively participate on various
    committees and "teams" that serve the holistic
    needs of the child within the school.  Through
    these formal and informal means, the teacher
    contributes to the understanding and acceptance
    that:  a child learns most effectively when
    mental and physical activities are congruous
    with ability; that social skills can be im-
    proved best when developmental opportunities
    are available and that problem solving skills
    are greatly enhanced when appropriate
    experiences are provided.  In essence, guid-
    ance committees or "teams" on which the class-
    room professional should become involved may
    be highly defined or loosely structured, but
    they are nevertheless a viable means for
    coordinating the child's total school program.

3.  The teacher should also be able and willing
    to become seriously committed as a teacher-
    advisor to students.  One such device is
    aptly named the "advisor-advisee" program.
    In this framework every student is assigned
    to a teacher who functions as the student's
    immediate affective resource person.  Commonly,
    the "frontline" teacher provides invaluable
    guidance to individual students or even an
    entire advisory group on such matters as peers
    relations, class scheduling, or career edu-

cation. It is not unusual for such conferences
to occur "on the spot;" however, flexible
homeroom periods are normally set aside for
this purpose. The teacher-advisor setting
should be advantageous to building rapport
between the teacher and the student, hopefully
to enable the youngster to feel free to discuss personal, social, and/or educational
problems or needs.

4. If teachers are to be effective contributors
   to the development of a strong middle school
   guidance program, they must be able to professionally interpret and apply basic academic
   and psychological test data for the purpose
   of assisting students. These skills are
   especially important in helping the middle
   school youngster with academic decision making
   along with career exploration and planning.
   Parents, too, can benefit from the teacher's
   explanation of such data as the student's
   standardized test scores and psychological
   referral information.

5. Besides being able to provide guidance to
   students through their knowledge of sound
   middle school guidance practices, data
   utilization, and professional involvement,
   the middle school teacher must also be able
   to recognize "atypical" student behavior such
   as abrupt changes in moods, attitudes, and/or
   work habits. Once it has been determined
   that a child needs "special help" for correct-
   ing personal-social maladjustment such as
   emotional instability or chronic physical
   illness, the teacher must be willing to take
   the time and effort to construct an informed,
   factual referral and see it through to
   completion.

6. The teacher should also have the desire to
   continue working toward gaining additional
   training in the affective area. Improved

effectiveness in this domain can come from
the acquisition of improved skills. The
teacher should be very willing to attend in-
service activities, take additional graduate
level classes, and attend professional
seminars and conferences to attain a higher
level of proficiency.

7.  Above all, the teacher can provide a tremendous guidance service by creating a classroom
atmosphere that is conducive to learning. In
this setting the youngsters not only can
receive academic instruction, they can be
encouraged to participate in extra-curricular
activities and other affective programs with
classmates. Moreover, it is within the classroom that the teacher can help the student
gain a feeling of responsibility and self-
worth. Thus, the teacher can contribute a
great deal of guidance through maintaining a
continuous, caring, and accepting attitude
toward students. When children feel good
about themselves, the realization of expectations is more easily accomplished.

## Counselors

The counselor in the middle school plays an
important and pivotal role in guidance. This person
assists parents in carrying out their humanistic responsibilities of the home, advises the school
administrator in matters relating to the school's
overall affective program, confers with teachers
concerning the performance of their guidance efforts,
and meets with student to help them with difficulties
or needs of a personal nature. It is within these
distinct relationships with parents, administrators,
teachers, and students that the primary task of the
counselor is synthesized: to provide direction and
support to the efforts of others in their involvement
with the guidance process.

The counselor must be able to "wear many hats."
This person functions as a consultant, advisor,
confidant, and friend. Special skills must be
utilized in applying knowledge and expertise, formulating programs, integrating curriculum, and
providing leadership to student development. It
becomes apparent, then, that the success of the
counselor is greatly dependent upon this person's
interactions with other faculty members; the
counselor must be able to support the various
personalities in the guidance network, and they
too, must be able to support the counselor.

Those areas of responsibility most common to
a middle school counselor are as follows:

1. The initial requirement of a middle school
   counselor is the ability to construct an
   appropriate guidance program. This is far
   from the counselor's former steretyped
   function of "talking with kids." Indeed,
   the most effective counselors spend less
   than half of their time in face-to-face
   contact with students. Their energies
   are applied to directly assisting in the
   planning, organizing, implementing, and
   evaluation of a broad-based affective
   program for the school. They realize that
   their knowledge and expertise can best be
   utilized in helping others to help
   children, rather than trying to "go it
   alone."

2. In sharing guidance knowledge and expertise with others, the counselor must
   remain acutely aware of the "fishbowl"
   syndrome. It is important that other
   personnel in the building as well as the
   parents and students view with favor and
   appreciation the contributions of the
   counselor. For this reason, attention to
   "public relations" is necessary if leadership is to be supportable and sustainable.

That the counselors, themselves, need self-
convincing to feel professional self-worth is
rarely an issue. A more plausible issue can
become: "What does the counselor do all day,
anyway?" Communicating with key people can
greatly dispel this all too frequent occupa-
tional hazzard.

3. The counselor should be a "high visibility"
   affective leader. This person should not wait
   for problems to come to his doorstep; rather
   he should use the assertively acceptable role
   of this position to seek out matters in need
   of attention--before they become crises. The
   wise counselor has a "nose for affective news"
   that provides a head-start advantage in resolving problems or needs, thereby increasing
   the likelihood of favorable support from
   others involved in the process of education.

4. As part of guidance development in the middle
   school, the counselor must be able and willing
   to demonstrate his professional/affective
   competency. In this effort, the counselor
   should seek to help individual faculty members
   as well as parents in their guidance roles.
   Generally, unobtrusive efforts such as informal
   observations avoid alienating those for whom
   support is intended. However, whether deliberate or not, the occasional "ruffling of
   feathers" could be but a small price to pay in
   view of the guidance objective: the fullest
   possible development of each middle school
   youngster's potential.

5. In addition to concern for his own professional
   self-improvement, the counselor must also
   encourage the continuous training and re-
   training of school personnel to meet the needs
   of the adolescent. Carefully planned periodic
   school in-service activities can be used to
   both inform and "re-charge" the school person-

nel's awareness and enthusiasm toward the
affective process. Other training possibilities that the counselor should consider
include role playing, demonstrating new
affective concepts, sharing innovative
techniques, critiquing teacher initiatives,
and organizing meetings with outside
"experts."

6.  The middle school counselor must be willing
    to participate in a multitude of student-
    related conferences. These meetings may
    involve a variety of "interested others:"
    parents, administrators, teachers, and
    specialized personnel, along with perhaps the
    students themselves. Attendance at these
    meetings will not only keep the counselor
    informed, but will give this person the
    opportunity to have input into the direction
    of the development of students.

7.  Likely, the most obvious counselor role—
    although certainly not the only important one—
    is that of "guidance counselor" for the stu-
    dents. Here, the counselor should engage in
    individual and/or group "developmental"
    strategies in which the student is given
    assistance in solving problems and/or ful-
    filling needs. To be both affective and
    effective, the counselor must be perceived by
    students as a "friend" who accepts them for
    who they are, regardless of circumstances.
    Consequently, the counselor should not be
    required to deal with student discipline.

THE GUIDANCE PROGRAM:
STRUCTURING THE CHANGE PROCESS

To be sure, there are numerous and varied
ways in which to initiate change in just about
any human endeavor. For the change process to
be effectively applied to a middle school guidance
program, an atmosphere of interactivity, under-

standing, and support is essential. Here, the
probability of acceptance is greater because
all those who share in its involvement are
given appropriate information and encouragement
to participate in its implementation.

## Implementing a Guidance Program

The guidance components described here—
parents, school administrators, teachers, and
counselors—are distinct, yet interacting. Each
is of vital importance; though, it is only when
they are integrated into middle school guidance
and applied to its child-centered philosophy can
their usefulness be fully appreciated. To
accomplish these ends, a systematic approach to
program development should be considered.

## Step 1—Needs Assessment

Aptly named, this initial step begins with
the administrator or designee creating a type of
task force to support investigation aimed at
initiating or expanding the middle school guidance
program. The committee, made up of a cross-
section of "key components" (parents, teachers,
administrators, counselors, and/or citizens)
along with the possible inclusion of students,
should ask if the current level of guidance may
not be meeting the needs of the students. With
support received from the larger school community,
the conducting of a "needs assessment" would be
warranted. The task force should utilize all of
its resources—both internal and external—to
devise an objective instrument for assessing the
need to establish/alter the guidance effort in
the middle school. Again, those most likely to
be surveyed would most certainly include the
parents, citizens, administrators, teachers, and
counselors—along with the students themselves.
With regard to the actual questionnaire, considerable research should go into its formation.

## Step 2--Develop Goals

After the results of the survey questionnaire have been compiled and analysis of these data indicates that development of guidance in the middle school is needed, goals should be established toward improving this affective curricular area. Without exception, every goal should be a written statement of intent. If a relatively large number of goals are formed, prioritizing their importance could be useful in setting-up a systematice approach toward accomplishment.

## Step 3--Goal Support

Development of goals, even by a representative cross-section of the school community, should not be erroneously construed as a mandate by the populace. Serious difficulties may result if the "tentative" goals are not aired in public. It is quite critical that interested persons are given the opportunity to act or even react to the work of the task force.

## Step 4--Establish Objectives

As statements of intent, goals are non-behavioralistic in nature. As corollaries to goals, "objectives" define what is to be accomplished, how they are to be measured, and the so-called "criteria for success." In formulating objectives to process goals for developing a guidance program for the middle school, the task force may wish to delegate or share the job of establishing written objectives with other staff personnel; those in the school who would be ultimately responsible for their success or failure.

## Step 5--Alternative Solutions Toward Achieving the Objectives and Reaching the Goals

The purpose of formulating goals and corresponding objectives is to provide a systematic

approach toward solving a problem or meeting a
need.  Step 5 asks the question:  "Of all of the
alternative solutions available, which is/are
the most viable for achieving the specified goals
and objectives?"  It then becomes the "task" of
the task force, and/or those to whom it delegates
such authority, to consider specified solutions
to attain the prescribed goals and objectives
leading to improvement in the middle school's
guidance.

## Step 6--Selecting the Most Appropriate Solutions

Great care should be exercised in selecting
specific solutions for developing a middle school
guidance program formulated by certain goals and
objectives as based upon the needs assessment.
Consequently, it is highly recommended to the task
force that rather than trying to "reinvent the
wheel" they would be encouraged to review for
possible adoption/adaptation--improvement quality
guidance programs from exemplary schools in the
area when choosing these "enablers."

## Step 7--Implementing and Assistance

Once the final objectives have been determined,
their implementation should be an immediate priority.  This undertaking may be an extension of the
task force's responsibility, or it may be delegated
to an administrator or someone else with authority
status.  In any case, the implementation strategy
should be one of both guiding and assisting.
Those accountable for implementation must provide
leadership for its process as well as resource for
its product.

## Step 8--Evaluation

Following a previously agreed upon trial
period for implementing the systematic goals-
objectives-solutions approach for developing a

middle school guidance program, an evaluation
should be undertaken to determine its level of
success. Such feedback would be based upon
pre-established criteria of success as indicated
within the content of the objectives. The type
of evaluation instrument most frequently used by
a task force is an anonymous survey questionnaire,
polling at least a cross-section of all those
involved in the trial program. As a final note,
the data feedback may (or may not) indicate a
need for even further refinement in the goals-
objectives-solutions used for developing the
middle school's guidance program.

## THE SECURITY FACTOR

The typical middle school youngster is a child
of many fears and to varying degrees, fears harm
the educational development of a middle school
student. A fearful child is frequently a slower
developing child, because fears have a way of
interferring with learning. A fearful child
cannot learn with a maximum efficiency and effectiveness. Fears at their minimum cause distrac-
tions; at their maximum: total learning blockage.
It remains, then, as one of the primary guidance
tasks of the middle school to deal with students'
fears and anxieties.

If student-centeredness is truly the philosophical core of the middle school, it follows that
any student need, including those associated with
fear, should be met. To merely describe middle
school students as fearful, is analogous to
describing a problem, but ignoring the need for
solution. That middle schoolers have fears is not
merely conjecture--it is fact. Yet, unless this
knowledge is applied to practical use, all the
verbiage printed up to this point may not meet the
test of: "So what?" So what if middle schoolers
have fears? So what if they are afraid of this
thing or that? So what if we are aware? The

answer is that something can be done to assist in
the development of these children. Attention can
be given to that which alleviates or eliminates
fear: security.

What actually is meant by "security" for the
middle school? Certainly, it isn't locks on the
classroom doors or the removal of all bullies from
the educational environment. Nor should security
be viewed as even a hint of promise of anything
representing a Utopian haven where youngsters can
enter, leaving all fears behind. But if these are
what security is not, what is it? Perhaps, put in
a brief, simple form security is attitudinal. It
describes feelings about the environment within
which the individual exists and functions.

Providing for student security is an important
consideration in the middle school philosophy.
But generally left unsaid is: who shall be concerned with providing for the security factor to
thereby meet the needs of the students? Should it
be the principal? Should it be the guidance
counselor? Should it come from the teams, the
homeroom and/or classroom teachers? Who should it
be? It should be provided by all of these and
wherever possible, the entire school staff through
a thoughtfully planned guidance program.

Not unlike a number of middle school efforts,
providing for the security of students must be a
total team effort. All staff members must be
involved to the extent of their abilities and the
limits of their time. No one's potential for
making positive contributions should be ignored;
all should contribute in some way to providing
for the security of students. This is illustrated
in the following examination of the changing role
of the guidance counselor--particularly at the
middle school level.

The one person in the school setting supposed
to have been responsible for providing student

security has been the school guidance counselor.
This person usually has been the one who has
endeavored to relieve the fears of the students.
Unfortunately, however, this person has sometimes
been the only one who ever has had this affective
responsibility. For example, when the students
outnumber the counselor by 300 to 1 and up to
600 to 1—even the most casual calculations would
reveal the ridiculousness of trying to effectively
serve even a small part of the students' affective
needs—let alone the vast security factor.

The modern middle school professional knows
that the only realistic solution for providing for
security lies in utilizing all the teachers to
meet the affective needs of students, rather than
exclusively relying upon the counselor. When all
the teaching members of the professional staff are
meaningfully included in a guidance capacity, both
the efficiency and effectiveness of the entire
school's affective efforts are increased, thereby
enhancing the security factor. Whether these
teachers assume their additional role under titles
such as: "Homeroom Teacher," "Teacher-Counselor,"
or "Student Advisor" is not critical. Their
function is what is important: to provide for
student security through attention to affective
education. Thus, by sharing the affective
responsiblity among the staff it becomes more
likely that all students in the middle school will
be able to have someone in the school whom they
may seek out for security.

To achieve an atmosphere of security for students, the efforts of the staff must be realistically conceived, properly planned, thoughtfully
organized and objectively controlled. Staff
involvement and commitment is needed: who is
going to do what and when. Along with this, some
sort of visible structure is necessary to insure
consistency, understanding and completion of the
fundamental principles relating to the security
factor.

## The Guide

The following presentation of one middle
school's initial attempt to provide for the
security factor reflects the uniqueness and
caring qualities of its staff. The staff in this
school, the Maltby Middle School in Brighton,
Michigan, has begun to develop an approach toward
providing for student-centered security that is
worthy of examination so that other middle school
educators may gain insights into their own situations from its initial structure. Except where
otherwise stated, the "Maltby Middle School
Affective Education Guide" will be presented in
italics, with commentary/explanation inserted
where necessary.

### *"Maltby Middle School Affective Education Guide"*

The title of this affective guide indicates
the nature of its aim:  it is a program to provide
for the security factor by bringing about affective education in the middle school. The "Guide"
seeks to create a tangible, objective means for
insuring that the affective domain will not be
neglected or overlooked in the process of educating the middle school youngster.

Although unstated in the title, unquestionably
of tremendous importance is the involvement and
commitment by the middle school teachers from the
very point of departure if the program is to be
successful. Thus, the school guidance counselor
would logically serve as general chairperson to
stimulate, coordinate and support the teachers'
affective efforts, particularly with regard to
the security factor. All need to become involved
in the formation of the "Guide," thereby obtaining
a feeling of ownership for the final product
produced.

In the Maltby case the guidance counselor did
serve as chairperson for the Affective Committee.
Initial communiques from that person were intended
to whet the appetite of everyone on the staff and
generally stimulate the interest of teachers toward
the formation of an affective program.  Subsequent-
ly, these efforts culminated in a well-planned
meeting in which three key teacher-leadership
segments were established to serve as benchmarks
in the sequential development of the "Guide."  At
the initial meeting three sub-committees were
filled and chairpersons determined—Phase I:
Philosophy; Phase II:  Component Areas, Goals,
Performance Objectives; and Phase III:  Evaluation.
It should be noted that these three divisions were
carefully extracted to divide the tasks of getting
the job done in such a way as not to overburden
those who voluntarily participated, yet gave
everyone enough responsibility to insure for
meaningful contributions toward the total group
effort.

Another vital motivator to enhance the group
effort was action.  Each phase was approached with
promptness and deliberation.  In the case of
Phase I, the task of developing an affective
philosophy for the middle school was undertaken
immediately.  The chairperson and other committee
members of the Phase I group, along with the
general chairperson, did their homework.  Much
data were gathered and assimilated and within a
relatively short period of time a philosophy
began to emerge.

During this emergence all staff were constantly updated via written communiques as to the
progress in the development of their middle school
affective philosophy.  This served three important
functions:  1) it kept all informed, 2) it sustained their interest and enthusiasm and 3) it
provided a vehicle for feedback from those not
directly involved in the Phase I work.  Within
four weeks from the inception of the Phase I work

the "final" draft of the Maltby Middle School
Affective Education Guide's Philosophy was
presented to and accepted by the Affective
Committee (the entire staff voluntarily served
on the Affective Committee!)

*Affective Philosophy for*
*Maltby Middle School*

*Whereas . . .*

*an effective human being is a harmonious blend*
*of cognitive, affective and psychomotor traits ...*

*affective education should be a major component*
*of a middle school philosophy ...*

*the middle school should recognize student's*
*transitional stage of development ...*

*the ultimate goal of education should be the*
*development of an effective human being ...*

*Therefore . . .*

*the middle school should seek to develop*
*students' personal identity through concern*
*for their self-concepts, values clarification,*
*self-evaluations, role explorations, and the*
*development of independence and autonomy ...*

*the middle school should strive to prepare*
*students to cope with a changing world ...*

*the middle school should endeavor to provide*
*students with goal-setting, problem solving*
*and decision-making skills ...*

*the middle school should attempt to instill*
*in students an acceptance, concern and respect*
*for and by others ...*

*the middle school should aim to develop*
*students' communication skills ...*

In Phase I the task was to provide a rationale
for the security factor vis-a-vis affective education within the entire educational process. The
resultant philosophy sought to give some worthwhile reasons for extending education beyond the
borders of the traditional 3 R's. In a sense
Phase I established, in principal, a fourth R:
Relationships—the substance of affective
education, especially as it applies to the
security factor.

While Phase I determined the theoretical
constructs for an affective education program,
Phase II is concerned with the practical
application of Phase I. Essentially, then,
Phase I is operationalized by Phase II. Phase II
sets forth the specific areas of responsibility:
Component Areas; the broad-based, non-behavioral-
istically stated aims: Goals; and the specific,
behavioralistic statements that describe teacher/
learner tasks: Performance Indicators.

The first Component Area is the Principal's
Responsibility. Since this area has only one
stated Goal it may be accurately inferred that
even though the principal has primary responsibility for all education within the school, much
authority is shared or completely delegated to
others:

*Component Area: Principal's Responsibility*

*Goal I: To establish affective education within*
*        the school*

*P.I. - 1: The principal and guidance counselor*
*         will jointly specify the goals,*
*         *performance objectives and activities*

that the guidance counselor should
achieve during the school year.

P.I. - 2: The principal, guidance counselor and
team coordinators will jointly determine
the goals, *performance indicators and
activities that the teaching teams should
achieve during the school year.

P.I. - 3: The principal, guidance counselor and
homeroom teachers will determine the
goals, *performance indicators and
activities that the teachers,
functioning as homeroom teachers,
should achieve during the school
year.

P.I. - 4: The principal, guidance counselor and
classroom teachers will jointly determine
the goals, *performance indicators and
activities that the teachers, functioning
as classroom teachers, should achieve
during the school year.

P.I. - 5: The principal, guidance counselor and
classroom teachers will jointly determine
the goals, *performance indicators and
activities that the teachers, functioning
as Unified Arts and enrichment teachers,
should achieve during the school year.

*NOTE: It should be emphasized that not every
performance indicator beneath a goal here or
elsewhere need be successfully undertaken to
assume the achievement of that goal.

Again, bearing in mind that providing for the
security factor is part and parcel of the affective
program, attention now turns to the second major
Component Area: the Guidance Counselor's Responsibility. It is at this juncture that the

influence of the middle school has an important
impact upon the differing role of the guidance
counselor within the affective program. Traditionally, under the junior high school, the
counselor was at the best involved in the development of students through direct contact; at
the worst as the school disciplinarian, inter-
rogator and truant officer. This role, viewed
as archaic by middle school standards, is
supplanted by more of an emphasis upon the
guidance counselor as a positive affective
leader among the staff and less as a negative
force mainly functioning to modify student
behavior through any means found to be effective.
The guidance counselor becomes a sort of quasi-
administrator, concerned with affective education
by providing for the planning, organizing and
controlling of affective programs, including the
direct assistance of the staff through procedures
dealing with motivation, stimulation and support.
While counseling students is not excluded, it
is somewhat restricted to the hard core cases.
A neo-counselor of sorts thus emerges:

*Component Area: Guidance Counselor's Responsibility*

*Goal II:   To develop and update a progressive
            affective program*

*P.I. - 1:   The guidance counselor will provide
             for a cooperative annual review/
             revision of the existing affective
             philosophy.*

*P.I. - 2:   The guidance counselor will
             provide for a cooperative
             annual review/revision of the
             existing affective goals.*

P.I. - 3: *The guidance counselor will provide for a cooperative annual review/revision of existing affective performance indicators and corresponding activities.*

Goal III: *To develop and implement an affective organization*

P.I. - 1: *The guidance counselor will help the homeroom teacher teams determine student homeroom groups, particularly to facilitate student affective growth.*

P.I. - 2: *The guidance counselor will help the homeroom teacher teams establish block schedules, particularly to provide for homeroom time.*

P.I. - 3: *The guidance counselor will help the homeroom teacher teams schedule students, particularly with regard to the affective needs of the students.*

P.I. - 4: *The guidance counselor will help the homeroom teachers select appropriate affective materials, particularly with regard to the transescent child.*

P.I. - 5: *The guidance counselor and media specialist will develop and maintain an affective resource center, particularly an affective library.*

Goal IV: *To develop and implement affective Communications*

P.I. - 1: *The guidance counselor will provide written communiques to all staff relating to affective education within the school at least once per 9-week period.*

P.I. - 2:   The guidance counselor will provide
            affective resource materials to homeroom
            teachers at least once per 9-week period.

P.I. - 3:   The guidance counselor will provide
            homeroom teachers with quarterly
            "updates" of problem students considered
            as "school" children and those who are
            receiving "special" guidance assistance
            such as referrals.

P.I. - 4:   The guidance counselor will conduct
            affective information/group guidance
            sessions during school hours for
            parents and other adults (e.g.:
            parent effectiveness training, etc.)

P.I. - 5:   The guidance counselor will organize
            affective information/group guidance
            sessions during non-school times for
            parents and other adults featuring
            outside speakers (e.g.: lecture
            series, encounter groups, etc.)

P.I. - 6:   The guidance counselor in cooperation
            with the homeroom teacher will organize
            a peer-counseling program.

P.I. - 7:   The guidance counselor will organize
            a cross-age tutoring program with
            input from teams and departments.

P.I. - 8:   The guidance counselor will coordinate
            a big-brother/sister program.

P.I. - 9:   The guidance counselor in cooperation
            with the homeroom teachers will provide
            for the orientation of new teachers.

P.I. - 10:  The guidance counselor in cooperation
            with the homeroom teachers will provide
            for the orientation of new students.

*P.I. - 11.* The guidance counselor in cooperation
with the homeroom teachers will provide
for the orientation of new parents.

*P.I. - 12:* The guidance counselor in cooperation
with the homeroom teachers will provide
for student exchanges with other schools.

*P.I. - 13:* The guidance counselor will provide for
the recognition of teachers' affective
efforts.

*P.I. - 14:* The guidance counselor will attend
to the moral needs of teachers.

*P.I. - 15:* The guidance counselor will coordinate
the sending of student test scores/data
interpretation to parents.

*P.I. - 16:* The guidance counselor will coordinate
the eighth grade team efforts toward
high school scheduling.

*Goal V:  To develop/maintain/support teachers'
affective instructional skills*

*P.I. - 1:* The guidance counselor will conduct
affective in-service training sessions
at least once per semester.

*P.I. - 2:* The guidance counselor will be
available, upon request, to critique
teachers' affective efforts.

*P.I. - 3:* The guidance counselor will write
affective mini-lessons for homeroom
teachers' group guidance sessions.

*P.I. - 4:* The guidance counselor will provide for
an annual evaluation of the state of

> *affective education within the school
> and publish these findings.*

*P.I. - 5:*   *The guidance counselor will identify,
list and describe for homeroom teachers
certain referral/service agencies in
the community.*

*Goal VI:*   *To provide personal/developmental
counseling for students with special
needs*

*P.I. - 1:*   *The counselor will conduct individual/
group counseling sessions as needed.*

Another unique feature of the middle school,
teaming, is a vital aspect of the affective program.
Here, the Component Area: Team's Responsibility,
plays a vital role in insuring that all members
of every teaching unit are meeting the affective
needs of their groups of students through attention
to planning and strategy sessions:

*Component Area:   Team's Responsibility*

*Goal VII:*   *For each teaching team to develop
affective education*

*P.I. - 1:*   *Teachers will include affective strategy
planning in their team meetings a minimum
of monthly.*

*P.I. - 2:*   *Teachers will discuss methods for
dealing with the affective needs of
children on their team a minimum
of monthly.*

*P.I. - 3:*   *Teachers will discuss plans for informing
parents regarding affective education a
minimum of once per semester.*

So far, the responsibilities of the principal,
guidance counselor and teams have been seen as vital
factors in the implementation of the security factor
through a meaningful middle school affective program.
Certainly, each of these three components has a
unique function within the operation of such a
program.  There is, however, another element within
the middle school that perhaps plays the most
important part of all in the success of the affective program.  This is the Component Area:  the
Homeroom Teachers' Responsibility.

The homeroom teacher (student advisor, etc.)
has the greatest impact upon a middle school
affective program because these professionals
collectively have the greatest contact with that
viable center of focus:  the middle school youngster.
In the middle school every youngster has a homeroom
teacher.  Hopefully, this person is a significant
other who is charged with the responsibility for
the welfare of each homeroom child.  Through the
homeroom teacher concept the child is given the
security enabling that child to develop to the
fullest extent.  As outlined in the following,
homeroom teachers are seen as providing the first
line of guidance through a wide range of methods
and strategies:

*Component Area:  Homeroom Teachers Responsibility*

*Goal VIII:   To provide for group guidance through
              extemporaneous student meetings*

*P.I. - 1:    Homeroom teachers will conduct
              "student involvement" meetings
              (e.g.: team meetings, etc.) as
              the need arises.*

*P.I. - 2:    Homeroom teachers will conduct
              student meetings to deal with
              current/relevant situations (e.g.:
              snowballing, name calling, etc.)
              as the need arises.*

P.I. - 3:   Homeroom teachers will conduct
            student meetings dealing with:
            self-control, behavior, attention,
            tolerance and personal strengths
            as the need arises.

P.I. - 4:   Homeroom teachers will conduct
            student meetings dealing with:
            roles, identification and self-
            concept as the need arises.

P.I. - 5:   Homeroom teachers will conduct
            student meetings dealing with:
            goal setting, decision making
            and success as the need arises.

P.I. - 6:   Homeroom teachers will conduct
            student meetings dealing with:
            friendship, trust, lying and
            self-disclosure as the need
            arises.

Goal IX:    For the homeroom teacher to implement
            group guidance through guidance mini-
            lessons dealing with students' self-
            awareness

P.I. - 1:   The student will identify at least
            five mood faces and will describe
            personal mood feelings through
            forced-choice selection from an
            ordered series of happy/sad faces.

P.I. - 2:   The student will construct a life-
            size silhouette and will personalize
            this body portrait according to his/her
            self-concept.

*P.I. - 3:* *The student will project various*
*facial expressions while speaking*
*and perceive these from "mirrored"*
*expressions by another student.*

*P.I. - 4:* *The student will verbalize that*
*he/she likes himself/herself*
*and complete the statement:*
*"I like myself because ..."*

*P.I. - 5:* *The student will recognize mood*
*words and will state at least*
*three words that describe*
*his/her mood.*

*Goal X:* *For the homeroom teacher to implement group*
*guidance through guidance mini-lessons dealing*
*with students' attitude/motivation/goal set-*
*ting.*

*P.I. - 1:* *The student will perform an exercise*
*in promoting positive self-development*
*by reciting the "Rx for Life."*

*P.I. - 2:* *The student will perform an exercise*
*in improving positive self-motivation*
*by verbalizing an understanding of*
*"The Price of Success."*

*P.I. - 3:* *The student will ascertain and display*
*a pictorialization of a specific*
*personal goal.*

*P.I. - 4:* *The student will relate the spending*
*of personal time by pictorializing a*
*"Daily Circle."*

The following guidance mini-lesson, written for
homeroom teachers by the guidance counselor is
typical of the kind of affective lessons that can be
developed for structured group guidance in the homeroom setting. This lesson refers to Goal X, P.I. 3:
"The student will ascertain and display a pictorialization of a specific personal goal."

*GUIDANCE MINI-LESSON "CONSCIOUS AND SUBCONSCIOUS MOTIVATION"*

PERFORMANCE OBJECTIVE:

*The student will ascertain and display a pictorialization of a specific personal goal.*

GENERAL OBJECTIVE

*To enhance personal motivation regarding a particular objective/goal.*

ACTIVITY

Preparation

*The teacher should briefly review the importance of goal setting as a means of motivation. Next, each student should be asked to write down three completely different objectives/goals he/she would like to accomplish. This should be done on a sheet prepared for this purpose.*

*THREE GOALS/OBJECTIVES I WOULD LIKE TO ACCOMPLISH:*

1. _____

2. _____

3. _____

*Next, each should think about the one he/she would most like to accomplish and circle it.*

*Following this, the one goal/objective selected should be pictorialized in 2 or 3 different ways in boxes provided on the same prepared sheet.*

| | | |
|---|---|---|
| | | |

*Finally, each student should decide which pictorialization best represents his/her goal/objective and recopy it onto the peel-backs -- in triplicate.*

*THREE PEEL-BACK LABELS SHOULD BE IN VITAL PLACES WHERE THEY WILL BE NOTICED MOST FREQUENTLY, SUCH AS INSIDE A LOCKER DOOR, INSIDE A WALLET OR PURSE FLAP, OR ON A MIRROR MOST OFTEN USED.*

*Sample:*

Read for
½ an hour
for the           =
entire
month of
October.

Goal XI: *For the homeroom teacher to implement group guidance through mini-lessons dealing with students' social awareness*

P.I. - 1: The student will perform an exercise in social skills by displaying various handshaking techniques.

P.I. - 2: The student will perform an exercise in sensitivity training by role playing at least one specific emotional situation(s).

P.I. - 3: The student will relate personal emotions and record these on an "Emotion Graph."

Goal XII: *For the homeroom teacher to implement group guidance through guidance mini-lessons dealing with students' group communication*

P.I. - 1: The student will reveal his/her feelings toward the group by verbally completing the statement: "I Feel ..."

P.I. - 2: The student will reveal his/her wishes toward the group's purpose by verbally completing the statement: "I Wish ..."

P.I. - 3: The student will reveal his/her perception of the group's direction by verbally completing the statement: "I See ..."

P.I. - 4: The student will reveal his/her knowledge of the group's achievement by verbally completing the statement "I know ..."

P.I. - 5: The student will reveal his/her intellectualizati toward broadening the group's purpose by completing the statement: "I think ..."

399 EFFECTIVE MIDDLE SCHOOL

*Goal XIII:* For the homeroom teacher to implement group guidance through guidance mini-lessons dealing with students' values

P.I. - 1: The student will perform an exercise in the personal development of humanitarian values by doing a "Values Hand Stack."

P.I. - 2: The student will perform an exercise in the personal development of school-related values by participating in the group construction of a "Values Tree."

P.I. - 3: The student will perform an exercise in the development of personal values by individually constructing a "Values Mobile."

P.I. - 4: The student will perform an exercise in the personal development of family values by individually constructing a "Values House."

P.I. - 5: The student will perform an exercise in the development of personal values by individually constructing a visual: "Values Hang-Ups."

*Goal XIV:* To provide for group guidance to focus upon the key aspects of the "Life and Career Education Curriculum Guide"

P.I. - 1: The homeroom teacher will infuse the ongoing Career Education instructional Component I: "Self-Awareness and Self-Assessment," particularly those dealing with 1) self-esteem, 2) self-appraisal, 3) self-concept, 4) self-confidence and 5) self-expression.

P.I. - 2: The homeroom teacher will infuse the ongoing Career Education instructional Component II: "Career and Life Roles Awareness," particularly those dealing with 1) life role model, 2) identification, 3) career role model, 4) self-determination and 5) values.

*P.I. - 3:* The homeroom teacher will infuse the ongoing
Career Education instructional Component III:
"Planning and Decision Making," particularly
those dealing with 1) critical thinking, 2)
conceptualization, 3) insight, 4) commitment
and 5) logical problem solving.

*P.I. - 4:* The homeroom teacher will infuse the ongoing
Career Education instructional Component IV:
"Goal Implementation" particularly those
dealing with 1) perception, 2) accomplishment,
3) motivation, 4) projection and 5) goal
setting.

*P.I. - 5:* The homeroom teacher will conduct student
meetings featuring Career Education speakers.

## Goal XV: To provide for individual guidance

*P.I. - 1:* The homeroom teacher will meet with each
advisee a minimum of once per 9-week period.

*P.I - 2:* The homeroom teacher will jointly plan an
advisee's schedule at least once per 9-week
period.

*P.I. - 3:* The homeroom teacher will maintain student
profile cards.

*P.I. - 4:* The homeroom teacher will prepare, publish
and display recognition roll lists.

*P.I. - 5:* The homeroom teacher will recognize students'
birthdays.

*P.I. - 6:* The homeroom teacher will assist students in
the celebration of special days/holidays.

Homeroom teachers, it has been seen, generally
set aside times from their academic classroom functions to deal with the needs of their homeroom
students.  Conversely, the final Component Area:

"Classroom Teachers Responsibility" seeks to infuse the affective into instructional activities during classtime.

*Component Area: Classroom Teachers' Responsibility*

*Goal XVI: To provide for the integration of the affective into the cognitive*

P.I. - 1: The classroom teacher will give evidence of affective activity in lesson plans at least once per week.

P.I. - 2: The classroom teacher will send every student a "happy gram" at least once per semester.

P.I. - 3: The classroom teacher will give evidence of the infusion of "life and career education" activity at least once per week.

P.I. - 4: A "student involvement" class will be conducted at least once every 9-week period.

*Goal XVII: To provide for the integration of the affective into the psychomotor*

P.I. - 1: The classroom teacher will give evidence of affective activity in lesson plans at least once per week.

P.I. - 2: The classroom teacher will send every student a "happy gram" at least once per semester.

P.I. - 3: The classroom teacher will give evidence of the infusion of "Life and Career Education" activity at least once per week.

P.I. - 4: Physical education classes will provide intramural sports for the total school population.

*Goal XVIII: To provide for the integration of
              affective education into unified
              arts and enrichment classes.*

P.I. - 1: The classroom teacher will give evidence of
          affective activity in lesson plans at least
          once per week.

P.I. - 2: The classroom teacher will send every student
          a "happy gram" at least once per semester.

P.I. - 3: The classroom teacher will give evidence of the
          infusion of "Life and Career Education" activity
          at least once per week.

Up to this point the discussion of the Guide
has focused upon: 1) a "Philosophy"—the when and
why relating to the security factor within affective
education and 2) the Component Areas, Goals and
Performance Indicators—the who and the how to get
it accomplished. Both of these aspects are certainly essential for meaningful and successful
implementation. There remains, however, one final
concern to make the Guide complete: that of
evaluation.

If the affective efforts of educators relating
to the security factor are to be fully realized,
the value of their product must be substantiated.
Does affective education, in general, and the
security factor, in particular, produce a desirable
change in a student? Or do these really have little
bearing upon youngsters? Only purposeful evaluation
can answer these questions.

Actual evaluation methods for measuring affective education and the security factor can run the
gamut from the very subjective to the very objective.
The former is typified by informal self-rating
teacher feedback surveys. The latter would include
non-projective tests complete with experimental and
control groups. Quite understandably, the degree of
objectivity befits both the needs and realities
of the situation.

In the case of Maltby, initial evaluation has been inclined to be perhaps more subjective than sound research techniques might dictate. This tact has been admittedly aimed at allowing the staff to become comfortable with the evaluation procedures, rather than risk the accountability bugaboo. Some first-time evaluative questions will include:

1. Do you feel that you pre-determined a sufficient number of affective goals?

2. Do you feel that you generally achieved your affective efforts?

3. Do you feel that your students benefitted from your affective efforts?

4. Were you given worthwhile affective resource materials from the supportive staff?

5. Were you given meaningful assistance from the supportive staff?

As the homeroom teachers become more comfortable with the evaluation of their affective efforts, evaluative focus will undoubtedly shift to the product: the learners. Students, themselves, will be objectively measured to determine the effect of their affective education. With regard to the security factor the key question will emerge: are they more secure because of certain affective measures?

Teachers are now considering some standardized instruments available to aid in this determination.

## AUXILIARY STAFFING

### I. A Definition

Overall staffing of the middle school has been termed an operation of the highest priority. In view of such an important consideration, it is appropriate to clearly delineate between the terms "staffing" and "auxiliary staffing." Within the context of middle school structure, staffing refers to the overall process of recruiting, selecting, and placing appropriately qualified and professionally trained personnel. Auxiliary staffing refers to the process of recruiting, selecting, and placing, highly diversified personnel that complement and assist the professional staff. These include volunteer parents, teacher aids, clerical aides, student volunteers, and other important categories of support staff.

### II. Why have auxiliary staffing?

Auxiliary staffing is needed to help provide the individual help students require.

Recent research has reinforced the realization of educators that large numbers of transescents begin the middle school years with significant instructional needs in several arts. Several causes contribute to the effect of such a problem. One is the reality that school financial structures, such as foundation programs, provide limited opportunities for first priorities within school programs. To combat such a problem of limitation, programs are frequently emphasized during the elementary school years by utilizing the resources of federal assistance. In such cases, the programs are for the most part funded by external-to-district dollars and therefore are usually restricted in operation to perhaps only the primary grade years of school. Students who have participated in such programs are

then frequently re-inserted into the regular classroom for the remaining elementary school years
thereby losing the individually focused attention
that was so vitally needed.  A typical pattern of
linear regression then follows and gives the result
of beginning the middle school years with significant educational disadvantagement.  Such disadvantagement is particularly severe in its future implications for learning unless there is some remedial
intervention.

Another rationale for auxiliary staffing concerns the need to focus services to students in the
most efficient manner possible.

Program variety tends to increase in the years
after the elementary school years.  In such years,
and particularly beginning with the middle school
years, a differentiation of staffing becomes possible
and feasible.  A resultant benefit of staff differentiation to students and taxpayers is that effective use of available staff resources is optimized.
Teacher aides, clerical aides, student volunteers,
and others provide the auxiliary services that are
most effectively met when considering auxiliary staff
training, background and peer association.

III.  Considerations for determining auxiliary
      staffing needs.

Let us assume that we are starting from "square
one" in analyzing auxiliary staffing needs for a
middle school.

1.  A first consideration would be to determine
the size of the student population to be served.
Included in such preliminary thinking would be how
many and what type professionals are available to
directly serve the students.  An appropriate ratio
of students to teachers can then be figured.

Second in priority would be the task of listing

students for consideration of auxiliary staffing services. Appropriate progressional staff should be given the responsibility of evaluating priorities of student needs. Such a needs assessment could, for example, be done by the guidance staff, teaching area team, central office professional staff, or individual teacher, to name but a few possibilities.

2. When analyzing the needs assessment data and when considering priorities for educational services, particular attention should be given to several areas of student historical information. Such information is frequently maintained in official student records. It is important to avoid overconsideration of a singular indicator, such as one test score, when determining needs priorities. Look for the total picture! By historical information, the reference here is to record achievement, absence data, examples of former homework, information concerning unusual physical or emotional problems, interest inventories, non-standardized test results, and teacher comments or evaluations. The overall objective, in determining needs priorities for students, is to analyze records for trends in student development so that a maximum utilization of program design is possible.

3. After specific needs have been determined, the next step requires that a weighting be given to each identified student need. Weighting refers to the importance attached to each need as determined by professional staff. The weighting may be determined by consensus of the evaluation group(s) or may be decided by the obvious nature of the analysis data.

4. The fourth step includes the construction of a needs profile. Such a profile would list in descending order the identified needs of a particular student.

5. The fifth step would involve assembling into groups those student needs profiles which have

similar characteristics. Group size will be determined by matching available resources with appropriate student numbers. It is important to match
the descending order of needs as closely as possible.
Such matching, for example beginning sounds or
inferred meaning in reading comprehension, will
facilitate the future assignment of auxiliary staff.

6. The recruitment, selection, and placement
of auxiliary staff will be greatly enhanced if steps
one through five can be accomplished prior to the
end of a school year at the time when auxiliary
staffing program(s) are planned for a succeeding
year. Why accomplish such steps one through five
before the end of a school year? The answer becomes
quite clear when one rethinks the confusion of school
year closing activities and further recognizes that
such tasks, as formerly outlined, may easily
encompass a four or five month period. Assemble as
many components of the auxiliary staffing program
in advance as possible and be prepared for finding
the solutions to unknown problems which will likely
arise. Advance preparation limits the number of new
problems and as a result will enhance the initial
operation of the program.

Following development of the needs assessment
profile, a study group should determine what student
needs should be set as priorities. The study group
may be composed of teachers, administrators, and
guidance department staff. It is also advisable to
include, if possible, a school psychologist. Such
an individual will assist in the interpretation of
psychological tests and may additionally be able
to provide invaluable insight into a student's
apparent needs.

Also important for inclusion in such an important group would be parent participants who may be
involved in analysis of student personally identifi-
able data. Take care to avoid violation of the
intent of Public Law 93-380 unless access to information is released by parent/guardian. Participants

could be involved in providing input when priorities
for service to students are determined. Parent
involvement in determining priorities for student
service will help to insure the overall effectiveness of the auxiliary staffing program. Such
involvement by parents will also serve to create
open lines of communication between and among school,
parents, and community at large.

One middle school community capitalized on
strong interest that parents have in their children's
schoolsin a positive, constructive way. With parent
leadership and teacher/principal cooperation, they
organized a WASP group (Women's Auxiliary for School
Programs) of volunteers who were willing to donate
one or more hours per week of time to serving as
unpaid volunteers. They even designed an inexpen-
sive emblem that each proudly wore while on duty.
The end of the school year saw their efforts
acknowledged in a modest but well attended luncheon
provided by the board of education. The benefits
to the school included better communication between
school and home, a stronger commitment of support
from parents for "their" school's programs, a
realization of middle school students that education
was a total community effort and therefore must be
important, plus many hundreds of hours of free and
needed assistance for teachers.

Following the setting of priorities for student
service, the task of determining type and number of
auxiliary staff can be initiated. Several questions
may be considered. Are teacher aides available?
Is an extension of teacher services necessary? Is
more individual attention to needs of the student
indicated? Are student peers likely to be beneficial
in such instance, as opposed to adult volunteers or
other auxiliary staff? Many other questions, of
course, are possible and likely. All questions
represent a point of view and should be considered
before final decisions are made.

When considering aides, it is important to
remember that teacher aides differ from so called

clerical aides.  Teacher aides usually are assigned
tasks that became an extension of instruction
planned and assigned under the direct supervision
of the teacher.  Clerical aides more frequently
assigned tasks involving the recording of data;
i.e., the scoring of tests made and administered
under teacher supervision, scheduling of student
library/media time, recess/playground/lunch supervision, etc.  The deciding factor between aide
description usually lies in the educational preparation and experience area of the aide.  Individuals
with some college preparation in education or education related areas, are frequently recruited as
educational teacher aides whereas individuals with
business related backgrounds are frequently
recruited as clerical aides.  In any event, place
your available aides into the area(s) where they
will complement the goals of the program and
additionally into the areas where good working
relationships with staff are likely to occur.

Some examples of tasks that might be assigned to
teacher aides in the middle school are these:

1. Work with small groups of students on work
   assigned by teacher.

2. Help in administering tests.

3. Set up and operate AV equipment as needed.

4. Tutor individual students under the teacher's
   supervision.

5. Assist students in library searches and the
   use of tapes, FS, etc.

6. Prepare basic materials for follow-up
   instruction.

7. Arrange displays of interesting materials
   related to topics of study.

8. Prepare charts, overhead transparencies, etc.

9. Grade papers as assigned by teacher and share evaluations with teacher.

10. Search out and secure supplementary material from library or IMC for use in classroom studies.

11. Supervise playground activities.

Some examples of tasks that might be assigned to <u>clerical</u> aides in the middle school:

1. Prepare and duplicate instructional materials - typing, dittoing, etc.

2. Help with record keeping - lunch money, attendance, test scores, etc.

3. General housekeeping chores - straightening bookshelves, etc.

4. Assist with classroom discipline.

5. Playground or lunchroom supervision.

6. Prepare charts, overhead transparencies, etc.

7. Set up and operate AV equipment as needed.

8. Supervise playground activities, lunchroom periods.

9. Assist teacher with field trip arrangements and supervision.

10. Cataloguing and organizing learning materials in the classroom and in the IMC.

11. Help students learn proper use of tools and equipment.

It will be noted that some duties are double-
listed as they may be handled by either teacher
aides or clerical aides.

Student volunteers are another valuable resource.
Particular advantages lie in potentially strong
peer relationships that are often developed among
students and this possibility contributes to a
desired increase in student motivation. Student
volunteers should be assigned tasks under the
direction of teachers or other auxiliary staff.
This might release a teacher from additional direct
responsibility and increases flexibility of the program as well. In any case of assignment, an adult
should be in charge of student volunteers. It is
wise to clearly establish in the student volunteer's
eyes who is boss. Avoid any confusion or potential
grief by clearly communicating this point to all
interested parties.

Student volunteers are sometimes chosen from the
same school where auxiliary services are being
offered to students. In other situations, student
volunteers may be chosen from a school of the same
type, located nearby, or may be chosen from a school
of a different type, for example, a middle school
student volunteer used in an elementary school.
School student volunteers are less frequently chosen
from a school of a lower type. In the latter case,
for example, elementary school students would not
be selected to assist students in the middle school.
High school volunteers would assist students in the
junior high/middle school and junior high/middle
school students would serve students in the elementary school. It is also freqment practice to permit students at the same grade or level to serve
students at the same level. For example, students
at the sixth grade level could assist other
students at the sixth grade level. In cases where
levels are the same, student volunteers should be
clearly superior students and should be self-directed in their ability to conceptualize an assignment
and follow directions, without argument, from a

supervisor.

The scheduling of student volunteers will be
helped if secondary or middle school student volunteers are selected to assist other students. Such
advantage is the result of study sessions/halls
which are frequently scheduled for the afternoon.
Scheduling for such times will be conflict free when
considering the expectations of the classroom or
area teacher. If elementary school student volunteers from middle schools are recruited, all
attempts should be made to avoid conflicts in those
students' schedules of required classes. Elective
classes or activity classes may offer less conflict
but still should be respected in terms of scheduling.
A possibility may be the scheduling of these student
volunteers for the elementary school either immediately before the school day or immediately after the
school day. This creates supervision problems but
this hurdle may be cleared if after-school professional staff are available to include in their
supervisory responsibilities the observation of
student volunteers. In cases of student volunteer
scheduling before or after school, the maximum
time per session should not exceed thirty minutes.
Parent resistance will likely become a problem if
parents feel that their offspring are being used to
that particular student's disadvantagement. This
should be cleared up in communicating with the
parents. Careful planning will likely insure benefits to the school and student resulting in an image
to parents and school that enhances the entire
operation.

One particularly interested group of student
volunteers may be found among those students
aspiring to become teachers. While the middle
school may be early for the formation of a chapter
of Future Teachers of America (F.T.A.) valuable
pre-formal training and pre-service experiences
become an advantage for such students. The opportunity for service as a student volunteer could
also be planned as a valuable component of the
guidance department's career education program.

Benefits for all concerned!

## IV. Program design

The following example of an auxiliary staffed program is suggested for inclusion into varied types of educational or physical-plant school structures. Variations on the following suggestions are certainly possible and it is realized that such variations are limited only by the creativity of the designer(s).

The components of this include utilization of the categories of auxiliary staff as follows:

1. Parent volunteers
2. Teacher aides
3. Clerical aides
4. Student volunteers.

Program design at this point also assumes that:

a. student population to be served has been determined,
b. student needs in service group have been analyzed,
c. student needs have been ranked in priority,
d. a needs weighting has been completed, and
e. a needs assessment profile has been constructed.

During the first days of the new school year, a meeting should be scheduled of all staff who have the responsibility for primary instruction in the needs assessment area selected for service. If reading is chosen as the area, then all teachers of reading would assemble as a group. The specific purpose of the meeting would be to collectively decide upon a scheduling plan and would additionally involve the working out of details and anticipated problems concerning communication. It may be helpful to have such a meeting chaired by the building

principal or appropriate deparement head. Overall
instructional plans for the school year should be
reviewed. Such review would include an analysis of
each quarter or period and short term and long term
goals. Goals of each type should be specifically
stated so that later evaluation will be more
realistically accomplished.

Following the discussion of short and long term
goals, the structure for educational services by
auxiliary can be discussed.

One type of structure is a concept called,
"Action Lab." The action lab is a designated area
within the middle school where students are scheduled for small group instruction and/or individual
supportive and/or remedial assistance. The lab is
staffed at all times during the school day with
available auxiliary staff. During the day, a rotation of such staff occurs. The early morning action
lab session should always begin with teacher direction and each late afternoon session should ideally
end with teacher closure. This is to say that a
service area teacher (perhaps reading) should be
present to welcome students along with the
auxiliary staff serving the first session. Such
an arrangement will give extra stability to the
day's activities and will also tend to remind students of the importance of the program. An example
of auxiliary staff rotation could be:

    a.  early morning session number one, parent
        volunteers,
    b.  session number two, teacher aides,
    c.  first afternoon session, student volun-
        teers,
    d.  last session, clerical aides.

1. During the first morning session, the
teacher(s) in charge would outline the activities
of the session. Such activities, in this or other
sessions, could include but not be limited to, seat
work, audio-visual presentations, monitoring or
oral reading, tachistiscope reinforcement,

rote-recall vocabulary building, etc. An advantage
concerning the scheduling of parents during the
early morning session comes from the reality that
many parents are most available for volunteer
service during the morning hours. Typically, the
parent has ushered the offspring out the door for
school or indeed have transported the offspring to
school. In the latter case, parents are already at
the school site so a special, duplicate trip is
avoided.

2. The second session involving teacher aides,
is complementary not only to the parent volunteers
but is an important extension of teacher directed
activities that have probably occurred in the classroom setting. Teacher aides are usually directly
assigned to teachers during the first part of the
school day. This occurs for many reasons. However,
one of the most important reasons is the fact that
language arts activities usually occur in the early
morning and here the teacher utilizes the teacher
aide to facilitate small group instruction. By
scheduling the teacher aides into the second session,
an extension of teacher direction is gained in the
action lab. Another advantage of scheduling teacher
aides into the second session occurs as a result of
two adult groups of auxiliary staff closely following each other in succession.

3. The third session (early afternoon) is probably the most appropriate time to schedule student
volunteers. The reason for this is consideration
for students who are volunteering for service and
additionally a consideration for other cognate area
professional staff. Concentrated cognitive activities are usually scheduled during the morning hours.
Elective subjects, art, music, study sessions, and
physical education are most likely to be scheduled
in the afternoon. Experience has shown that staff
conflict is more easily resolved if student volunteers are scheduled during the more flexible times.
Student achievement will not suffer in the cognate
areas and make-up work possibilities will be more
easily planned if student volunteers are scheduled

for auxiliary staffing services in the afternoon.
Avoid staff conflicts to insure the significance and
impact of the program!

Student volunteers may need to be supervised
depending on their ages and maturity levels. Each
situation will be different so appropriate solutions
will be necessary.

4. The fourth (closing) session is scheduled
utilizing clerical aides. Such aides may serve at
least a two-fold purpose during the final session.
First, they will be involved with recording necessary
data from all sessions as supplied by volunteer staff.
Additionally they will be responsible for assisting
the professional teacher with whatever tasks become
necessary for closure of the educational activities
of the day. Data collection may involve the recording of seat work results, taking attendance for
each session, media center, library recording keeping,
etc. Another valuable task for clerical aide
assignment becomes the changing of bulletin boards.
Suggestions or coaching supplied by the teacher will
be helpful here in supplying ideas for the clerical
aide staff. Don't be afraid to give the clerical
aides some leeway in supplying ideas for bulletin
board illustrations. If inconsistency develops
between program design and bulletin board illustration, the remedy between teacher and clerical aide is
simple. Tactifully re-instruct the aide perhaps
giving a few extra examples or illustrations and new
ideas will likely be generated as a result of
teacher direction, tact, and interest.

## V. Evaluation

With an educational program, it is important to
provide a planned evaluation design. The following
design is suggested as one measure for evaluating
program effectiveness. Careful analysis of program
effectiveness will give help to give direction to
changes necessary in improving the total auxiliary

staffing program. Evaluation data should be used to strengthen program elements which may appear to be only marginally meeting student needs. It is important to consider the sharing of evaluative information with other professional staff. Such sharing will facilitate total educational planning within the school. It will also tend to reinforce or refute other data thereby creating another dimension to the information gathering process concerning student achievement.

When possible, it is an advantage to include objective testing within the auxiliary staffing program. Such testing should of course be within the stated purposes of evaluation in the school district. Restrictions may exist in the district concerning the number or kinds of tests administered so it is important to be in tune with the district philosophy. If appropriate and consistent with direct testing practices, objective testing within the auxiliary staffing program will "wax as advantage" with other staff members who may see such testing in the action lab, for example, as supportive of the need to monitor student performance. Such testing will also assist guidance staff as such individuals plan educational programs for action lab students. In any case, be careful to clearly state or communicate the purposes of the action lab testing to avoid concept that schools test for limited or unsound educational reasons.

The evaluation design should include at least three elements:

1.  Auxiliary staff written and oral feedback to teachers concerning their observations of students. Such observations will need to be directed and will likely be included on printed forms. Directed information will vary with the situation, but will be determined early in the school year when analyzing priorities to be considered for service. Examples of observation could include study habits, behaviors, eye problems, emotional indicators of potential

problems, etc.

2. Teacher evaluation of assigned student seat work as supplied to teacher by auxiliary staff members.

3. Teacher made tests and the administration of standardized tests.

The written and oral feedback from auxiliary staff should be structured as indicated above. Structure will assure the uniform collection of data and will apply the evaluative model more fairly to all students.

Indications of feedback structure might include for each group:

1. Parents-behavior records

2. Teacher aides-seat work corrections and preliminary data on such to the teacher(s)

3. Student volunteers-right response records for teacher made tests and resultant administration of such

4. Clerical aides-general housekeeping records as may be assigned. Included here would be the record of bulletin board changes inclusive of the topical area of instruction.

Professional teachers should be totally responsible for the evaluation and control in quality of student seat work. The work habits of students, determined by teachers and aides, may be helpful in analyzing student needs and how improvements in achievement may likely be attained. Finally, all tests, whether teacher made or standardized, should be considered as another indicator or element of the evaluation design. In no case should a single test alone be interpreted to be the absolute indicator of student performance. Sound testing practices

dictate that when inconsistent test data are
obtained, other measures of student achievement
(including different tests) should be administered.
Such opportunities for insight should be provided
at periodic intervals for the purpose of insuring
an adequate sampling.

When standardized tests are a part of the
total school testing program, every attempt should
be made to correlate testing of students in the
action lab program with the total school testing
sequence.  Such a decision to uniformly test will
be cost effective and will additionally serve to
limit disruptions during the school year.

A consideration should be given to testing for
aptitude as well as achievement.  If both measures
are obtained, and particularly at the same time, a
comparison is possible in that student performance
may be compared with individual student aptitude.
Advantages in such a testing design will be
especially realized when, for example, school
administration personnel or school board members
compare student performance in one school with the
performance of students in another school.

Let us remember that the bottom line for any
middle school testing program is to maximize student actualization of innate abilities into skill
development.

## STUDENT SERVICES

Auxiliary student services basically have only one
function in the school organization—to make the
total learning environment as efficient and effective
as possible. This can primarily accomplish three
things:

1. permit the middle school teacher to humanize
   education as well as effectively diagnose
   learning progress, prescribe group and
   individual lessons and evaluate the student's
   total growth. In order to achieve this, the
   teacher must be relieved of some unskilled
   trivia tasks.[1]

2. supplement the classroom teachers' data
   collection by use of an auxiliary specialist.

3. provide special auxiliary aid whenever
   classroom conditions cannot accommodate the
   disparity among individuals or when special
   problems exist which are beyond the classroom
   teacher's expertise.

Embedded in the structure and philosophy of the
middle school are several major needs for auxiliary
student services or support systems. These provide a
wide range of aid and assistance to the students,
teachers, and parents. Such services are geared to
special and unique needs of the middle school age
students who find themselves physically, socially,
emotionally, and academically making the transition
between the earlier developmental stages of elementary school students and those of more mature
secondary students.

The elementary school has provided for a large
segment of the five through eleven year population

[1]Overly, Donald E., Kinghorn, Jon Rye, Preston,
Richard L. The Middle School: Humanizing Education
for Youth. Worthington, Ohio: Charles A. Jones Publishing Company, 1972, pp. 195-198.

with the fundamentals of a general education. The
middle school student finds himself in a society which
is now demanding more of him as a student and as an
individual attempting to make the change from childhood to adolescence and then to adulthood. The rapid-
ity and diversity of technological and social change
are placing a great deal of stress on the individual
in making this transition. It is in this transitional
period of exploration into the preadult world that the
middle school concept is attempting to individualize
not only the academic but the total growth of the student. The departmentalized patterns of the junior
high school and the self contained classroom of the
elementary school seem less than adequate to meet the
changing needs of this age student. Diagnosing, planning units based upon interest as well as needs and
ability, evaluation, and recording and the multitude
of minor expectations of the teacher become excessive
even for the team teaching organizational pattern.[2]
It seems apparent, then, that an organizational pattern that can utilize auxiliary services to supplement
the basic classroom learning environment can become
more effective in meeting the needs of the middle
school student both in and out of school.

In light of the characteristics of the middle
school students and their school, a number of services
may be beneficial in maintaining the school in the
most efficient and effective manner. Reviewing the
salient characteristics of the middle school, each one
the subject of a chapter in this book, affords us the
opportunity to examine the potential auxiliary student
services a school could develop. The number and types
of services a school would have depends upon different
variables controlling each school or school system.
These include size of the district, financial status,
philosophy of education, teacher receptiveness, community support, availability of auxiliary assistance,
and others.

---

[2]McCarthy, Robert J. The Ungraded Middle School.
West Nyack, New York: Parker Publishing Company,
Inc., 1972.

By definition, auxiliary student services are
those special services which normally cannot be
handled solely through the basic classroom educational program.  Since the philosophy of the middle
school is student-centered with a strong emphasis on
individual growth and development, it becomes
increasingly difficult for classroom teachers to
accommodate the wide expanse of learning problems,
levels of progress, and rate of learning that confront
them each day.

The very nature of auxiliary student services
implies a type of differentiated staffing.  In some
cases there will be personnel obtained on a volunteer
basis or paid basis to relieve the teacher or teaching
team from a great number of non-learning tasks such as
secretarial assistance, lunchroom assistance, grading
papers (objective answers), playground duty, small
group instruction, preparation of instructional
resources, improving classroom physical environment,
bus duty, and assistance with individualized instruction allowing teachers to spend their time more
efficiently and effectively on the learning environment.[3]  On the other hand, some professional decisions
for service may necessitate calling upon auxiliary
personnel with a different degree of specialization
than that of classroom teachers—the psychologist,
nurse, reading specialist, etc.—for additional diagnostic data or remedial aid.

If we accept the definition of readiness as having
the minimal prerequisites to complete an assigned task
successfully, the role of the teacher changes from a
subject-centered approach to a student-centered
diagnostic-prescriptive approach.  In this prescriptive role, auxiliary services become a valuable classroom instructional aid and means to diagnostic and
remedial assistance.  Prescriptive learning environments are based upon the known strengths and weaknesses of the students in general as well as in

---

[3]Ornstein, Alan C., Talmage, Harriet, and Juhasz,
Ann W.  The Paraprofessional's Handbook.  Belmont,
California:  Fearon Press, Inc., 1975, pp. 69-72.

specific skill areas. The auxiliary services available to the teacher can give valuable insight into
the academic, emotional, social, mental, physical,
and experiential background of the student. When
using a diagnostic-prescriptive approach, teachers
can cluster students based upon common needs, interests, or skill development. Flexible scheduling
plus adequate diagnostic information and auxiliary
staff provides means for regrouping students across
grade and age categories. In addition these auxiliary services provide personnel to work with
students who need specialized help beyond the classroom teacher's expertise.

Auxiliary student services cluster themselves
in three major categories which are reflected in the
characteristics of a middle school.

1.  Instructional Services

            teacher aides (teacher assistants)

            parent helpers

            paraprofessionals

            remedial reading programs

            reading consultants or specialists

            learning disability programs

            special tutors

            hometown tutors

            educable mentally retarded programs

            emotionally disturbed classes

            gifted programs

            enrichment programs

        instructional learning centers

        media specialists

        instructional consultants

        speech therapists

        supervisory staff

        parents with special talent

        business and industry specialists

2. <u>Counseling and Guidance</u>

        counselors

        psychologists

        psychometrists

        social workers

        principals

        assistant principals

        nurses

        community agencies

3. <u>Extracurricular Activities</u>

        interschool physical and social activities

        intramural activities

        special interest and club activities

        special need groups

        exploratory programs

Need is sometimes the catalyst for creativity. In a
U.S. Air Force Dependent's School some years ago,
parents realized how difficult it was to teach their
own children—because of the emotional bonds. A
recommendation was made to form parent teaching
pools where parents agreed to work with someone
else's son or daughter under the direction of
several interested faculty members.[4] The program
was both a success for students and a relief to the
anxious parents.

The emphasis given to the use of auxiliary
aides must be consistent with the willingness of the
classroom teacher to use auxiliary help properly and
for the teachers to perceive their roles somewhat
differently. Rather than viewing one's self as the
exclusive dispenser of knowledge, the teacher
increasingly moves toward a position as a planner,
programmer and evaluator of learning.

In the advent of computer assisted instruction
becoming a reality in schools and society, the idea
of teachers as dispensers of knowledge is becoming
less and less significant. It is in the retrieval
and acquisition of information and in the process of
how these young people will use this knowledge to
solve their personal and social problems that will
indicate whether or not the schools built around
a middle school concept are more successful than
their predecessors.

Parents, teachers, and communities must search
and work together to provide auxiliary student services wherever they are needed.

As promising as auxiliary services may seem to
be, a school wishing to initiate such a program
should consider the following.

---

[4]Schubert, Delwyn, and Torgerson, Theodore.
*Improving the Reading Program.* Dubuque, Iowa: Wm.
Brown Company Publishers, 1981, p. 103.

1. Before any program of auxiliary services is started, those who have the ultimate responsibility should be involved in the planning and evaluation of the program. This includes administration, teachers, parents, etc.

2. The role of each auxiliary service should be spelled out carefully in order to avoid misunderstanding of job expectations.

3. It must be remembered the overall purpose of auxiliary services is the enhancement of student learning, not just the reassignment of responsibilities.

4. Auxiliary services should result in the most effective use of time and talents of all personnel.

5. Effective use of auxiliary help takes time, preplanning and inservice preparation before and after its initiation.

6. Constant study and evaluation should be made as to the value of auxiliary services.

Larger and more affluent school systems are more likely to have the resources for a comprehensive program of auxiliary services whereas smaller districts may need to apply for special temporary funding, depend more upon volunteers, or develop cooperative arrangements with other school districts to provide the services desired. In this regard, intermediate school district or county school offices often offer some services upon request, but such arrangements can also be made by several school districts pooling their limited resources and sharing them.

One specific example of auxiliary student services offered in the middle schools of a local school district is indicated below.

## <u>CENTERVILLE CITY SCHOOLS (OHIO)</u>

## Pupil Personnel services

I. School Nurses and School Health

II. Psychological Services

III. Visiting Teacher and Home Instruction Coordinator

IV. Speech and Hearing Therapy

V. Guidance and Counseling

VI. Special Education

    A. Learning Disability Programs

    B. Low Incidence Programs

       1. Developmental Disabilities

       2. Trainable Mentally Retarded

       3. Hearing Impaired

       4. Visually Impaired

       5. Physically Handicapped

       6. Severe Behavior Disorder

       7. Severe and Multiple Impairment

    C. Learning Enrichment Program (Gifted Students)

VII. Additional Services/Responsibilities

    A. Work Permits

B.   Student Records

C.   Child Accounting


Services offered may be organized differently in several school districts.  Here is another listing.

FOREST PARK MIDDLE SCHOOL

   I.   School Health Service

  II.   Psychological Services

 III.   Home Instruction Service

  IV.   Speech and Hearing Therapy

   V.   Guidance and Counseling Service

  VI.   Instructional Specialist Services

 VII.   Assessment Center Services

VIII.   Special Education Services

        A.   Learning Disability

        B.   Developmental Handicapped

        C.   Trainable Mentally Retarded

        D.   Visually Impaired

        E.   Hearing Impaired

        F.   Physically Handicapped

        G.   Severe Behavior Disorder

        H.   Multi-Handicapped

    I.  Autistic Program

    J.  Gifted Programs

IX.  Project Center

    A.  Student Records

    B.  Student Teaching Coordination

    C.  Inservice Coordination

    D.  Special Project--Outside Funding

    E.  Annehurst Curriculum Classification
       System Service

The county or intermediate school district unit offers a convenient way of providing needed auxiliary services.

### BUTLER COUNTY BOARD OF EDUCATION OFFICE

Pupil Personnel and Leadership Services

    I.  Curriculum Development Services

   II.  Administrative Services

  III.  Legal Services

   IV.  School Health Services

    V.  Home Instruction Coordinator

   VI.  Speech and Hearing Therapy

  VII.  Social Work Services

VIII.  Psychological Services

IX.  Special Education

    A.  Learning Disability Programs

    B.  Developmental Handicapped Programs

    C.  Trainable Mentally Retarded

    D.  Hearing Impaired

    E.  Visually Impaired

    F.  Orthopedically Handicapped Program

    G.  Severe Behavior Disorder

    H.  Multi-Handicapped

    I.  Work Study Coordinator for Handicapped

X.  Special Services

    A.  Work Permits

    B.  Child Accounting

    C.  Attendance Officer Services

The following student auxiliary service program suggests a wide diversity of assistance that can enhance the learning environment.

### Auxiliary Student Services

   I.  School Health and School Nurse

  II.  Psychological Services

III.  Guidance and Counseling Service

 IV.  Evaluation Service

  V.  Tutorial Service

VI. Visiting and Home Instruction Coordinator and Faculty

VII. Community Resource Coordinator

VIII. Instructional Resource and Learning Center and Faculty

IX. Special Interests and Needs Advisor

X. Instructional Aides and Paraprofessionals

XI. Special Education

    A. Learning Disability Program

    B. Gifted Program

    C. Speech and Hearing Therapy

    D. Low Incident Programs

        1. Developmental Disabilities (EMR)

        2. Trainable Mentally Retarded

        3. Hearing Impaired

        4. Visually Impaired

        5. Physically Handicapped

        6. Severe Behavior Disorder

        7. Severe and Multiple Impairment

XII. Special Programs

    A. Enrichment Programs

    B. Environmental Education Program

    C. Remedial Reading and Mathematics Programs

D.  Instructional Learning Resource Center
    (self instructional center)

E.  Work Study Programs

XIII.  Managerial Auxiliary Services

A.  Lunchroom Supervision

B.  Study Hall Supervision

C.  Corridor Supervision

D.  Child Accounting

E.  Student Records

F.  Work Permits

AUXILIARY STUDENT SERVICES IN THE COMMUNITY

Each community shares the educational responsibility for its students by providing access to three
types of auxiliary services.

1.  The exploratory nature of the middle school
    suggests an instructional function to supple-
    ment the day to day classroom program.
    Educationally, the community can offer stu-
    dents an extensive exposure to its vast
    resources such as the commercial, industrial,
    professional, and technical facilities.
    Field trips and more longitudinal observation
    and participation in numerous experiences
    help provide readiness for each individual
    to make personal career decisions later at
    the high school level.  Secondly, a society
    which is finding that a college education is
    not the only route to success in life demon-
    strates that other viable options are open
    to students.

2. The second type of auxiliary services the community can offer are those specialized services which contribute directly or indirectly to the students' total growth. Directly, by having agencies provide out-of-school diagnostic, counseling, and supportive aid to individual students. Indirectly, they offer support and guidance to students by educating and counseling parents and teachers concerning the uniqueness of problems facing the preadolescent such as drugs, sex, behavior problems, learning disabilities, etc.

3. The third type of auxiliary services are those services which community individuals can offer students in a school setting. There are many people who are willing to share their time, talents, training, and experiences with young students. These educational experiences can range from unique hobbies and specialized skills to professional training of various types. The opportunity to work in the community with the very young and to interact with the aged is, in itself, a rewarding educational experience for the preadolescents as a way of satisfying their strong missionary zeal.

The following is a partial sampling of community auxiliary services which may be available locally.[6] In each community these same services may be offered by a variety of organizations. It is recommended that some type of social service directory be developed in each community making these services more widely known and accessable to schools, students, and parents. The more obvious services of the police, Lions and other service clubs, and Church services, etc. were not included due to wide recognition of their services.

---

[6]White, Virginia, Editor. Directory of Community Services. Published by The United Way of Hamilton, Fairfield, Ohio and Vicinity. January 1978.

Directory of Community Services, Published by The
United Way of Hamilton, Fairfield, Ohio and vicinity

Alcoholism Services
    Alcoholics Anonymous

    Function:  Alcoholics Anonymous is a fellowship
               of recovering alcoholics whose primary
               purpose is to continue sobriety and
               help alcoholics to achieve it.

ALANON (Friends and Relatives of AA's)
ALATEEN (Teenagers with Alcoholic Parents)
    Alanon and Alateen function similarly within
    their target groups.

Alcoholism Council of Butler County, Ohio, Inc.
    Function:  To increase understanding of alcohol-
               ism, its nature and treatment, for
               the purpose of alleviation, the damage
               of alcoholism and reducing the inci-
               dence of alcoholism.

               Types of Service:

               1.  Education
               2.  Community organization
               3.  Consultation
               4.  Case Coordination
               5.  Out-patient counseling
               6.  Detoxification and treatment faci-
                   lities

Behavior Problems of Children
    Family Service of Butler County, Inc.

    Function:  To strengthen family life, to promote
               health personality and satisfactory
               functioning of various family members
               through professional case service work
               to individuals and families, through
               family life education.

Types of Service:

1. Family and individual counseling
2. Family life education
3. Home aid service

## Mental Health Center

Function: Out-patient psychiatric and psychological services to children and
adults unable to afford private care.

Types of Services:

1. Out-patient psychiatric services
   to children and adults
2. After care treatment and services
   discharged from public and private
   hospitals
3. Diagnostic, evaluation, and consultation services to courts, schools,
   and community agencies
4. Mental health education and pre-
   vention programs

## Ohio Youth Commission

Function: (1) To provide rehabilitative services
directed towards assisting delinquent
youth returning to the community and
satisfactorily adjusting to society,
and to enable these youth to avoid
recidivism. (2) A preventive program
to get at those conditions which breed
delinquency, keep youth from becoming
involved with the juvenile justice
systems, and to prevent youth from
committing new offenses.

## Dental Services
Children's Dental Care Foundation

Function: To provide dental services for the
physically and mentally handicapped

child and the preschool child.   To
train dentists in the problems of
pediatric dentistry.

Types of Services:

1.   Render dental care to the cerebral
palsied, cardiac, hemophiliac,
cleft palate, and retarded patients.

Drug Education and Counseling
     Middletown Drug Treatment Center

     Function:   Drug treatment and preventive drug
                 education

     Types of Services:

     1.   Out-patient drug free services
     2.   Drug related counseling
     3.   Preventive drug education services

Together, Inc.

     Function:   (1) Crisis intervention information
                 and referral.   (2) community outreach
                 education (mental health and drug
                 related.   (3) Community development--
                 improving the quality of life of the
                 disadvantaged.

     Types of Services:

     1.   Crisis intervention--emotional,
          drug, sex

     2.   Individual counseling

     3.   Outreach education program--
          includes workshops, discussion
          groups, speaker's bureau, lending
          library, and inservice training.

437

Educational Facilities
  Fair Acres School, Butler County Board of Mental
  Retardation

  Function:  To provide a comprehensive and habili-
             tative program for mentally retarded
             and developmentally disabled school-
             age (6-21) individuals.

             Types of Services:

             1.  Classroom instruction
             2.  Supportive programs

Butler County Council for Retarded Citizens, Inc.

  Function:  To promote the general welfare of the
             mentally retarded. To advise and aid
             parents in the solution of their
             problems and to coordinate their
             efforts and activities. To develop a
             better understanding of the problems
             of mental retardation by the public.

Chilren's Diagnostic Center

  Function:  To provide interdisciplinary diagnos-
             tic and prescriptive services to
             children with suspected developmental
             disabilities, and to initiate treat-
             ment.

             Types of Services:

             1.  To provide a comprehensive diag-
                 nostic service which examines
                 the components of the child's
                 functioning possibly related to
                 his present condition.

             2.  To serve as a central resource for
                 collection and dissemination of
                 information pertaining to excep-

tional children to parents,
physicians, educators, service
agencies, and others.

Speech and Audiology Department, Mercy Hospital

Function:    To provide speech, language and
             hearing evaluations and services to
             the populace in our service area.

Speech and Hearing Clinic, Miami University

Function:    The clinic serves as part of the
             training program for students majoring
             in speech and hearing therapy.

             Types of Services:

             1.  Speech and hearing evaluation
                 and therapy.

Mental Health and Mental Retardation
   Psychology Clinic, Miami University

Function:    A training clinic established as a
             part of doctoral education in clinical
             psychology.

             Types of Services:

             1.  Short or long term psychotherapy
             2.  Psychological evaluation and
                 assessment
             3.  Consultation

Rollman Psychiatric Institute, State of Ohio

Function:    To provide short term intensive care
             psychiatric treatment.

             Types of Services:

             1.  Evaluation of patient needs
             2.  In-patient service
             3.  Community information service

Minority Problems
  Middletown Citizen's Council on Human Relations

    Function:    (1) To investigate charges of alleged
discrimination, analyze facts, and
make recommendations to parties involved.  (2) To initiate studies in
areas which could give rise to
serious intergroup tensions.  (3) To
launch programs designed to reduce
tensions, prejudices, and discrimina-
tions and promote cooperation among
the various groups in the community.

# COMMUNITY RELATIONS

Every school has a community relations program whether it wants one or not! The days are long since past, if indeed they ever existed, when the school can survive as a self-contained educational enclave. Things that occur in school have impact in the community the moment children arrive home from school at the end of the school day. For that reason, a good community relations program begins with consistent professional behavior on the part of school staff members. No "P-R" program can effectively overcome unprofessional behavior, and a child who has been academically abused by such behavior will not be a good-will ambassador for the school.

Teachers, counselors, cooks, secretaries, janitors, nurses and all other school people affect school-community relations by their behavior. The best planned community relations programs begin with inservice programs for all staff. Does a middle school teacher who says at a meeting of her student's parents, "I don't know just where my science class is going yet, but. . ." really serve the school well? What message is being received concerning that teacher's competency?

The public receives "messages" about the school and its staff on every occasion of public or private contact with school personnel. An effective community-public relations program begins with accepting the reality that a planned approach will be more effective than a random one which relies upon chance encounters. Inservice education is a good place to begin the plan. But what is this thing called "community relations" about which the staff needs to be formally educated?

Edward Bernays offers a useful view of community (public) relations by suggesting that they include a) information given to the public, b) attempts to

persuade the public to a particular attitude or
action, and c) efforts to integrate the attitudes
and actions of an institution with those of its
public.[1] Certainly, public relations programs are
meant to increase public confidence in the schools
and to generate support for school programs and
activities.

However, community relations programs are not
solely driven by the kinds of definitions suggested
above. There are crucial attitudes concerning the
public that are basic to successful programs.
Those attitudes develop by accepting 1) the community
has a need to know, 2) the community wants to know,
and 3) the community has a right to know. Accepting
the three premises leads to programs that are continuous and ongoing and that utilize the public sector
in planning. Without the attitudes, public relations
programs are doomed to concentrate on explaining
crises and on requests for public help for financial
support.

An additional reason for mobilizing community
support is academic. When parents are involved in
educational programming, academic achievement
rises.[2] If involving parents as integral parts of
the community relations program can pay dividends in
improved learning, then that option must be considered in planning the progam. Parental involvement
may require educators to reconsider "roles" in their
building in favor of fostering improved student
performances.

---

[1]Bernays, Edward. Public Relations (Norman:
University of Oklahoma Press) 1952, p.3.

[2]Coleman, James, et. al., Equality of Educational Opportunity (Washington, D. C.: U.S. Department of HEW, U.S. Office of Education), 1966.

## Public Relations as Communication

Much can be said for considering your public relations program as a problem in human communications. That kind of conceptualization requires your attention to not only the nature of the messages you send to the community but also to the messages your community is sending to you. No community relations program can succeed without paying heed to both sides of the communication network.

Messages. If we define "true" communication as perfect congruence between the message sent and the message received, then such a condition seldom occurs. Even when we try to be precise, extraneous elements get in the way. Suppose, for example, a witness to an auto accident tries to be absolutely explicit by saying, "The bicycle was struck by a red, 1983 Oldsmobile." You may visualize a fire engine red, two-door hardtop, full-sized sedan, but the witness saw a maroon, four-door compact. It is precisely because our vocabularies are insufficient to accommodate the many nuances of perceptions and images that the best communications are two-way.

The ability (and the inclination) to seek additional information in pursuit of message clarity pays handsome rewards of understanding. The political candidate often uses vocabulary to confusing advantage. Using a calculated ambiguity, messages are sent intentionally which the different receivers can perceive in different ways. Meanings which were never intended can be read into the message. In that way the candidate seeks to gain favor with the largest possible audience while alienating the smallest possible number. Candidates so inclined abhor reporters or others who would probe the words with vigor to expose the real position being hidden.

Educators seldom have need for the functional ambiguity of the politician. Rather, they need to seek all avenues which facilitate clarity, and this

requires frequent opportunities for questioning.
The general principle of messages remains. . . don't
send a message when you can deliver it.

As a receiver of a written message or the
listener to an oral one, ask yourself some recurring
questions:

1.  Does the message contain everything
    I need to know?

2.  Is it clear as to what is required?

3.  Do I know enough background to put the
    message in perspective?

4.  Is the meaning clear?

5.  Do I understand the intent or am I
    impuning the sender's motives?

Messages can be made more clear if you can
answer for yourself the reporter's questions: who?
what? when? where? why? and how? As a receiver the
obligation for clarity is as much upon you as the
sender. When unclear, seek answers. To do otherwise is to presume, or guess, or rely on the perceptions of others who are as fallible as you.

Both senders and receivers engage in their
respective acts through many "filters." Because the
sender's filters are never the same as the receiver's,
perfect congruence is seldom achieved. The filters
have nothing to do with honesty or integrity, but
they can do great damage to both. Suppose that in
the final stages of employing a teacher, the
teacher's current principal is called for a reference.
If you are told reluctantly that the teacher is unfortunately an alcoholic, you may choose not to offer
the position. In fact, the message about alcoholism
may come from one whose honest definition of an alcoholic is one who drinks any alcoholic beverage even
in great moderation. How much different it might

have been if the conditions which lead to the conclusion regarding the teacher's "alcoholism" had
been described; for example, "I know _____ has
been seen drinking publicly." Under that circumstance, the receiver might have gotten a different
message or sought additional data.

A final example of mixed messages is common to
all administrators. When the principal asks a
faculty for written input concerning almost anything,
different advice will be forthcoming from the
membership. Teacher A may suggest, "The money
should be spent for more audio-visual equipment, but
don't waste any more on teacher aides." Teacher B
may say, "Get some more teacher aides, but don't
waste the money on any more A-V equipment." When
the decision is made to buy a new video-taping
system, teacher B repeats the oft heard line, "You
didn't listen to me!" As a matter of fact, the
principal may have heard and understood perfectly,
but in weighing all options found one choice to be
more appropriate at the instant. When you are likely
to receive conflicting advice, take time to share
your reasoning with those whose advice you could not
accept. In that way, understanding is increased,
and the avenue for subsequent messages is kept open.

Written Messages. From the foregoing, it is
apparent that written messages must be couched with
great care because they are one-way unless the
reader chooses to actively seek further clarification. The first principle seems self-evident; write
to your audience.

Newspapers and magazines are very careful to use
a language level suitable to their "average" reader.
The Wall Street Journal's vocabulary is quite different from that used in comic books. Unfortunately,
clarity comes from shades of meanings not available
in primary level vocabularies as in the difference
between "red" and "cerise." Thus the message sender
often must choose between words which are easy to
understand but not very precise and others which are

precise but not known to all readers as in
"agreement" vs. "consonance." Try to find a
reader of the kind you seek to communicate with,
and ask for their understanding of your message.
That may mean a cook, janitor, P.T.A. member, or
teacher. Remember, using words larger than necessary can get you accused of being hyperpolysylla-
bicsesquipedalianistic!

In addition to vocabulary, format should also
change with your audience. For formal, recurring
publications, mastheads are in order to help the
reader quickly identify the source of the message.
Wide margins and plenty of "white space" will help
encourage the person to read the material. Black
copy is overwhelming, and no message is received
until it is read. Use a type face that is open,
neat, and clean in appearance. The duplication
process you choose should be the best your budget
can afford, because the physical make-up of a
written message sends a secondary statement to the
receiver about you and your style.

Great care must be taken to insure that language
details are in proper order. Schools are a primary
agent in language development and in matters of
grammar and punctuation. If the messages you send
to the community are not representative of the best
in language mechanics, you may lose more in educational credibility than you gain through the substance of message.. Proofread carefully, for typo-
graphical errors cannnot easily be distinguished
from spelling ignorance.

Carelessness with details can also be disaster-
ous to the message itself. For example, consider
the plight of the caring husband at a convention who
wishes to send to his wife a telegram reading,
"Having a wonderful time. Wish you were here."
It may be a small detail, but the meaning is dramatically changed if the telegraph operator should
inadvertently omit the final "e" in the telegram!

Or consider the governor who wishes to commute a death sentence, and at the eleventh hour sends to the warden a message reading, "Spare him, not kill him." What happens if the comma gets misplaced to change the message to, "Spare him not, kill him."

Or consider the language damage done by dangling participles and placed modifiers. What is the reader to assume when your letter to the P.T.A. contains a sentence telling the membership, "The chairman met with the mayor explaining the parking problems." Did the chairman or the mayor do the explaining? From the preceding examples, it should be clear that proofreading cannot be overdone.

There are times when handwritten notes are more effective than typed ones. A handwritten note's secondary statement is that the writer took time from a busy schedule to pen a personal note and thereby I, the reader, and what is happening to me are important to the sender. That perception may be as important as the message. Thank you notes, congratulations and condolences are good candidates for personally written messages.

Oral Messages. · Many of the rules of written messages apply as well to oral ones. Vocabulary and grammar rules are just as much in order, and care in preparation and presentation are requisite to a clear understanding.

Every formal oral presentation starts by considering the purpose of the message.

1. What do I want the audience to know?

2. How can I reinforce the major points?

3. How will I hold their interest?

4. How can I actively involve the audience in the communication?

The best messages are parsimonious in the points to
be made and the time spent in making them. Three
points well made are better than a "laundry list" of
items which might better have been distributed by
memo, and ministers know "no souls are saved after
twenty minutes!"

The Chinese proverb of a picture being worth a
thousand words carries much truth, and many speeches
could be dramatically enlivened by effective visual
aids. The schools teach "speech" and should be
examples of the best practice.

When a community audience is invited to participate in an oral interchange, their comments and
questions deserve respect. If you assume that each
speaker is sincere and that each has a right to an
opinion and the right to express it, then you can
receive each remark with graciousness regardless of
the hostility you may suspect permeates it. The
hostile comment or question has provided the speaker
with catharsis, and if you turn away the wrath by
your own graciousness, communication will continue.
Belittling and derisive responses will elevate the
hostility and close off future avenues of communication. Such responses also send nonverbal messages
to all other listeners.

A final principle of messages concerns the credibility of the message sender. Numerous research
studies have shown that the power of a message is
directly proportional to the credibility of the
sender. Regardless of how careful you may be to
protect your own credibility, you cannot be expected
to be the most credible person with every member of
your audience. Therefore, in planning for oral
presentations, you should seek to match maximum
credibility with the nature of the message. Should
the principal talk about student adjustment problems
or would the counselor be more credible? Should the
principal or the school's primary teachers discuss
the values being derived from the new reading program?

## Public Relations as Mutual Interchange

For many years teachers have been encouraged to participate in community activities. Scouting organizations, churches, fraternal organizations, hospitals and various community boards have all profited from teachers' willingness to contribute time and talent to community improvement. More and more often parents and other citizens are being drawn into school operations as valued participants in the school program.

Teachers in the Public Arena. Teachers play a unique role in every society, and society continues to honor their dedication and their contributions. Expectations for teachers are high. Some minor proof can be seen in the local news stories which so often cite an arrested culprit as the son or daughter of a teacher but seldom identify the parent's occupation if it happens to be carpenter, salesperson, or bus driver. Precisely because of the esteem in which teachers are held, visible community contacts need to be done in particularly good taste consonant with high community expectations. "Is that what I pay taxes for?", "Is that what my child is subjected to in school?", and "Is that what educators stand for these days?" are only three common questions raised by witnesses to questionable behavior.

Recognizing that questionable behavior may be indeed in the eye of the beholder, and recognizing that teachers are not very different from other humans, you might try to ignore this aspect of public relations. Unfortunately the public will not, and the public behavior of school personnel will ever be a factor in the quality of relations between the school and its society.

The Public in the Schools. The range of activities in which parents and interested citizens can participate is limited largely by the ingenuity of the administrative staff. For years "library

mothers" have filed books, pasted in pockets, and
supervised student behavior. They can also read
stories, and they can develop special resources for
use by children. Both library and classroom bulletin boards have profited from their volunteer
labors. Like other people, these volunteers like
to feel appreciated, and public relations programs
should provide opportunities for appropriate expressions.

Parents can also be used in activities more
directly related to instruction. For students who
have a primary language other than English, bilingual parents can serve as an important resource to
accelerate bilinguality. Bilingual teachers continue
in short supply, and with careful orientation to
language objectives and programs, parents can participate in many language development activities.

The school staff cannot begin to encompass the
array of talent represented in the broader community.
Invitations to selected citizens can improve occupa-
tional information programs, can introduce middle
school students to new hobbies, crafts, and recreational activities. Sports activities, so important
to middle school students, can also profit from
demonstrations and exhibitions from parents more
skilled than the staff may be. Clubs can be spon-
sored by interested community people.

Tutoring is also a possible place to utilize
external talent.[3] Dougherty suggests a two session
preparation period prior to assigning parents to
tutoring tasks. The first session should focus on
orienting the tutors to the school, the tutoring

_____

[3]Dougherty, Michael and Mary Dyal, "Community
Involvement: Training Parents as Tutors in a Junior
High," The School Counsellor, May, 1976, p. 353+.

programs, and to the uniqueness of middle school/
junior high school students. The second session
should focus on the techniques available to the
tutor in effectively helping young persons.

In fact, orientation should precede all activities in which parents are invited to participate.
Some kinds of school activities require, by law,
certified personnel in positions of responsibility
or control. Therefore, a clear delineation of
duties and expectation is required if professional,
paraprofessional, and nonprofessional activities are
to be meshed into an effective educational program.
Job descriptions and role restrictions put into
place after a problem arises will not be well
received, and well conceived programs resolve role
conflict problems before the action is begun.

## Formal Organizations and Public Relations

Parent Teacher Associations, Parent Teacher
Organizations, Music Parents, and Booster Clubs are
examples of formal organizations which can be
important assets to the community relations programs.
In each case they can serve as important vehicles
for receiving and dispensing information and for
building a reserve of good will strategically
located throughout the community. Poorly conceived
and poorly led they can become irrational pressure
groups focusing on narrow and selfish needs.

School personnel who abdicate their role in
influencing the parent organizations can expect the
worst. On the other hand, skillful participation
can generate excellent support which can be called
up in time of need. To some extent at least, good
will can be "banked."

Parents are as busy as the professional middle
school staff, and another meeting will not be
attractive unless several conditions are met:

1.  the meeting helps them meet some of
    their needs;

2.  they are respected participants in the
    activities of the meeting;

3.  the meeting moves crisply from the
    beginning to end; and

4.  some meeting activities are of interest
    to them.

Parents must therefore be actively involved in the
planning of meetings for they know the underlying
conditions requisite to meeting parental concerns
and interest.

The school personnel can be effective in some
agenda items such as those related to explaining
middle school programs.  Effective participation
requires careful attention to attitude and language.
Speaking to parents as respected partners is a good
place to start.  Parents, like others, know when
they are being spoken down to, and, like others,
they resent it.  Effective participation also
requires careful planning and attention to language
details.

### The School Conference as Public Relations

The Parent-Teacher conference was discussed in
an earlier chapter on evaluation.  The following are
additional suggestions dealing with PR aspects.
Because of its one-to-one nature, the school conference is an intense experience.  The conference provides great opportunity to improve home-school
relations, but poorly done, the conference can
generate strong negative reactions.  A workshop for
principals, counselors, teachers, and other staff
members who confer with parents can greatly improve
the quality of conferences.  Dealing with confron-
tation should be a major item on the workshop agenda.

Teach-Parent Conferences.  Before every conference, the teacher should establish a short list of
objectives to be met during the meeting.  Have in
mind what you want to discuss and what you hope the
parent will learn in the process.  Because the conference is two-way, the teacher should be prepared
to answer the most likely kind of questions, and to
listen to the messages being sent by the parent.
The parent may have some legitimate objectives for
the meeting too!

Good listening is particularly necessary when
the conference involves an agitated parent.  Until
the agitation is vented, no good conversation can
proceed.  Voice and body language usually will hint
at a deeper distress.  Some conferences, particularly those generated by behavior problems, are
almost certain to contain some stress on the part
of the parent, and good listening will provide not
only a vent for the parent but may also provide
useful clues as to sources of the difficulty.  An
insecure teacher who wants to fill conference time
with "teacher talk" lest the conference get out of
control will miss the opportunity to learn from the
parent.

The conference should begin with a relaxed
attempt to establish rapport.  If the parent is
known, this usually takes care of itself by a short
discussion of things of past or present mutual
interest.  With a stranger, a few questions
designed to elicit information about the parent
usually helps, particularly if the teacher is truly
interested in the answers.  Rapport is also a matter
of a relaxed setting and style.  A fresh cup of
coffee and a broad smile are time tested ice breakers
and important tools in making a parent feel welcome
to your environment.

With rapport established, move into the agenda.
Item one should be positive if at all possible.  All
items should be laid out frankly with plenty of
opportunity for parent response.  In responding to

questions, try to explain rather than defend, for
defensiveness tends to destroy good conversations.
Parental questions and responses must be accepted
at face value. Too often parents are asked for
their opinion and then told why they should not have
such an opinion. Their responses must be accepted
as true reflections of their perceptions, attitudes,
or beliefs. To belittle a response in any way is to
lose the opportunity to learn from it.

Try to meet parent needs in the conference.
Find out what they would like to know and make a
conscientious effort to secure the information. If
it may take some time to secure, later delivery can
be another opportunity to solidify a good relationship. When the information requested is about the
child, the parent has a very great vested interest.
In fact, it is hard to find information about a
child to which a parent does not have a greater
right to know than the teacher.

In explaining student behavior, it is usually
better to describe the behavior rather than to
interpret it. For example, showing the hidden note
card you took from the student during a test is far
better than calling the student a "sneaky cheat."
Parents do not want others passing judgments and
labeling their children, but they can be led toward
their own conclusions.

The conference should use a "we" approach whenever possible. What can "we" do to help maintain
the good start of the student? What can "we" do to
plan a remedial attack on the learning problem?
What can "we" do to make a mutually supportive
attack on the behavior problem? The "we" approach
has a better chance of success, it spreads the
responsibility, and it removes the necessity for
establishing blame. In follow-up conferences, the
"we" strategy can be examined; and since "we" agreed
to it, there can be mutual joy in success or mutual
concern for revising an unsuccessful approach.

Every conference should end with recognizable closure. The information shared in the meeting can be summarized, unfinished items identified along with plans to complete them, and the accepted approaches to the resolution of continuing problems can be reviewed. Parents should leave each meeting feeling that they learned what they came to learn and that there is hope for the problems which were shared. Satisfied parents are crucial elements in every public relations program.

Counselor-Parent Conferences. The counselor-parent conference is very often a follow up to an earlier teacher conference. In such instances, the counselor must begin preparation for the conference by a thorough discussion with the teacher to determine all necessary background data which came to light in the teacher's meeting with the parent. Consistency between teacher and counselor comments is important unless there is reason to send disparate messages.

Counselors often deal with delicate matters of confidence. The role of counselor is seriously damaged by discussing student confidences with parents. Nevertheless parents have a strong need and right to know, and evasiveness can destroy parent confidence in the counselor who is perceived as "keeping secrets." The case of the pregnant young teenager is a classic example.

In many cases, an adroit counselor can convince the reluctant student to confide in the parents or to let the counselor play the role of intermediary in resolving or alleviating the problem. If neither of those two approaches is acceptable to the student, the counselor can non-directively get the parents to evaluate clues in the home environment in ways designed to generate correct conclusions without the counselor having to expose the child's confidence. Improved home relations generated by the counselor is good public relations for the school.

The counselor also has a unique opportunity to build bridges between home and school by using frequent home visits as an ordinary adjunct to the counseling role. "Dropping in" is unacceptable because parents may be unduly ashamed of the conditions, and the opportunity to prepare is always appreciated. Home is a good place to conduct joint parent-counselor-student meetings because of the comfort provided by familiar surroundings. These conferences need to abide by the same principles mentioned for teacher conferences, and they should end with each party clear in the course of action that will be required of them in the days, weeks, and months ahead.

Counselors also serve an important role in test interpretation to parents. Test data are often sensitive when a student is assigned to a below average status on some scale. Parents are bombarded by popular press exposes about the fallacies of standardized tests. In meeting with parents, the strengths and weaknesses of tests should be explained in simple terms. After test results are interpreted, focus should be on the more productive possibilities of the conference; namely, how can home and school develop positive approaches to moving forward from the measured positions. Focusing on positive steps can help send parents home with positive feelings about the school.

Several objectives can be met by counselors (and teachers) who look for reasons to comment positively to parents about their children. Not only does positive response reinforce desired behavior, but public relations are improved as well. Positive comments are particularly potent when counseling sessions have earlier been focused on negative, norm-violating behavior.

Principal-Parent Conferences. The preceding comments concerning teachers and counselor are certainly applicable to building principals.

However, the principal's unique role, and the
nature of the office does affect the conference.
Because the principal occupies a power position, the
incumbent can often require or force a particular
action to occur. For example, "If you can't see
that your child stops abusing other children, I will
seek suspension through the school board!" Power
contained is power retained, and the exercise of
power should be severely limited. Rationality makes
for long term solutions while power solutions are
likely to feed the ego of the wielder at great
expense to the ego of the recipient.

As an executive officer of the school board, the
principal is obliged to faithfully execute the
policies of the board and the rules and regulations
derived therefrom. The implementation and execution
of policy in conference settings can be done in ways
which reinforce good relations or in ways which are
destructive. When in a parent conference the
principal finds a situation requiring a particular
policy-driven response, several options are open:

1.  The principal can say, "The policy
    says. . .and that's the way it must be.
    because my hands are tied."

2.  The principal can say, "Well, I don't
    agree with the policy that says. . .
    but we must follow it to the letter
    anyway."

3.  The principal can say, "There is a policy
    covering these kinds of cases. It says
    that. . .and I would like to share the
    board's thinking at the time the policy
    was enacted. . ."

In the first case, the principal has dealt with
the parent in a brusque way and then hidden behind
the policy. In the second case, the principal is
seeking weakly to keep parental respect by blaming
a mutual culprit. In the third case, the principal

executes the policy but takes the time to make
helpful explanations. Respectful listening after
explaining can do much to increased understanding
and acceptance by the parent.

Finally, when principal-parent conferences are
of an appeal nature following parental dissatisfaction with prior teacher or counselor conferences,
a particularly delicate set of conditions prevails.
Such conferences must begin with careful preparation. The principal must be fully informed about
all prior contacts. The nature of the problem, the
nature of the prior conferences, and the pertinent
policy issues must be clearly in mind before the
conference. The time it takes to prepare can be a
cooling-off period which can work to the principal's
advantage.

Principals cannot blindly support improper
actions by teachers and counselors nor are parents
always right because they are applying heat and
pressure at the instant. In conflict resolution the
principal must be above the fray and must maintain a
caring demeanor to all persons involved. When the
appeal decision is reached, careful complete explanations and rationales are deserved by all parties.

Public relations cannot always be served in
appeal driven conferences because the principal has
other publics (teachers, counselors, superintendent,
and school board) to serve. But public relations can
be served by the style exhibited by the principal in
rendering a decision and in informing affected
people.


### Community Relations and Controversy

Schools inevitably must deal with controversial
issues. In their role as leaders in society they
will occasionally move beyond the norm of the community. Schools can also be involved in controversy
when they reflect the majority of the community

particularly when the majority is a very narrow one.
Classic battles between liberals and conservatives
often use the schools as the arena for their conflict.  The battle is often for the mind of the
child.

Controversy is everywhere, and choosing moderate
positions often is viewed as fence straddling.  A
civil war soldier who put on grey pants and a blue
tunic was shot at by both sides!  Common controversial issues include:

1.  Sex education

2.  Religion and/or prayers

3.  Cross town bussing

4.  Neighborhood school closings

5.  Communism

The appropriate arena for addressing controversial issues is the school board meeting.  The middle
school P.T.A. cannot resolve the issue, but strong
leadership is required to keep the boiling issues
from destroying an otherwise productive association.
The truth is that far left and far right factions
cannot convince the other extreme to leave its
position.  Debate only makes each extreme more sure
of the rightness of its own position.

Hearings and debates may be held in neighborhood
school buildings, but they should be under the aegis
of the board, not of the school or a parent association.  The board is the peer group of the community,
and it has both the power and responsibility to
examine the positions, the policy, the law, the
economics, and the feasibility of accepting any of
the alternatives offered to it.  The presence of a
district-adopted philosophy of education can do much
to place the controversial issues in perspective.

School boards that act and that explain their
actions retain wider community respect than those
who act behind closed doors. Generally, the responsible school board can retain good press relations
through good operating style, and the press as an
ally can do much to serve the public relations
concerns of the board.

When the press gets into the act, several rules
seem to apply. First, when the news is true though
bad, school responses are out of order because
response keeps the bad news in front of the public
longer, thereby exacerbating the situation. Nothing
is older than yesterday's news, and tomorrow (with
its replacement news) is almost here! Secondly,
when you disagree with an opinion taken by the press,
you have the right to disagree. However, the press
always can have the final word. Thirdly, when the
facts are wrong, response is required with documen-
tation to support the corrected facts. A correctly
informed public is an asset even when the topic is
controversial.


Community Schools in Community Relations

Middle schools make ideal community education
centers, and their use for that purpose can serve
vital objectives in a community relations program.
As the number of tax paying adults without children
in school increases, commitment to educational
support of schools diminishes, and demographic data
paint a dismal picture for the coming decades.

Fortunately, the aging population is returning to
formal education in massive numbers. Opening the
doors to the non-parent population can help to meet
demand for educational programming, can increase the
utilization of school plant, can increase adult identification with the school, and can improve financial
support for all levels of education.

At least three kinds of adult programs are already enjoying great popularity. Formal credit courses offered by community colleges and universities are enjoyed by those seeking new licensure, by those seeking a mid career change, by those pursuing a first degree, and by those who simply enjoy learning. Non-credit adult education courses which promote avocational and hobby interests also attract large numbers of adult citizens. Recreation programs using school facilities are favorites of other adults.

As enrollments decline, parts of a middle school building might be leased at token cost to open a branch library in a different neighborhood, and the local park district might coordinate its programs in ways to utilize the middle school facilities. Community organizations also seek space for such programs as Alcoholics Anonymous and Parents Without Partners. The school cafeteria facilities might get extended use as a site for subsidized meals for senior citizens.

The only limit to the community use of school facilities is the imagination and inclination of school officials. Any use which increases adult identification, adult participation, and feelings of "ownership" in the school enterprise will pay public relations dividends. Help adult citizens get a real and personal dividend from the tax investment they make in schools, and they are more likely to continue the investment!

## Ten More Places for Community Relations

The preceding sections of this chapter have dealt with general aspects of creating the larger climate for public relations programs and has suggested some serious matters of style. This final section will identify some specific public relations activities appropriate to a middle school.

1. <u>Attendance</u>. Too often attendance taking is limited to an inhouse function unless a specific trouble spot arises. If the school's program includes home telephoning every day for every absence, that call can be used in positive ways. The caller can express sincere empathy when illness or grief is identified, and the call can be used to make personal invitations to an upcoming school event. A personal, "I hope you can come to our. . ." will be received more warmly than the paper announcement sent home with the child.

2. <u>Athletic, Theatrical, and Music Events</u>. Parental participation in the students' cocurricular events can be encouraged in many ways including the times at which they are scheduled. Booster clubs are commonly used to encourage attendance. P.T.A.'s and similar organizations can be used to educate parents to the enormous need of middle school youngsters to have the active support of the very parents they are psychologically moving away from. When parents are present, breaks in the action can be used to advertise other events of personal interest.

3. <u>The Media</u>. The media are largely disinterested in becoming an announcement center for your programs. They are interested in news. By their nature, the press has more space for school news than do radio and television. Even so, the vast majority of school news appears only on the sports page or on page one when controversy or skulduggery is suspected.

To get space or time in the media, you must be alert for the new or the different which will appeal to the mass audience. When the school chorus sings for an assembly, that's not newsworthy, but if the chorus gives up its Christmas Eve to sing for the infirmed at the County Hospital, that's of greater interest. Getting into the media requires thinking as the media think and notifying them of possible newsmaking events far enought in advance to permit their coverage.

You might try to get a continuing column in a
local paper on a weekly or monthly basis devoted to
education. The schools are often a community's
largest business, and the local press may be glad
to have your byline particularly if it is free.

In larger urban centers, the number of educational and public television channels may identify
the station's philosophy and the means whereby your
district and your school might occasionally be
featured in their broadcasting schedule.

4. Orientation to the School. The orientation
of the parents of elementary school students about
to enter the middle school can be conducted in
phases. In the first phase, parents can be met in
the neighborhood feeder school, and in the second
phase they can be made familiar with the middle
school facility and the educational program through
onsite orientation meetings. The orientation should
be conducted by teachers, counselors, the principal,
and middle school parents who can explain (in positive terms) the opportunities of parental involvement.

5. Parent Handbook. When a parent buys an elec-
tric knife for $29.95, a handbook is provided to
describe the product and to tell how it can be used.
Unfortunately the purchaser of educational services
seldom gets a handbook which deals with an investment
many times more expensive.

Organize interested parents to design the handbook. Let them decide what they would like to know
about the school, its policies, its opportunities,
its programs, its philosophy, its requirements, or
the like. Staff can help to get materials together,
but in large measure it can be a book from parents to
parents about things which parents view as important.

6. Rumor-Information Phone. Rumors are insi-
diously destructive of good relationships. By designating one person on the staff as responsible for
getting and dispensing facts, rumors can be quelled

and information put forth which is useful to evaluating citizens. The attitude of the staff member must be helpful and concerned, and they must be dedicated to getting factual information. Following through with a return call is essential if a delicate situation is not to be made worse. The same rumor phone number can be used to dispense information about upcoming events.

7. School Census. An annual school census provides administrators with vital planning data about preschool children in particular. To reduce costs and to provide additional opportunity for active involvement, parent volunteers can effectively conduct a census. If volunteers are strategically located, they can serve the school from their own neighborhood.

The census takers provide a direct link to the schools, and they can be a source of information about the schools to citizens who would otherwise be outside of school information networks. Census takers should be briefed about important school issues, and when not prohibited by law, they can be distributors of public relations brochures about the schools. Dispensing information about adult education programs is particularly appropriate as an adjunct of the census process.

8. Teacher Orientation. Commitment is very often strengthened through programs of active participation. The community can make an investment in the schools by participating in teacher orientation programs. Teachers need orientation to their role, to their school, and to the educational system. However, they also need orientation to the school community. Jaycees, fraternal groups, churches, business, and other community organizations may wish to participate in an orientation luncheon and in sponsoring a trip through the community. Bridges built by these kinds of cooperative ventures are useful in meeting public relations objectives.

9. <u>Trilateral Collective Bargaining</u>. Although
not yet widespread, a few cities are experimenting
with community involvement in the collective
bargaining process. Thus, a master contract takes
shape in a manner involving a three way discussion.
Properly conceived, representation by the public
sector can satisfy the general public that their
interests have been a serious consideration in
reaching the final conclusion. Even a partial
clearing of the mystery which surrounds the collective bargaining process which often eventuates in
increased taxes has a positive public relations
effect.

10. <u>Welcome Wagon</u>. The Welcome Wagon programs
offer a unique opportunity to positively influence
new parents. Information about the schools and
their programs can be a part of the information
packet about the community which is distributed to
newcomers. New parents can gain information they
need to know, and nonparents can be influenced by
high quality materials about how the schools impact
the quality of their lives.

## Summary

Community relations in any school is first of
all a cultivated attitude about a school-community
relationship which must be positive if needed
support for the schools is to be generated and maintained. Programs must include sending information to
the community and receiving information back. Thus,
community relations is a two way process designed to
make both groups beneficiaries.

Community relations is a style of doing business.
The participants are good listeners, and they behave
in ways which overtly reflect their respect for
others. Working to insure that people can gain
access to the information they want, need, and deserve solves most community relations problems
before they arise.

Community relations is also a series of programs and techniques. While no program or technique is a panacea for every community, there are ways and means of serving public objectives which must be known and implemented by all school administrators including the middle school principal.

BIBLIOGRAPHY

Anselmo, Sandra. "Parent Involvement in the
     School," The Clearinghouse, March, 1977, pp.
     298-9.

Byrne, Robert and Edward Powell. "Planning School-
     Community Relations," The Education Digest,
     November, 1976, pp. 52-6.

Carr, David and Clifford Chaffee. Readings for the
     Principal in School-Community Relations,
     Danville, Ill.: Interstate Printers, 1975.

Conference Time. Washington: National School
     Public Relations Association, 1970.

Dougherty, Michael and Mary Ann Dyal. "Community
     Involvement: Training Parents as Tutors in a
     Junior High," The School Counsellor, May, 1976,
     pp. 553-6.

Holloway, Ken. "Parent/Teacher Conferences: What
     do Parents Think?" School and Community, Decem-
     ber, 1976, p. 10.

Jenkins, Kenneth. "Community Participation and the
     Principal," NASSP Bulletin, November, 1976,
     pp. 70-2.

Lordeman, Ann and Sandra Reese, Robert Friedman.
     Establishing and Assessing Two-Way Communication,
     Paper Read at AERA Convention, New York, 1977.

Morris, Robert and George Vrabel. "The Role of the
     Principal in Public Relations," Theory into
     Practice, February, 1979, pp. 50-2.

Sills, James. "The School Principal and Parent In-
     volvement," Contemporary Education, Fall, 1978,
     pp. 45-8.

Tobey, Thomas and Sally Martinez. "Involvement of
    the Parent in the School Program," Contemporary
    Education, Winter, 1979, pp. 93-4.

Working with Parents. Washington: National School
    Public Relations Association, 1968.

Unruh, Adolph and Robert Willier. Public Relations
    for Schools, Belmont, Cal: Fearon Publishers,
    1974.

# INDEX

## ABOUT THE AUTHORS

Nicholas P. Georgiady is presently Professor of Educational Leadership at Miami University, Oxford, Ohio. He has served as Deputy State Superintendent of Schools for Michigan. His background includes experience as a teacher and administrator in elementary and middle level schools.

He helped to charter the National Middle School Association. A visiting professor at several major universities, Dr. Georgiady is also author or co-author of over 110 books in addition to numerous articles for leading professional journals. Active in research projects and professional societies, he received his degrees at the Milwaukee State Teachers College and the University of Wisconsin at Madison.

James E. Heald is Professor of Education at Northern Illinois University, DeKalb, Illinois. He has served there as Vice-President for Academic Affairs and as Dean of the College of Education. Prior to that he was with the University of North Carolina and Michigan State University.

Dr. Heald has been a planning consultant to numerous school districts as well as to the U.S. Department of Defense, other federal agencies and to foreign governments. His publications listings include many articles in noted professional journals as well as a number of professional books. He has been a participant and major contributor at state, regional and national conferences. His degrees were earned at Illinois State University and the Ph.D. at Northwestern University.

Louis G. Romano, Professor of Education at
Michigan State University, was formerly Superintendent of Schools at Wilmette, Illinois. A pioneer
in the middle school movement, he helped to found
the Michigan Association of Middle School Education
and presently serves as its Executive Director.
He has also served as President of the National
Middle School Association.

His published writing includes many articles
and over 100 books. He has been a consultant to
middle schools in countries of five continents
and to U.S. school districts ranging in size
from 1,500 to over 1,000,000 students. His
Ph.D. degree was earned at the University of
Wisconsin.